LANDSCAP CHILDREN'S LITERATURE

Children's Literature and Culture
Jack Zipes, *Series Editor*

For a complete series list, please go to routledge.com

Constructing the Canon of Children's Literature
Beyond Library Walls and Ivory Towers
Anne Lundin

Youth of Darkest England
Working Class Children at the Heart of Victorian Empire
Troy Boone

Ursula K. Leguin Beyond Genre
Literature for Children and Adults
Mike Cadden

Twice-Told Children's Tales
Edited by Betty Greenway

Diana Wynne Jones
The Fantastic Tradition and Children's Literature
Farah Mendlesohn

Childhood and Children's Books in Early Modern Europe, 1550–1800
Edited by Andrea Immel and Michael Witmore

Voracious Children
Who Eats Whom in Children's Literature
Carolyn Daniel

National Character in South African Children's Literature
Elwyn Jenkins

Myth, Symbol, and Meaning in Mary Poppins
The Governess as Provocateur
Georgia Grilli

A Critical History of French Children's Literature, Vol. 1 & 2
Penny Brown

Once Upon a Time in a Different World
Issues and Ideas in African American Children's Literature
Neal A. Lester

The Gothic in Children's Literature
Haunting the Borders
Edited by Anna Jackson, Karen Coats, and Roderick McGillis

Reading Victorian Schoolrooms
Childhood and Education in Nineteenth-Century Fiction
Elizabeth Gargano

Soon Come Home to This Island
West Indians in British Children's Literature
Karen Sands-O'Connor

Boys in Children's Literature and Popular Culture
Masculinity, Abjection, and the Fictional Child
Annette Wannamaker

Into the Closet
Cross-dressing and the Gendered Body in Children's Literature
Victoria Flanagan

Russian Children's Literature and Culture
Edited by Marina Balina and Larissa Rudova

The Outside Child In and Out of the Book
Christine Wilkie-Stibbs

Representing Africa in Children's Literature
Old and New Ways of Seeing
Vivian Yenika-Agbaw

The Fantasy of Family
Nineteenth-Century Children's Literature and the Myth of the Domestic Ideal
Liz Thiel

From Nursery Rhymes to Nationhood
Children's Literature and the Construction of Canadian Identity
Elizabeth A. Galway

The Family in English Children's Literature
Ann Alston

Enterprising Youth
Social Values and Acculturation in Nineteenth-Century American Children's Literature
Monika Elbert

Constructing Adolescence in Fantastic Realism
Alison Waller

Crossover Fiction
Global and Historical Perspectives
Sandra L. Beckett

The Crossover Novel
Contemporary Children's Fiction and Its Adult Readership
Rachel Falconer

Shakespeare in Children's Literature
Gender and Cultural Capital
Erica Hateley

Critical Approaches to Food in Children's Literature
Edited by Kara K. Keeling and Scott T. Pollard

Neo-Imperialism in Children's Literature About Africa
A Study of Contemporary Fiction
Yulisa Amadu Maddy and Donnarae MacCann

Death, Gender and Sexuality in Contemporary Adolescent Literature
Kathryn James

Fundamental Concepts of Children's Literature Research
Literary and Sociological Approaches
Hans-Heino Ewers

Children's Fiction about 9/11
Ethnic, Heroic and National Identities
Jo Lampert

The Place of Lewis Carroll in Children's Literature
Jan Susina

Power, Voice and Subjectivity in Literature for Young Readers
Maria Nikolajeva

"Juvenile" Literature and British Society, 1850–1950
The Age of Adolescence
Charles Ferrall and Anna Jackson

Picturing the Wolf in Children's Literature
Debra Mitts-Smith

New Directions in Picturebook Research
Edited by Teresa Colomer, Bettina Kümmerling-Meibauer, Cecilia Silva-Díaz

The Role of Translators in Children's Literature
Invisible Storytellers
Gillian Lathey

The Children's Book Business
Lessons from the Long Eighteenth Century
Lissa Paul

Humor in Contemporary Junior Literature
Julie Cross

Innocence, Heterosexuality, and the Queerness of Children's Literature
Tison Pugh

Reading the Adolescent Romance
Sweet Valley and the Popular Young Adult Romance Novel
Amy S. Pattee

Irish Children's Literature and Culture
New Perspectives on Contemporary Writing
Edited by Valerie Coghlan and Keith O'Sullivan

Beyond Pippi Longstocking
Intermedial and International Perspectives on Astrid Lindgren's Works
Edited by Bettina Kümmerling-Meibauer and Astrid Surmatz

Contemporary English-Language Indian Children's Literature:
Representations of Nation, Culture, and the New Indian Girl
Michelle Superle

Re-visioning Historical Fiction
The Past through Modern Eyes
Kim Wilson

The Myth of Persephone in Girls' Fantasy Literature
Holly Virginia Blackford

Pinocchio, Puppets and Modernity
The Mechanical Body
Edited by Katia Pizzi

Crossover Picturebooks
A Genre for All Ages
Sandra L. Beckett

Peter Pan's Shadows in the Literary Imagination
Kirsten Stirling

Landscape in Children's Literature
Jane Suzanne Carroll

LANDSCAPE IN CHILDREN'S LITERATURE

JANE SUZANNE CARROLL

NEW YORK AND LONDON

First published 2011
by Routledge
711 Third Avenue, New York, NY 10017

Simultaneously published in the UK
by Routledge
2 Park Square, Milton Park, Abingdon, Oxfordshire OX14 4RN

First issued in paperback 2014

Routledge is an imprint of the Taylor & Francis Group, an informa business

© 2011 Taylor & Francis

The right of Jane Suzanne Carroll to be identified as author of this work has been asserted by her in accordance with sections 77 and 78 of the Copyright, Designs and Patents Act 1988.

All rights reserved. No part of this book may be reprinted or reproduced or utilised in any form or by any electronic, mechanical, or other means, now known or hereafter invented, including photocopying and recording, or in any information storage or retrieval system, without permission in writing from the publishers.

Trademark Notice: Product or corporate names may be trademarks or registered trademarks, and are used only for identification and explanation without intent to infringe.

Library of Congress Cataloging in Publication Data
Carroll, Jane Suzanne.
  Landscape in children's literature / Jane Suzanne Carroll.
    p. cm. — (Children's literature and culture series ; v. 84)
  Includes bibliographical references and index.
  1. Children's stories, English—History and criticism. 2. Landscapes in literature. 3. Setting (Literature) I. Title.
  PR830.C513C37 2012
  823.009'9282—dc23
                          2011048722

ISBN13: 978-0-415-80814-9 (hbk)
ISBN13: 978-1-138-79425-2 (pbk)

Typeset in Minion
by IBT Global.

For Lisa and for John

Contents

List of Illustrations		xi
Series Editor's Foreword		xiii
Acknowledgements		xv
	Introduction	1
1	The Sanctuary Topos: Sacred and Domestic Spaces	17
2	The Green Topos: Gardens, Farms, Wilderness	49
3	The Roadway Topos	91
4	The Lapsed Topos: Caves, Graves, and Ruins	133
5	Applications	169
Notes		185
Bibliography		225
Index		237

Illustrations

1.1	Houses at Abergnowlyn, Wales.	16
1.2	St. Cadfan's Church, Tywyn, Wales.	25
1.3	The Nine Maidens, Cornwall.	30
1.4	Llyn Barfog, Cwm Maethlon, Wales.	36
2.1	Mountainside at Tal y Llyn, Wales.	48
2.2	Cottage garden in Mevagissey, Cornwall.	51
2.3	Farmland near St. Austell, Cornwall.	59
2.4	View from Dynsynni Valley, Wales.	68
2.5	Riverbank at Pentewan, Cornwall.	69
2.6	Mist at Cader Idris, Wales.	81
2.7	Green man in St. Cadfan's Church, Tywyn, Wales.	83
2.8	The 'Mud Maid,' by Sue and Pete Hill, at The Lost Gardens of Heligan, Cornwall.	85
3.1	Track near Tintagel, Cornwall.	90
3.2	Street at Mevagissey, Cornwall.	95
3.3	Pathway through Cwm Maethlon, Wales.	107
3.4	Ghostly track leading towards the Nine Maidens, Cornwall.	127
4.1	Ruined house in Cwm Maethlon, Wales.	132
4.2	Stratified layers of rock, Boscastle, Cornwall.	137
4.3	Cave at Pentewan, Cornwall.	140
4.4	Ruined house at Pentewan, Cornwall.	157

Series Editor's Foreword

Dedicated to furthering original research in children's literature and culture, the Children's Literature and Culture series includes monographs on individual authors and illustrators, historical examinations of different periods, literary analyses of genres, and comparative studies on literature and the mass media. The series is international in scope and is intended to encourage innovative research in children's literature with a focus on interdisciplinary methodology.

Children's literature and culture are understood in the broadest sense of the term children to encompass the period of childhood up through adolescence. Owing to the fact that the notion of childhood has changed so much since the origination of children's literature, this Routledge series is particularly concerned with transformations in children's culture and how they have affected the representation and socialization of children. While the emphasis of the series is on children's literature, all types of studies that deal with children's radio, film, television, and art are included in an endeavor to grasp the aesthetics and values of children's culture. Not only have there been momentous changes in children's culture in the last fifty years, but there have also been radical shifts in the scholarship that deals with these changes. In this regard, the goal of the Children's Literature and Culture series is to enhance research in this field and, at the same time, point to new directions that bring together the best scholarly work throughout the world.

Jack Zipes

Acknowledgements

I am grateful to Susan Cooper for kind permission to reproduce material from her work and to Kate Glennon who was particularly helpful in preparing this volume. I wish to acknowledge The Lost Gardens of Heligan for permission to use the image of the Mud Maid in Chapter 2. I am grateful for permission to reproduce material from The Journal of Children's Literature Studies in Chapter 2. Thanks are due to Pauline Adams, Librarian and Archivist, Somerville College, Oxford for her kind help in sourcing information. I also wish to acknowledge The Irish Research Council for Humanities and Social Sciences for their generous support for this project in an earlier form.

This book is the product of many years' work but I could not have done it alone. I would like to thank my colleagues at Trinity College Dublin and at The Sussex Centre for Folklore, Fairy Tales and Fantasy and the University of Chichester, and all my family and friends for their help and support while I was researching and writing. I would especially like to thank Professor Amanda Piesse who gave me invaluable support, advice, and passion from the very beginning; Professor Peter Hunt who encouraged me to publish; Professor Bill Gray who was especially enthusiastic; Helen Conrad O'Briain for her help with the translations and editing, and for all the tea and books; my fearless proof-readers, Trish Ferguson, Dara Downey, Sorcha Ní Fhláinn, Hanna Hoorenman, and Derek Dunne; Jenny McDonnell, Anne Markey, Pádraic Whyte, and Patricia Kennon for their good advice; and C.P. who made a space for children and their books.

Many thanks are due to Karl Kinsella for his kindness, tireless encouragement, and for listening to me talk about landscapes when no one else would. I am also extremely grateful to Beth Rodgers, Jessica Longland, Adam Rudden, and Dermot Byrne for laughter in moments of despair and support in difficult times. I would also like to mention Marcus Hamilton because he said I had to.

I would like to thank Professor Jack Zipes, Elizabeth Levine, and Julie Ganz at Routledge for their patience and their hard work in getting this book to print and Eleanor Chan and the Page Composition team at IBT/Hamilton.

Finally, I want to thank my family for all their help and support; Alex Conroy, the best god-brother anyone could ask for; my sister, Laura, who reminded me that there was more to life; my dad, Fran, who drove me all across Wales and Cornwall and England taught me the value of hard work; and my mam, Linda, who introduced me to Mr. Jackson and taught me to love books.

PERMISSIONS

THE DARK IS RISING. Reprinted with the permission of Margaret K. McElderry Books, an imprint of Simon & Schuster Children's Publishing Division from THE DARK IS RISING by Susan Cooper. Text copyright © 1973 Susan Cooper; copyright renewed 2001 Susan Cooper.

GREENWITCH. Reprinted with the permission of Margaret K. McElderry Books, an imprint of Simon & Schuster Children's Publishing Division from GREENWITCH by Susan Cooper. Copyright © 1974 Susan Cooper; copyright renewed 2002 Susan Cooper.

THE GREY KING. Reprinted with the permission of Margaret K. McElderry Books, an imprint of Simon & Schuster Children's Publishing Division from THE GREY KING by Susan Cooper. Copyright © 1975 Susan Cooper; copyright renewed 2003 Susan Cooper.

Excerpted from OVER SEA, UNDER STONE by Susan Cooper. Copyright © 1966 Susan Cooper, and renewed 1994 by Susan Cooper Grant. Used by permission of Harcourt Children's Books, an imprint of Houghton Mifflin Harcourt Publishing Company. All rights reserved.

SILVER ON THE TREE. Reprinted with the permission of Margaret K. McElderry Books, an imprint of Simon & Schuster Children's Publishing Division from SILVER ON THE TREE by Susan Cooper. Copyright © 1977 Susan Cooper; copyright renewed 2005 Susan Cooper.

The Mud Maid" created by Sue and Pete Hill at The Lost Gardens of Heligan. The Lost Gardens of Heligan, Pentewan, St Austell, Cornwall. PL26 6EN. Open daily all year round from 10am daily (closed 24th and 25th December) Telephone: 01726 845100   Website: www.heligan.com

Introduction

Landscape is a central concern of canonical British fantasy for children,[1] and the emergent and 'increasingly complex'[2] nature of children's literature within the academy makes it ideally suited to the development of a new methodological approach to the landscapes of literature. Peter Hunt asserts that in children's literature 'places mean.'[3] However, even though this meaningful relationship with landscape is endemic in children's literature, it is by no means confined to children's books; Stephen Daniels and Simon Rycroft have observed that 'as a literary form, the novel is inherently geographical [...] made up of locations and settings, arenas and boundaries, perspectives and horizons.'[4] Landscape is a vital aspect of almost every text; action cannot take place in a void and so all texts contain some elements of landscape, be these elements urban or rural, public or domestic, artificial or organic, realistic or fantastic, positive or negative. Landscape shapes literature both contextually and textually and the same geographical, cultural, and socio-political concerns which affect real territories also form the contextual substrata which underlie any work of fiction. Robert Dunbar comments that 'all fiction, children's fiction included, is indicative to one extent or another of its geographical origins, even when it goes out of its way to ignore or to mask them.'[5] Landscape, then, provides not just the background against which the narrative is played out 'but the very stuff with which the story will be woven.'[6]

Whereas time was the chief concern of the Victorian fin-de-siècle and the early years of the twentieth century,[7] space has been the chief concern of the late twentieth and early twenty-first centuries and interest in landscape has increased exponentially since the Second World War.[8] In the early 1980s, Foucault suggested that 'the present epoch will, perhaps, be above all the epoch of space.'[9] Foucault's comments are not prophetic, merely observant, as in the late twentieth and early twenty-first century a shift in literary perspective has refocused critical attention away from narrative structure or character and towards the geographical settings of texts. The rise of landscape criticism can be traced to the end of the Second World

War when there was an inexorable rise in landscape studies—increased transport, tourism, and a sense of nationalism all contributed to a growing awareness of, and interest in, landscapes. For the first time, landscape has been acknowledged as a vitally important and 'inextricable'[10] part of the text. Now, as Siddall has pointed out, 'landscapes are more popular than any other subject.'[11]

Despite this popularity, recent critical approaches to landscapes in literature have been criticised as 'theoretically dormant.'[12] Whereas 'over the last twenty years geographers have become increasingly interested in various forms of literature as ways of investigating the meaning of landscapes'[13] many contemporary literary critics still overlook the work of geographers and landscape theorists.[14] As many children's texts 'originate in a sense of place'[15] such work may be especially useful in opening up new approaches to the study of children's literature. Tony Watkins suggests that geographical studies and particularly cultural geography which explores 'ideas of landscape, spatiality, utopia, globalisation, heritage and national identity, and geographies of gender and of race [...] could prove vital for the cultural study of children's literature and media.'[16] Of these factors, Watkins suggests that landscape is the 'most relevant'[17] for scholars of children's literature and advocates a renewed interest in the interpretation and interrogation of landscape in children's texts. In this study I will bring some of the elements of cultural geography to bear on fictional landscapes. But before a new critical approach to the landscapes of literature may be developed, the great divorce between what landscape means to geographers and what landscape means to writers and critics of fiction must be addressed.

Landscapes are at once geographic and historical, natural and cultural, experienced and represented, and present a spatial interface between human culture and physical terrain. Landscape is a perceived spatial area comprising of distinct topological features which are integrated to form a coherent and unified whole. The unique variation of these features gives each landscape a particular character which distinguishes it from others. Landscape is, then, a construct; a portion of land or territory that is shaped and given order either physically (through cultivation or building) or imaginatively (through art or literature). The interaction between geography and human culture transforms land into landscape. As Gussow and Wilbur suggest, 'the catalyst that converts any physical location—any environment if you will—into a place is the process of experiencing deeply.'[18] Human experience of territory—be it inhabited, viewed, remembered, or imagined—focalises and changes the nature of the site.

Despite their obviously artificial nature, literary landscapes may be considered in the same terms as any real territory; they too are influenced by historical and cultural factors and exist as shifting palimpsests on which 'traces of successive inscriptions from the complex experience of place'[19] may be read. Like real environments, literary landscapes are composed of a series of identifiable topological commonplaces—topoi—and the literary representations of such elements conform with traditional, morphological forms which make use of the same physical features and symbolic functions and support the same kind of narrative action. These topoi are embedded in the canonical tradition of landscape representation and have been distilled through centuries of repetition and use. Topoi are pure elements of landscape, irreducible in their basic components and unchanging in their significance. These morphological and topological elements are the focus of my study.

Tracing the correspondences between early twentieth-century morphological studies of both spaces and texts, I propose a new, critical relationship between literary and geographical studies which acknowledges the cultural, historical, and intertextual substrata which inform the appearance and function of landscapes in literature. Thus, informed by a range of disciplines, this new approach—topoanalysis—will provide a solid interdisciplinary basis for the future study of landscapes in literature.

In 1925 the American geographer Carl Ortwin Sauer published an essay called *The Morphology of Landscape* which sought to provide a structure for the analysis of landscapes by breaking landscape down into its component elements. Sauer suggests that all landscapes, no matter how distinctive, are shaped by a series or combination of these factors and forms. In 1928, scarcely three years later, Vladimir Propp published his *Morphology of the Folktale* which sought to show how stories, especially folktales, were made of interlinking, and often interchangeable, 'recurrent constants.'[20] Considering Propp's work alongside Sauer's has led me to consider that the morphological study of elements—be they elements of a landscape or elements of a narrative—can provide a readily adaptable critical framework which enables the systematic study of a wide range of subjects. Furthermore, as morphology is not simply 'the study of the component parts' but also the study 'of their relationship to each other and to the whole,'[21] it requires recognition that 'the phenomena that make up an area are not simply assorted but are associated, or interdependent.'[22] Thus, morphology—as a critical scaffold—allows both for the study of individual features in the landscape and their relationship to surrounding features.

This relationship inculcates an awareness of the history underlying the textual landscape. The objects within a landscape—and within a text—not only bear a relationship to contemporary objects, but also bear a relationship to objects that have gone before. Sauer suggests that 'we cannot form an idea of landscape except in terms of its time relations as well as of its space relations,'[23] and so any true study of landscape must consider 'the series of changes which the cultural landscape has undergone.'[24] The study of the changes in the landscape which take place over time is a discipline in its own right: landscape history.[25]

Treating landscape not simply as a backdrop to human action,[26] or as a surface that can be apprehended in a single gaze,[27] but as a complex series of strata where human culture and geographical space intersect, landscape history seeks to understand and account for the influence of the past upon the present territory. This interdisciplinary approach to landscape, combining the fieldwork of geography with the documentary research of history, gained popularity in the years after the Second World War, especially in Britain where W. G. Hoskins, Jacquetta Hawkes, and Sir Cyril Fox were among the most influential figures of the movement.[28]

The principles of landscape history are straightforward. As Hoskins puts it, 'everything in the landscape is older than we think,'[29] and so we cannot begin to understand a place until we first acquire an understanding of the history of that place. Whereas space was once treated as 'the order of co-existing things' and time as 'the order of successive things,'[30] landscape historians began to view landscape as an embodiment of both space and time, not just layers of rock and clay but complex strata of time and history, where one could see 'the ghostly outline of an old landscape beneath the superficial covering of the contemporary.'[31] For landscape historians, unlike archaeologists or geographers, the primary aim is not to study the past in isolation but to see how the past has influenced the present age. For Hawkes, 'the continued presence of the past'[32] is manifested in the landscape in which 'dark, rarely disturbed layers [...] have accumulated, as mould accumulates in a forest, through the shedding of innumerable lives since the beginning of life.'[33] Thus, landscapes began to be viewed as historical texts, as deep palimpsests on which the traces of the past are still visible even when the present age is being inscribed.

The residues of the past are not simply physical. Simon Schama asserts that landscapes are 'built up as much from strata of memory as from layers of rock.'[34] To trace the history of a place and to see that history reflected in the present time 'is to be made vividly aware of the endurance of core myths.'[35] Thus, the principles of landscape history are not confined to physical or geographical territories but may be extended to include imaginative, figurative, and even fictional landscapes. In adapting and developing the principles of landscape history to accommodate fictional landscapes I propose that if one is to understand a fictional landscape—a literary landscape—one must also understand the fictional antecedents and literary histories which inhabit the text. Indeed, as Ackerman suggests, 'the best way to understand the nature of a convention is to discover for what reason and under what circumstances it originated.'[36] Curtius proposes that all fictional landscapes 'are to be understood in the light of a continuous literary tradition.'[37] To my mind, all texts are part of a continuous cultural tradition and the topoi of modern fictional landscapes are best understood in terms of their intertextual provenances.

Regarding modern texts as the surface of the literary landscape and treating older texts as the cultural substrata which exert influence over the shape and nature of the surface, I will demonstrate the multi-layered nature of fictional landscapes. By tracing the origin and development of four individual topoi, I will show that whereas landscape is central to twentieth- and twenty-first-century children's literature, the forms and functions of those landscapes are embedded in much earlier literature.

In tracing landscape topoi, it is important to acknowledge that literatures from around the globe have their own distinct canonical models and their own unique set of topoi. The continuous tradition is strongest among texts which emerge from and engage with the same geographical territories. Although classical texts such as Virgil's *Eclogues* and *Georgics* provide the exemplar for Mediterranean landscapes, medieval vernacular literature offers the first articulations of vernacular Northern European landscapes and so provides a more obvious source for the landscapes of modern British children's fantasy. Indeed, there is evidence that the very concept of landscape may be traced to these texts. Although 'landscape' is commonly thought to originate from '*landschap*', a Dutch painters' term which entered the English language sometime in the seventeenth century[38] the word '*landscipe*' is native to English and appears in the Anglo-Saxon *Genesis B*, when Satan, addressing the fallen angels, declares '*Ne ic geseah swich ladran landscipe*'—'I have never seen such a loathsome landscape'.[39] Here, the word 'landscape' clearly refers to a perceived geographical territory. The word is, most likely, a compound of the noun '*land*' which means much the same as it does today and the verb '*Scippan*' meaning 'to make' or 'to give shape to.' Thus, for the medieval mind, landscape was a construct which united ideas of nature and culture. The Anglo-Saxon origins of both the word and the sense of 'landscape' as it is used in English today further validates the use of Anglo-Saxon literature and other contemporary Northern European literature as a touchstone for any discussion of the textual representations of landscape in modern children's fantasy.

The Limits of the Present Study

Whereas topoanalysis is applicable to all literary landscapes, it is simply not possible to trace all aspects of all landscapes in all traditions within such a small space. Elsewhere I have examined imaginary landscapes and mindscapes but here I will focus exclusively on physical and tangible spaces.[40] For the purposes of this study, it is necessary to draw sample texts from a closed geographical and temporal frame. Based on the footfall approach advocated by Sauer—which advocates close contact with the landscape achieved through slow exploration and personal observation—and the closely detailed work of landscape historians such as Hoskins and Hawkes, it is appropriate to demonstrate the value of my methodology by the application of these theories to a limited number of texts. Also, given that an authentic reading of landscape must take both the horizontal and vertical aspects of space into consideration, the texts chosen must demonstrate an awareness of the source texts in which the topoi are first presented and must also have a close relationship with contemporary literature. The texts selected are contemporary and originate from the same geographical area, and also portray a similarly closed fictional landscape. This increases the likelihood of identifying correspondences between these texts and, in turn, makes it easier to identify the intertextual sources for the fictional landscapes. The ideal subject will be acknowledged as representative of a wider range of texts and as having made a significant impact upon the tradition of children's literature; that is to say, it will be canonical both in its attitude and in its reception. Above all else, the chosen texts must have a strong sense of landscape. The fictional landscape should comprise a variety of interconnected topoi and, within the texts these topoi should be treated in a conscious, consistent, and coherent fashion. Based on these criteria, I have selected Susan Cooper's *The Dark Is Rising Sequence* (1965–1977) as the ideal test case for this study.

Cooper's *The Dark Is Rising Sequence*

Cooper's *Sequence* is central to the canon of British children's literature. Written during the 'Golden Age' of British children's literature, it has remained popular and influential since the first of the five books appeared in 1965.[41] In 1977, *The Dark Is Rising* and *Greenwitch* were highlighted by *The English Journal* as exemplary fantasies for young readers[42] and in 1980 a group of academics reflecting on the children's canon singled out *The Grey King* as a potential classic of the fantasy genre:

> Written in an exquisite style, treating a beautiful rural life with reverence while finding under it an exciting and satisfying sub-structure of universal meaning, the entire series of *The Dark Is Rising*, but especially the glorious *Grey King*, suggest that Susan Cooper has created a fantasy classic.[43]

To date there have been nine complete reprints of each title and three reprints of the collected edition since its publication in 1983.[44] The second book of the *Sequence*, *The Dark Is Rising*, was dramatised for BBC radio in 1995 and various audio-book editions of each title appeared between 1995 and 1997. In 2007 a special collected edition of the *Sequence* was published to coincide with the release of *The Dark Is Rising: The Seeker*, a film by Walden Media.[45]

These numerous reprints and adaptations attest to the sustained popularity of the texts among the general public, but Cooper's work has also been well received critically. The *Sequence* has been awarded two Carnegie medals, two Tir Na N'Og awards, a Newbery Prize, and a Horn Book Award.[46] The popular and canonical position of Cooper's work means that the *Sequence* reflects many of the dominant generic trends, not just in terms of landscape, but in terms of narrative structure, character, and theme to the extent that it is 'almost a ground plan for modern epic fantasy.'[47] Therefore, it may be said to be unusually representative of children's literature as a whole, making it an ideal arena for the investigation and development of a new critical approach to children's literature.

In spite of its prominence and popularity, there has been little critical work dedicated to the *Sequence*. Cooper has been the subject of a biographical study, Nina Mikkelsen's *Susan Cooper*, which is 'designed to extend our awareness of the special talents [Cooper] brings to readers'[48] rather than to provide a formal, critical engagement with her fiction. Whereas reviews of Cooper's work have been extremely positive, such critical essays as exist misalign and even misrepresent it. She has been accused of being anti-feminist[49] and overly nostalgic[50] and, in spite of the fact that *The Dark Is Rising Sequence* was completed in 1978 and Cooper was by then living and working in America, of upholding the xenophobic ideologies of 'Thatcherite, conservative Britain.'[51] Elsewhere, Cooper's work has been the subject of comparative studies and theme-based criticism including Timothy Rex Wadham's 1994 dissertation "Light from the Lost Land: A Contextual Response to Susan Cooper's *The Dark Is Rising* Sequence" and Charles Butler's *Four British Fantasists: Place and Culture in the Children's Fantasies of Penelope Lively, Alan Garner, Diana Wynne Jones and Susan Cooper*. Wadham's dissertation focuses on the influence of background and environmental factors—experiences of the war, contemporary art and music—on Cooper's writing, and relies on finding direct and often partial correspondences between elements in Cooper's texts and contemporary movements in music and art. For example, he cites M. C. Escher as an influence on her depiction of the Lost Land but neglects to trace the influence of fantasy literature or Welsh folklore on the same scene, thereby providing a somewhat incomplete approach to the context which gave rise to the texts.[52] Butler's *Four British Fantasists* also provides a contextual reading of Cooper's work, and places her firmly in among the canon of British authors, drawing out many of the common thematic and generic qualities of British children's fantasy written in the 1960s and 1970s, but the comparative nature of the study necessarily limits its depth and detail concerning Cooper's work.

Cooper and Landscapes

The central role of landscape in Susan Cooper's fiction is well recognised. Dick Abrahamson and Barbara Kiefer note that a sense of place is 'necessary to the best fantasy and [a] vital [...] part of *The Dark Is Rising* and *Grey King*.'[53]

Colin Manlove states that 'Cooper's sense of place is one of her strongest suits: her fantasy is continually bound up with geography.'[54] Similarly, Wadham remarks that Cooper's work is distinguished by a 'remarkable sensitivity to setting'[55] and elsewhere Margaret Esmonde asserts that 'her strong point [...] is an absolute and unfailing familiarity with the landscape'[56] of Cornwall, Buckinghamshire, and North Wales. Cooper herself is acutely aware of the importance of landscape and speaks eloquently of how her relationship with landscape informs and affects the representations of space in her fiction. In a personal interview she says that she is 'very conscious [of geography] all the time, whether or not I'm writing [...] the places are a part of me.'[57] Elsewhere, she describes the central importance of landscape to *The Dark Is Rising Sequence*, particularly to the last four books which were written after she emigrated to America:

> I was extremely homesick, and the landscapes of the last four books are all my places in England. I would go into them in my head, even though I was actually sitting in Winchester, Massachusetts [...]. First, Buckinghamshire, where I grew up and where Will Stanton and his family live. And then mid-Wales [...] I've always been obsessed by the place [...] I think the Welsh part of me is very powerful, and to this day when I go to Wales, I feel I'm going home. My third place is Cornwall [...] and if there were such a thing as Old Magic, these are the places—Wales, Cornwall—where it would be.[58]

Even though Cooper speaks of these remembered landscapes with fondness, she resists romanticising them, regarding 'Wales as tough and mysterious and secret, not romantic.'[59] Thus, she ensures that her relationship with the places in the *Sequence* is an authentic one in spite of the homesickness which prompted her detailed topographical descriptions.[60]

Cooper's sense of landscape also encompasses many of the key elements of landscape history identified earlier. Charles Butler traces her interest in landscape back to her reading of Jacquetta Hawkes's *A Land* (1951) in her teens.[61] Hawkes—and her husband J. B. Priestley—made a distinct impression on Cooper as a young author. Cooper writes of the 'huge influence' Hawkes had on her as a girl, recalling 'walking over a piece of Warwickshire with her and watching bewildered as she picked up a fossil here, a potsherd there, told me casually what they were, and tossed them away again.'[62] Hawkes's influence is significant because it provides a direct and indelible connection between Cooper's work and the Landscape History movement which was so prevalent in post-war Britain. Hawkes made a significant contribution to the movement, publishing practical texts such as *A Guide to the Prehistoric and Roman Monuments in England and Wales* (1951) as well as theoretical works such as *A Land* (1953) which encouraged amateur interest in landscape history. A contemporary reviewer saw *A Land* as 'an epitome of the geological and archaeological history of the British Isle, presented in a form attractive to a wide circle of readers who would probably never open a book on geology.'[63] Hawkes's work is still regarded as having seminal importance to the discipline,[64] and Charles Butler describes her *Guide* as 'the perfect guide, indeed, with which to tramp around the Neolithic henges and Iron Age hill forts of Britain.'[65]

The key idea here, although Butler does not explicitly acknowledge it, is that of tramping around, that is to say, acquiring footfall knowledge of the landscape. Although Cooper's recollection of Hawkes is apparently casual, it reveals that in taking Cooper, then a schoolgirl, on this walk through Warwickshire, Hawkes introduced her to the footfall method, and thus encouraged her to form a direct and symbiotic relationship with landscape. Hawkes inculcated in Cooper a rich 'sense of the continuum of place and time'[66] and 'a strong sense of the mythic history of the land [and] an awareness of the past.'[67] For Cooper, as for Hawkes, 'place implies time.'[68] Thus, for Cooper, landscape is not merely a background factor in her fiction but a vital and richly resonant setting. Cooper's relationship with Hawkes puts her—and her work—firmly in connection with the landscape history movement which forms the basis of my methodology.

The embedded nature of landscape within Cooper's fiction makes her work ideally suited to landscape-based study and although a concern for landscape is reflected in all of her fiction,[69] it is strongest in *The Dark Is Rising Sequence*. The very first line of *Over Sea, Under Stone*, the first book of the *Sequence*, expresses a concern for the figure in space; Barney Drew, disembarking from the train in St. Austell and looking for Merriman Lyon asks 'where is he?'[70] This opening line recalls the opening line of Shakespeare's *Hamlet*—'Who's there?'—in that it could almost be taken as a synecdoche for the whole text. Just as *Hamlet* is centrally concerned with identity, the 'where is he?' that opens Cooper's *Sequence* is indicative of a primary concern with space, landscape and the position of the human figure within geographical space. Each subsequent book shares this concern for space, a concern which is reflected in the quintet's topographical titles. The first in the quintet, *Over Sea, Under Stone*, evokes not only a sense of place but, as is revealed in the novel, a sense of a very specific place. *The Dark Is Rising* examines how atmospheric conditions impact upon the landscape. The Greenwitch who provides the title of the third book is a wicker-work folklore figure connected with the harvest sacrifice. The title of the fourth book, *The Grey King* refers to Cader Idris, a mountain range in North Wales near the Dyfi estuary. *The Grey King* was originally titled *Fire on the Mountain*, a title which appears to suggest the landscape connection more strongly but is, on consideration, rather weaker than *The Grey King* as it disregards the symbolic relationship between the landscape and the mythological figures that inform its meaning.[71] The title of the final book, *Silver on the Tree*, refers to the image of mistletoe on oak. Cooper's settings are fictionalised but have their roots in the reality of faithfully observed, 'specific'[72] geographical places. Trewissick, the Cornish fishing village where the Drews and Will Stanton spend the holidays, is loosely based on Mevagissey.[73] Cooper takes liberties with the topography, adding a stone circle to one of the nearby headlands and imposing the three-storey Grey House on the hill beside the harbour where no such building currently exists, but the descriptions of the harbour and the village streets are relatively accurate. Cooper does not alter the names of the towns that appear in *The Grey King* and *Silver on the Tree*, the Welsh books of the quintet. Tywyn and Aberdyfi are transcribed directly from reality, down to such details as the interior of St. Cadfan's church with its stocky pillars and recumbent knight.[74] It is interesting to note that Cadfan's Way, the magic ley-line which Will follows over the mountains, existed in the form of Llwybr Cadfan, (lat. 52°38'37", long. 3°58'47"–57'18") 'a clearly marked pathway [that] is still used by miners, and its name is well known' in the 1920s.[75]

However, the geographic origins of the *Sequence* are not my focus here. My purpose is not to find simple correspondences between real places and imaginary ones, but to use the fictionalised landscapes of Cooper's *Sequence* as a framework with which to trace the origin and development of literary topoi. As I have established, Cooper's awareness of landscape is firmly tied to the landscape history movement and, therefore, to an awareness of the historical and cultural substrata of any given place. Topologically, there are significant physical joins and overlaps in Cooper's landscape, but it is also full of temporal and mythic seams. The physical topoi meet over temporal fault-lines where the reader can mine for history, myth, and analogue. Embedded within Cooper's landscapes is a profound sense of the landscapes of traditional and canonical work.

Cooper and Intertext

Drout notes that 'although critics have focused on Cooper's reworking of Celtic and Arthurian legends, they have missed or ignored a third strand of the author's "magical medievalism" (the phrase is Peter Goodrich's), her use of Anglo-Saxon source materials.'[76] Indeed, as Donna R. White notes, 'Cooper uses almost nothing of the Mabinogi in her books.'[77] Accordingly, my study will primarily focus on the medieval, and especially Anglo-Saxon, intertexts of Cooper's work which she became familiar with as an Oxford undergraduate in the 1950s although I will refer to Welsh literature where relevant. Cooper's connections with the canon and her awareness of early English literature in which the landscape topoi relevant to British children's literature are first articulated are easily established. She read English at Oxford, graduating in 1956. There she attended lectures by C. S. Lewis and J. R. R. Tolkien which Charles Butler claims had 'a significant effect' on her later literary efforts.[78] Cooper notes that Tolkien's lectures on Anglo-Saxon Literature were an especially significant part of her undergraduate career.[79] Butler traces direct correspondences between Cooper's work and Tolkien's but admits that 'the influence, real or imagined, of Tolkien and Lewis has [...] probably [...] had a distorting effect, and obscured the importance of other, arguably more relevant literary influences, such as John Masefield and E. Nesbit' on her work.[80] Whether or not Tolkien and Lewis have obscured literary influences on the *Sequence* they have certainly masked other academic influences on Cooper's career. A significant and tangible impact—apparently overlooked by Butler—stems from the women academics who tutored Cooper from term to term at Somerville College: Ursula Brown (later Dronke) and Joan Turville-Petre for Old and Middle English; Rosemary Syfret for seventeenth-century literature; Catherine Ing for nineteenth-century literature; and Mary Lascelles for Shakespeare, Elizabethan literature, and eighteenth-century literature.[81] Even though Mary Lascelles was Cooper's main contact before coming to Oxford, it seems likely that it was Ursula Dronke, a 'brilliant but remote scholar'[82] and a celebrated medievalist and former Reader of Old Norse at the University of Oxford, who had the greatest impact on the young Cooper.

Until now, the extent of Dronke's influence on Cooper seems to have gone unnoticed by critics but it is something that Cooper herself freely acknowledges. In 1967, Cooper sent Dronke a copy of *The Dark Is Rising* 'and she wrote a nice letter back saying she'd always thought I had promise. Perhaps she liked the fact that I had tucked inside the story a quotation from the line written in Anglo-Saxon around King Alfred's Jewel, the greatest treasure of Oxford's Ashmolean Museum.'[83] Cooper's reference to the Alfred Jewel and its Anglo-Saxon inscription is indicative of two things—first, that Cooper understands Old English. This may seem a very basic point but it does mean that Cooper remembered the Anglo-Saxon texts which she studied under Dronke. These texts, as I will demonstrate, underlie much of the intertextual background for the *Sequence*. Second, it indicates that Cooper deliberately constructed relationships between her texts and the cultural and mythic history of Britain, acquired and learned through footfall knowledge of the literature as well as the landscape.

Cooper's interest in Old and Middle English, and, to an extent, Old Norse is clearly evidenced in her fiction. The Anglo-Saxon texts, more than those of any other literary period, form the intertextual basis which underlies each of the five books in the *Sequence*. The reference to the Alfred Jewel 'tucked into' *The Dark Is Rising* is only one of many such borrowings. Michael Drout notes that sources for the *Sequence* 'include Beowulf, the Anglo-Saxon Chronicle, various Old English poems, and the persona of King Alfred.'[84] Over the course of this book I will discuss the intertextual position of these medieval texts, specifically when Cooper draws on them as sources for landscape and setting. Perhaps the most significant of Cooper's references to Anglo-Saxon literature comes early in the first book, *Over Sea, Under Stone*, when Merriman Lyon explains the nature of the conflict between the Light and the Dark to the three Drew children. He says that

> In the old days [...] the struggle between good and evil was more bitter and open than it is now. That struggle goes on all around us all the time, like two armies fighting. And sometimes one of them seems to be winning and sometimes the other, but neither has ever triumphed altogether.[85]

His words are not an empty formula but a complex allusion to the Old English Maxims which Cooper studied under Dronke. The Maxims express a series of universal truths which must be accepted because they will never change. Among other things, the poet states that

> Good shall struggle against evil, youth against age,
> Life shall strive against death, light against darkness,
> army against army, one enemy against the other,
> foe must fight against hated foe, wrangling over the land,
> inflicting injury.[86]

Merriman's words closely resemble the form and the sentiments of the Maxims and it is clear that Cooper's vision of the Light and Dark, not as abstracts, but as solid entities which struggle against one another 'like two armies fighting' derives directly from the poem. That the intertextual position of the Maxims—and by extension of Old English literature—is firmly in place in *Over Sea, Under Stone* refutes the popular notion that this text is somehow thematically and structurally unrelated to the others in the *Sequence*.[87] Thus, the central idea of the *Sequence*, the struggle of the Light against the Dark, and the ethos with which it is expressed, is fundamentally rooted in Anglo-Saxon literature.

Just as Jacquetta Hawkes connects Cooper with the landscape history movement, Ursula Dronke provides the link between Cooper and medieval literature. Thus the connections between Cooper's work and earlier literature are established. Cooper is acutely aware of these connections, saying 'every beginning, every opening page, has in it an echo of what has gone before. Literature is a chain in which every link is connected to the one before it and the one after. And so is life.'[88] For Cooper, an ability to navigate the geographical landscape is bound up with an ability to navigate its embedded mythic and historical past. Drawing on the techniques of landscape history I examine the intertextual substratum of the five texts in the *Sequence*. Thus, a major part of this study is the identification and interpretation of such elements in Cooper's *Sequence* as are analogous to the landscapes of canonical children's literature and medieval literature. For example, the ruined buildings and crumbling graveyards of Cooper's fiction have their foundations in the *dústscéawung* poetry of the Anglo-Saxon period, such as *The Ruin, The Wanderer, Seafarer*,[89] but also recall modern children's texts such as Penelope Lively's *The House in Norham Gardens* (1974), Lucy M. Boston's *The Children of Green Knowe* (1954), J. K. Rowling's *Harry Potter and the Prisoner of Azkaban* (1999) and Neil Gaiman's *The Graveyard Book* (2008). Having identified such analogues, I conduct a comparative analysis of the landscape elements which are common to both historic and modern texts and so determine the features which are intrinsic to and which typify each topos.

The Structure of this Book

Taking the principles of landscape history and combining them with the earlier morphological studies, I develop a new approach to the study of fictional landscapes. These theories enable a study of landscape in literature, where the landscape is not merely an unnoticed background to the text but is a powerful medium in the production of meaning and action in a text. This project springs from the studies described above, thus asserting an organic and interactive relationship between narrative meaning and geographical space within literature. Through my first four chapters, I hope to address a series of crucial questions, using Cooper's *Sequence* as a test case; can the methodologies used to decipher the meaning of the physical landscape inform the production and understanding of literary landscapes? Can fictional landscapes be understood in terms of topoi? What is the function of each individual topos and how are these topoi established? How do children's texts interact with and relate to these established topoi? Most importantly: how can topoanalysis be adapted as a useful critical tool for students of literature? My fifth chapter demonstrates how these questions, and topoanalysis, can be used to analyse a wide range of texts.

Combining Sauer's interest in the physical appearance of landscape elements with Propp's interest in the narrative function of his elements, I categorise the elements of literary landscapes in terms of their physical form and symbolic function. I identify four main landscape elements or topoi which are distinguished by their physical and symbolic attributes and which are central to the landscapes of British children's fantasy: the sanctuary, the green space, the roadway, and the lapsed space. The term *topos* is chosen for several reasons. First, the term refers not only to a place but to the actions occurring in that place. Second, it is already a commonplace in landscape criticism in works such as Curtius' *European Literature and the Latin Middle Ages* and Bachelard's *The Poetics of Space* (1958). Bachelard also proposes the word

14 • Landscape in Children's Literature

'topoanalysis' as 'the systematic psychological study of the sites of our intimate lives.'⁹⁰ As a phenomenologist, Bachelard's interest lay in the relationship between real places and the human consciousness. Taking Bachelard's idea of a systematised study of the relationship between humanity and environment, I suggest that topoanalysis may be adapted to provide a means of understanding the influence of fictional locations upon fictional characters (in which psychological analysis is all but defunct). Combining this topoanalysis with morphological studies and landscape history, I provide a new approach to fictional landscapes.

The first part of each of the first four chapters is devoted to the morphological study of the physical forms and symbolic functions of one of these topoi. The second part of each chapter, the landscape history aspect, traces the origins of these four topoi back to their earliest inception—to the earliest literature which relates to the same geographical territory and thus contains references to the same range of topoi—showing how the topos functioned within medieval and pre-modern literature (for example: *Beowulf*, the *Mabinogion*, *Snorra Edda*). I have particularly focused on those medieval texts which are widely available in both their original forms and in translation. All translations are my own, unless otherwise stated. The third part of each chapter examines the role of the topos in canonical children's texts; having identified the origins of the topos, I then trace the development of these spaces in late nineteenth, twentieth, and early twenty-first century children's literature (such as Wilde 1888, Pearce 1958, Lively 1972). The fourth and final section of each chapter is dedicated to a detailed analysis of the topos and its symbolic and literary functions as manifested in the *Sequence*, with particular emphasis on the ways in which it upholds or subverts these topological elements. The identification, interrelation and interpretation of topoi are thus established.

Chapter One investigates the function of the sanctuary topos in its two manifestations, the domestic space, and the sacred space. The physical and symbolic liminality of these spaces is reflected in their dualistic connotations, such as those of safety and danger. This chapter investigates how these spaces allow for moments of safety and danger and examines the intertextual background and origins of the topos.

Chapter Two compares cultivated and spontaneous green spaces, analysing the dichotomous tensions which underscore the green space and examining especially the relationship between death and the green space in the *Sequence* and in canonical source texts.

Chapter Three treats roadways and railways as subversive spaces and examines the relationship between physical journeys, temporal journeys, and metaphysical journeys with special emphasis on the effect of the roadway topos upon personal identity.

Chapter Four examines lapsed spaces. Ruins and chthonic spaces—caves and graves—expose the palimpsestic layers of history and myth in the landscape and mediate between the past and the present. This chapter examines the significance of time in these spaces and analyses the literary antecedents of the topos.

In Chapter Five I propose topoanalysis as a rich critical method for the study and understanding of children's literature and indicate how my findings may be expanded upon. I provide brief topoanalytical studies of three other children's texts; John Masefield's *The Box of Delights* (1935), Alan Garner's *The Owl Service* (1967) and Meg Rosoff's *How I Live Now* (2004), demonstrating the generic value of such a methodological critical approach and demonstrating that whereas Cooper's *Sequence* is the test case, the methodology holds good when applied elsewhere.

Figure 1.1 Houses at Abergnowlyn, Wales. ©Jane Carroll.

Chapter One
The Sanctuary Topos
Sacred and Domestic Spaces

The desire to shape and order land and to create landscape may be expressed, at its most basic, as 'the passion for building enclosures.'[1] Enclosed, bounded, and limited spaces dominate the built environment and, accordingly, are among the most common features in literary representations of landscape. Yi-Fu Tuan suggests that 'nature is too diffuse, its stimuli too powerful and conflicting, to be directly accessible to the human mind and sensibility'[2] and so must be mediated through architectural forms which 'demarcate and intensify forms of social life.'[3] Focusing on sacred spaces, on enclosures which are set apart from other aspects of the built environment and distinguished from the rest of the landscape by virtue of their sacred nature,[4] this chapter will examine the role of enclosed spaces in children's literature. Positing the home as a sanctuary, I suggest a new way of reading the domestic dwelling spaces as they are represented in such texts.

The architectural characteristics and symbolic functions of the sanctuary topos are closely related. Three main attributes, which signify metaphysically and are expressed physically, characterise the topos. First, the sacred space has a strong vertical dimension. Whereas landscape, just like the format of a paper document, is generally imagined and represented as horizontal, the sacred space transcends the basic geometric plane by extending on a vertical as well as horizontal axis. As we shall see, this verticality is not unique to the sacred space. The lapsed topos, which is the focus of Chapter Four, also makes use of vertical—albeit chthonic—directional aspects. This verticality is spiritual as well as physical and the space 'allows for passage between different levels of reality,'[5] thus providing an interface between the mundane and the sacred. Second, the sacred space has strongly demarcated boundaries.[6] Sharon Gerstel notes that whereas there are 'material expression[s] of [...] visual limits' there are also sensory and emotional barriers in place around the sacred zone, and that 'prohibition, sanction and fear also establish boundaries.'[7] Third, and perhaps most importantly, the sacred space has a central chamber or space which is, in effect, the heart of the topos. This central space may hold an object 'vested with real and symbolic importance in and beyond the act of worship, an object that compels notice and demands response [...] a book, or a scroll, an image, a relic, even a sacred stone.'[8] Thus, the space has a central focal point. By extension, the sanctuary may represent 'the centre, the axis or the navel of the world,'[9] and so becomes a focal point for the surrounding community. Even if it is not located at the direct centre of the civic space, it is a site 'on which the feelings and senses of the people [are] deeply engaged.'[10] These spaces are sanctified through their form, contents, and attitudes and reactions of the community towards them.

The Home as Sacred Space

Sacred space is often closely conflated with domestic space as the same physical and symbolic elements which distinguish sacred spaces also characterise domestic spaces. The sanctuary is 'a house of the gods'[11] and the boundaries of the sacred zone may be likened to the walls of a house.[12] As Hamilton and Spicer have observed, the Indo-European sacred space is closely modelled on the shape of the house; for instance, in Celtic societies which favoured round dwellings with a central hearth, the typical temple is also circular with a altar or sacred fire placed at the exact centre; and the style of churches and cathedrals across Northern Europe generally reflects the hall-style dwelling common in medieval times.[13] Just as the domestic space provides a frame of reference which enables a greater understanding of sacred places, the paradigms associated with such sacred places may, in turn, enable a greater understanding of domestic spaces.

Our understanding of the home is authenticated only if it is considered as a sacred space and as part of the sanctuary topos. Edward Relph cautions against the dilution of the symbolic function of the home by treating it as synonymous with the term 'house' which brings about a 'splitting of the functions associated with it.'[14] The mass-produced desacralised house which results from and is expressed by modernist and post-modernist architecture often deliberately subverts the dialectical relationship between interior and exterior space. By embracing these 'homogenous and neutral' spaces, the structure becomes a secular 'machine for living in.'[15] Whereas the function of the house may be narrowly defined as 'a shelter against heat, cold, rain, thieves and the inquisitive' and 'a certain number of cells appropriated to cooking, work and personal life'[16] the function of a home—as an aspect of the sanctuary topos—is far broader.

The home is sanctified because it reflects, on a microcosmic level, the world as a whole. Humans, as made in their god's image, sacralise a space by making it their own, by shaping it according to their needs and desires. Eliade notes that

> to settle in a territory is [...] equivalent to consecrating it. [...] Establishment in a particular place, organizing it, inhabiting it, are acts that presuppose an existential choice—the choice of the universe that one is prepared to assume by 'creating' it. Now this universe [the home] is always a replica of the paradigmatic universe created and inhabited by the gods; hence it shares in the sanctity of the gods' work.[17]

As the human body may be read as a version of the cosmos, the home which houses, shelters and protects that body acquires similar associations. Thus, home is at once a personal, localised place and a microcosmic version of the world. For Edward Casey, it is the 'first universe'[18] where, as Eliade suggests, 'the roof symbolizes the dome of the sky; the floor represents earth, the four walls the four directions of cosmic space.'[19]

The home shares in the physical and symbolic attributes of the sanctuary topos; it too is characterised by verticality, strict boundaries and an intense, interiorising central focus. Like other sacred spaces it 'is imagined as a vertical being. It rises upwards,' and this verticality is confirmed by 'the polarity of cellar and attic.'[20] Like other sanctuaries, the domestic space is is secured and distinguished from the rest of the world by a series of clearly delineated boundaries, causing it to stand 'apart from the wilderness'[21] and from the profane world. The space is often partitioned internally too; thresholds, walls, windows, doors, roofs, hearths, attics, basements, and stairwells demarcate areas of the home which have their own distinct function. These demarcations affect the behaviour of the occupants. Irene Cieraad points out that 'domestic borders are not just materialised in brick and mortar, but are also confirmed and expressed in the residents' behaviour towards visitors.'[22] The rituals enacted on crossing the threshold of the domestic space serve to remind us that the borders of the home are also the borders between public and private, family and community, self and other.[23] The dialectic of self and other is especially important as the home is a highly exclusive zone, and the things gathered there form a carefully selected collection. The group of people admitted is similarly select. Thus, the threshold 'filters the crudities of nature, the lawlessness of society, and produces an atmosphere of temporary well-being, where vigour can be renewed for contact with the outside.'[24] These boundaries allow the centre of the home to become 'a concentrated being'[25] and an 'idealised'[26] rarefied space.

Whereas the majority of sacred places are appropriated to a special purpose, the home is appropriated to some person or persons. So whereas temples and churches and standing stones provide a link between a deity and the mundane world, the home, as a centre of human identity, acts as a nexus between the world and the Self. Home is the 'focus of personal sentiments [and] the meanings associated with it lie at the core of a persona's identity.'[27] As a place of profound attachment, the domestic space has, for many people, 'socially endowed and shared meanings that touch on all aspects of their lives, helping shape *who* they are by virtue of *where* they are.'[28]

In literature, 'landscape and identity reinforce one another'[29] to the extent that 'place is identity'[30] and setting is 'inextricable from character.'[31] In literature, where all places are significant, the relationship between location and identity reaches its climax in the representation of the home which becomes 'a logical extension and reflection of the self.'[32] Moreover, as John Rennie Short suggests, the home—the true sacralised house—functions as a meeting place between the self and the world. It is

> a nodal point in a whole series of polarities; sanctuary-outside; family-community; space-place; inside-outside; private-public; domestic-social; spare-time-work-time; feminine-masculine; heart-mind; Being-Becoming. These are not stable categories; they are both solidified and undermined as they play out their meaning and practice in and through the home.[33]

The key element of Short's vision of the home as sacred space is play: the fluctuating interactions, differences, challenges, and games and rituals which are enacted at the threshold, on the meeting point between the private cosmos and the universe. These negotiations and interactions are central to the narrative function of the home in literature.

The Symbolic Function of Home

Whereas Pauline Dewan sees the built environment and nature as 'incongruous elements'[34] in the landscape, the home, when considered as a sacred space, becomes a site of integration, of communion between the Self and the wider world. Just as the sacred place provides a point of contact between the earth and the gods, the home is also a point of contact—it is the nexus between the individual and the physical environment. Providing a point at which the human body, the built environment and the natural landscape come together, the home is the site where the connection between human and landscape is at its most intense, where the boundaries between person and place, between the Self and the landscape, dissolve altogether.

Although it may be 'hermetically closed,'[35] the borders of the home are not completely inviolable, lest the dwelling-place becomes a prison. The boundaries between home and universe are, as Gaston Bachelard notes, 'painful on both sides.'[36] In the sacralised home, the threshold acts as 'the limit, the boundary, the frontier that distinguishes and opposes two worlds—and at the same time the paradoxical place where those worlds communicate, where passage from the profane to the sacred world becomes possible.'[37] These liminal areas are, as Homi Bhabha suggests, 'the connective tissue that constructs the difference.'[38] They both separate and join adjacent spaces and, as such, allow the home to operate as a sanctuary, a site which allows communication to a physically and symbolically higher place. The borders of the home are, in truth, interfaces.

These physical and symbolic attributes may be readily traced in the representations of sacred and domestic spaces in literature. All aspects of the sanctuary topos are characterised by clearly demarcated boundaries set around a central space or precious object. They are sites of identity, liminality, and sacred communion with the rest of the world which connect human characters with their geographical and cultural environments. These functions are evident in the representation of sanctuaries, sacred spaces and homes throughout literature. I will trace the primary features of the topos from its earliest inception in medieval literature through to modern children's literature before analyzing the form and functions of the topos as expressed in Susan Cooper's *Dark Is Rising Sequence*.

The Sanctuary Topos in Medieval Literature

In Northern European medieval literature the sanctuary topos is a common and readily recognisable aspect of the fictional landscape. Whereas sacred spaces are seldom described in the fiction and poetry of the period, halls, homes, and dwellings of all kinds may be categorised as sanctuaries and may be seen to uphold the physical and symbolic conventions of the topos which I have identified. Many of the castles in *The Mabinogion* are enclosed by walls and gates which both exclude unwanted visitors and protect the people living within. In *The Lady of the Well*, it is ironic that Owain should become trapped between the portcullis and the gate of one such castle, unable to get in or out without help.[39] Here, the marginal areas of the castle are sites of juxtaposition, not only between outside and inside, but also between safety and danger.

However, it is the hall, as a 'metonym for the society centred in it,'[40] and a focal point for the community as well as the dwelling place of a family, which is the most common manifestation of the topos. The narrative and dramatic action of many texts centres on the hall and, in some cases, action is generated when the sanctity of the hall is somehow compromised. For instance, the halls in the *Finn* episode in *Beowulf*, and in the *Saga of the Niebelungs* become the locations of calculated murder and horrific violence.[41] Perhaps because they are concerned with familial relationships and feuds, the narrative action of many of the Icelandic sagas focuses on halls. In *Njal's Saga*, the burning of Njal's hall is universally condemned as a wicked and cowardly act.[42] It seems that even if the people who shelter within it are despicable, the hall itself should be respected and its sanctity maintained and defended at all costs.

In literature narrative action is generated when the boundaries of sacred spaces are threatened, transcended, or transgressed. For characters within the space—who hold the space dear or sacred—such incursions constitute a direct attack and must therefore be resisted. This tension between invasion and resistance leads to the creation of one of the great narrative set-pieces in English literature: the defence in the doorway. The defence in the doorway is the narrative expression of a tension between the sacred, enclosed, demarcated space of the hall or the house and the undifferentiated wilderness that lies beyond. It is a common motif in medieval literature: it can be seen in "Grettir's fight with Glám" in *The Saga of Grettir the Strong* and in the parody "Boðvar Bjarki at the Court of King Hrolf" from *Hrolfs Saga Kraka*.[43] The trope is so popular that it has even coloured literary representations of historical battles, from *The Battle at Stamford Bridge* to *The Battle of Maldon*, to the short piece from the chronicles known to students of Old English as *Cynnewulf and Cynneheard*.[44] However, the exemplar for the Defence in the Doorway is the fight between Beowulf and Grendel.

Read in terms of landscape, the first section of *Beowulf*, which concerns Grendel's attacks on Heorot, a gift hall built by Hrothgar for his people, is essentially the story of the desecration and reclamation of a hall. From the outset, it is clear that Heorot is a sacred space. It rises vertically; it is high and 'horn-gabled.'[45] The poet places great emphasis on the margins of the building and Grendel's attack is very much depicted as a violation of these boundaries. In the moments leading up to the attack, the poet creates a tension between the inside of the hall and the monster outside, coming towards them in the dark: the space where these opposing forces meet, where inside and outside touch, is the doorway. Grendel lays his hand on the door-frame, causing it to buckle inwards:

> The door soon retreated
> The fire-forged bars fast, after his hand touched it,
> He threw it open, evil-minded. Then he was swollen
> In the mouth of the building.[46]

Once the limits of the hall are breached, its function as a safe space is utterly negated. Consequently, Beowulf fights and defeats Grendel, re-establishing the hall as a sanctuary, not only by overcoming the monster but also by reasserting the boundaries of the space. He pins Grendel's severed arm to the lintel above the doorway, reclaiming the doorway by destroying the arm that broke it down.[47] When Hrothgar arrives at the Heorot the next morning, the newly established boundary causes him to hesitate in the doorway: 'he stood on the stoop and stared the gold-decorated, steepled roof and Grendel's hand.'[48] Daniel Donoghue notes that Hrothgar's moment of hesitation while he stares at the arm 'dramatizes a threshold moment physically, poised as he is between the inside and the outside of the hall.'[49] Hrothgar's hesitation recalls the 'numerous rites [that] accompany passing the domestic threshold—a bow, a prostration, a pious touch of the hand, and so on'[50] which mark the domestic space as separate to the rest of the world.

The Sanctuary Topos in Children's Literature

The sanctuary topos is among the most important spaces in the fictional landscapes of children's literature. As a site in which human culture combines with geographical landscape, the topos is commonly expressed as part of the built environment or as a natural place which has been sanctified through human use and worship. Penelope Lively uses this to great effect in *The Whispering Knights* (1971), where the stone circle above the village is the only place which is safe from Morgan le Fay's malign influence. Similarly, in Alan Garner's *The Weirdstone of Brisingamen* (1960) the children are kept safe from harm once they reach the Fundindelve, a place sanctified through its contents—King Arthur and his Seven Sleepers—and through its magically reinforced boundaries. In both texts, the significance of the Whispering Knights and the Fundindelve has been largely forgotten by the local community. Only children recognise—or in the case of *The Whispering Knights*, learn to recognise—the power inherent in these sites. In the other cases, such as David Almond's *Clay* (2005), sacred spaces are an acknowledged focal point for the surrounding community.

Given its central value to the lived environment, both as a locus for identity and a nexus for personal effects, the home is by far the most common manifestation of the topos, providing the setting for the opening and the closing of many stories.[51] Pauline Dewan observes that

> throughout children's literature houses dominate the novels in which they are found. [...] Even though domestic settings play an important role in fiction for all ages, the house in children's literature is the preeminent place of importance. For children, home is charged with great emotional significance as the focus of all that is most important and influential in their lives.[52]

Thus, the home becomes synonymous with personal identity. In modern children's literature, the home is consecrated by being appropriated to a certain person and thus a character's home is frequently taken as an outward and visible embodiment of their personality. Examples of this direct relationship between character and setting, identity and appearance include Kenneth Grahame's *The Wind in the Willows* (1908) in which Mole expresses a deep longing to return to his own home, to a place which properly reflects him and all of his moods, Beatrix Potter's *Tale of Mrs. Tittlemouse* (1910), whose tidy little house reflects her fussy, neat personality, and J. R. R. Tolkien's *The Hobbit* (1937), where the round comfortable Bilbo Baggins lives in a round, comfortable little house. In Catherine Storr's *Marianne Dreams* (1958), Marianne draws, and dreams about, a house which reflects both her fears about her illness and her desire to be safe and well again. Her moods and actions have a direct effect upon, and a physical reality within the dream-house.

Many children's texts emphasise the liminality of the home through references to doors, hallways, windows, and thresholds. For instance, in *The Children of Green Knowe* (1954), Lucy Boston draws the reader's attention to the doors, windows and ceilings of the house, and especially of Tolly's bedroom, allowing these borders to become the sites of contact between Tolly and the ghostly children who live in the house and their agents; the horse Festa, the little mouse, and the birds. Similarly, in Penelope Lively's *The Ghost of Thomas Kempe* (1973), the reader's attention is repeatedly called towards the windows and doors of the house as the ghost makes his presence known by blowing doors shut or banging on the walls. In *Howl's Moving Castle* (1986) and *The House of Many Ways* (2008), Diana Wynne Jones calls attention to the temporal and physical instability of the wizard's houses by describing dwellings that have no apparent centre. Yet these moving, dislocated homes still reflect the identity of their inhabitants. Here, the characters' relationship with their environment proves to be shifting and unstable, which both reflects and is reflected by, the instability of the home. Therefore, even though Jones's houses appear radical, they uphold the traditional conventions of the sanctuary topos.

Canonical children's texts often stress the exclusivity of the domestic space. In Nina Bawden's *Carrie's War* (1973) Mr. Evans believes that the home must be kept free from dirt and even from excessive use. When Mrs. Tittlemouse's 'nice clean house'[53] is invaded by a series of insects, arachnids, 'creepy-crawly people'[54] and, worst of all Mr. Jackson the toad, she can only restore order by making the door of her home too small for the toad to get through and by conducting 'a spring cleaning which lasted a fortnight.'[55] Her obsessive cleaning equates the exclusion of dirt with the exclusion of unwanted visitors. The motif of exclusion is also manifested in reworkings of the defence in the doorway trope, as in Marcus Sedgwick's, *My Swordhand Is Singing* (2006) and Patrick Ness's *A Monster Calls* (2011). The set-piece is so common that there are even parodies of it. For instance, in Shirley Hughes's *Alfie Gets in First* (1981), Alfie is so eager to prove himself the master of the space that he slams the front door behind him, locking his mother and sister outside and shutting himself within. Another parody is found in J. K. Rowling's *Harry Potter and the Philosopher's Stone* (1997) in the moment when Hagrid bursts into the little shack where Harry and the Dursleys are staying. Like Beowulf, Harry is the only one left awake. Like Grendel, Hagrid approaches in the dead of night and when he lays his hand upon the door it falls inwards. But there the monsters diverge: Grendel's eyes burn with '*a ligge gelīcost lēoht unfæger*'[56] an 'unholy and an unlovely light,' whereas Hagrid's shine like black beetles.[57] Grendel stuffs things he wants to eat into his '*glōf*' but Hagrid takes food out of his pockets to share with Harry.[58]

As with 'Boðvar Bjarki at the Court of King Hrolf,' these parodies indicate that the sanctuary topos and its associated tropes are widespread and readily recognisable. Thus, it suggests that the sanctuary topos has been deliberately adopted and unconsciously subsumed by many children's authors. The examples I have discussed here illustrate the extent to which the sanctuary topos is adopted into and adapted for the representational landscapes of children's literature and further demonstrates how topoanalysis may be used to find connections between seemingly diverse and unrelated texts.

Figure 1.2 St. Cadfan's Church, Tywyn, Wales. ©Jane Carroll.

The Sanctuary Topos in *The Dark Is Rising Sequence*

The sanctuary topos is among the most common spaces in Cooper's *Sequence*, and it is manifested both through the built environment and through natural spaces where humans can come into contact with the supernatural. Whether public, ritual spaces or private, domestic spaces, in each instance the topos is characterised by the same physical and symbolic elements as had been first articulated in medieval literature and further established through canonical literature; each is a clearly delineated space separated from the rest of the world both by its borders and by virtue of its connection with something beyond the normal, profane world. This interplay between the mundane and the fabulous has special significance in fantasy literature. In high fantasy, the narrative action takes place in a single, fantastic universe. In domestic fantasy, the narrative action is spread out over two or more worlds. The world to which the protagonist belongs is the 'primary' or 'domestic' world. The secondary world is often a binary opposite of the primary world; an inverse, or mirror-image of the consensual reality of the text. The two worlds may differ in terms of landscape, flora, fauna, time-frame, culture, society, ideology, and language. The secondary world often provides a space in which the magical elements of the fantasy may unfold.

The *Sequence*, like many other domestic fantasies written for children, is rooted in its primary, domestic spaces and in the homes which act as touchstones for the primary world as a whole.[59] It has been suggested that the primary function of sacred spaces is to connect the mundane world to a divine world through hierophany; that is through the 'irruption' of the sacred into the normal world.[60] Drawing on this idea of hierophany Cooper adds an innovative twist to her representations of sacred spaces. The sacred spaces in the *Sequence* not only act as a threshold between the public sphere and the private realm but also provide a connection between the primary world and the secondary world. In this way Cooper amends the sacred space, not to connect with a God or a Christian ideal of heaven, but to provide a nexus between the primary world of consensual reality and the fantastic, supernatural secondary world.

Both domestic and non-domestic aspects of the sanctuary topos act as interfaces between the primary and secondary worlds of the *Sequence*. In these spaces, the primary world of consensual reality is brought into conjunction with the fantastic secondary world inhabited by the forces of the Light and the Dark. The use of the sanctuary topos as a bridge between the primary and secondary worlds is not unique to Cooper's work but it is relatively rare in children's literature. Some other examples include Rudyard Kipling's *Puck of Pook's Hill* (1906) where a fairy-ring allows Una and Dan to first contact Puck; C. S. Lewis' *The Lion, the Witch and The Wardrobe* (1950) where Narnia is accessed through a wardrobe in a spare room, and

Philip Pullman's *Northern Lights* (1995) where the aurora borealis brings Lyra out of her world into parallel world. Whereas in these examples and many others, the secondary world is a place the protagonists visit, Cooper enables the secondary world to encroach on the primary reality. She further subverts the expected paradigms of the topos by presenting 'irruptions' from the secondary world as unwelcome and dangerous. The boundaries of the sacred and domestic spaces in the *Sequence* are frequently attacked, and often breached by forces from another world. Cooper shows that the boundaries of the topos are not absolute, not inviolable, but may be compromised from within or attacked from without. Thus, Cooper's use of the sanctuary topos is informed by the traditional paradigms established through medieval literature as well as by the representations of the domestic and sacred space in contemporary children's fiction.

Because this chapter aims to examine the importance of the sanctuary topos within the *Sequence* and to demonstrate how Cooper both upholds and subverts its conventions, rather than treating the texts sequentially, I will discuss the more straightforward, conventional manifestations of the topos before moving on to the more subtle and subversive treatment of sacred and domestic spaces in *The Dark Is Rising*. Given the foundational importance of the home to the identity of its inhabitants, I shall also question what impetus forces a character like Will Stanton, whose identity seems to be wholly tied up with his home, to leave the domestic space behind and move out into the wider landscape.

Over Sea, Under Stone

As the first book in the *Sequence, Over Sea, Under Stone* presents many of the paradigms of character, narrative, and space which are upheld throughout the series. Cooper uses two different aspects of the sanctuary topos; the Grey House which typifies the private, domestic dwelling, and the stone circle on Kenmare Head which is a public, ritual space.

With its clearly demarcated external boundaries and an abundance of internal liminal spaces, the Grey House typifies Cooper's use of domestic space as an aspect of the sanctuary topos. Although it is not the Drews' home, the space is clearly appropriated to a person, in this case, the absent Captain Toms. Here, Cooper forges a direct link between human identity and its physical expression in space; Captain Toms has mapped his own identity onto his home. The bookshelves are filled with charts and books about sailing and the bedroom, the absolute centre of the home and the most individual, private space, looks like the inside of a ship and the objects found there may also be found on board a ship.[61] However, it is through the repeated emphasis on liminal and transitional spaces—landings, stairwells, halls, and doors—that Cooper posits the Grey House as a sanctuary.

Like several of the other sanctuaries in the *Sequence*, the Grey House comes under attack. Cooper describes, with great emphasis on liminal areas, the moment Simon comes downstairs to discover the house has been burgled:

> It was not until he reached the flight of stairs leading down into the hall that Simon first noticed something was wrong [...] as Simon glanced along the wall of pictures down the stairs he saw there were several more gaps [...] He found several strange, naked-looking patches where pictures had been taken down [...] then he noticed that at the far end [of the hall], where the sun was streaming in from the kitchen through the open doorway, several of the blocks had been wrenched out and were strewn all over the floor.[62]

Even though the Grey House is not their home, but only a holiday home, the Drews' feelings towards the space are intense and protective. When Simon runs shouting for his father, Mr. Drew immediately assumes that there has been a fire—a sure indication that any violation of the sacred borders of the house is akin to its destruction. The intrusion of strangers and unwelcome visitors is more frightening to Jane than the thought of something being stolen. Barney, being highly imaginative, suggests that the house has been attacked by a poltergeist.

Barney's suggestion is not as bizarre as it may first appear; given the sacred nature of the space and that any violation of such as space is *unheimlich* (unhomely and uncanny), it follows that such invasions may easily carry a supernatural quality.[63] However, it soon becomes clear that the invasion of the Grey House is of a strictly mundane nature; the thieves enter through the unlatched kitchen window and the print of a shoe remains on the kitchen counter.[64] Nevertheless, because its borders are breached, the Grey House no longer seems like a safe place and the three Drews want to go somewhere else, somewhere safe and so Merriman brings them to an alternative sanctuary; the stone circle on Kenmare Head.

The circle of five standing stones has many of the characteristics of the sanctuary topos and features prominently in both *Over Sea, Under Stone* and *Greenwitch*.[65] As it is situated on the edge of Kenmare Head, the geographical liminality of the stone circle is immediately apparent; on the horizontal axis it is the limit between land and sea and on the vertical axis it is the limit between earth and sky. The circle is 'lonely' and 'miles from anywhere'[66] but its seclusion makes it a safe place. When the Drews first visit the stone circle with Merriman, Cooper draws on established motifs to fix this site firmly within the traditions of the topos:

> They turned again and scrambled up the slope, and at last they were at the top of the headland, with the line of surf laid out like a slow-moving map below them on either side, and beyond it the great blue sweep of the sea. [...]

the land before them was unfamiliar, a silent, secret world of mounded peaks and invisible valleys, all its colours merging in a haze of summer heat.[67]

Here, Cooper draws attention to the edges of the space—the hill is bounded on either side by the ocean—but also emphasises the sense that this is an enclosed, secret place; a place held apart from the rest of the world. This is undoubtedly a sanctuary.

Cooper's allusion to 'invisible valleys' reiterates the function of the sanctuary as an axis between the primary world and the secondary world. The stone circle connects the primary world of consensual reality to the fantastic secondary world and the 'merging' of the colours reflects the merging of these two worlds within this space. Indeed, the stone circle marks the boundary between familiar and unfamiliar territory—even though it is a safe place, its liminality makes it strange and awesome—and it has a strong defamiliarising effect upon the people within it. Here, the Drews are shaken out of their ordinary routines as they realise their lives are connected with a mythic and magical world. Within this space, their familiar uncle Gumerry becomes the Old One, Merriman Lyon:

> The children stared at him, awed and a little afraid. For a moment he was a stranger, someone they did not know. Jane had a sudden fantastic feeling that Great-Uncle Merry did not really exist at all, and would vanish away if they breathed or spoke.[68]

Like Jane who, in *Silver on the Tree*, is transformed by the defamiliarising power of the sanctuary, Merriman also becomes strange. Here, the force of the secondary world almost overwhelms the ordinary world. Jane, who at this point has had few dealings with the supernatural, becomes aware that there is something strange about this place. She has a 'fantastic' feeling which is totally at odds with her normal, stoic and practical behaviour which leads her to question to solidity and reality of her world. Thus, the stone circle enables the characters to connect to something beyond the mundane present; they connect to a mythic past and, however unwittingly, to the secondary world, the world of the Old Ones. Cooper reiterates the otherworldly nature of the site later in the novel, particularly in her description of the stones at night:

> Magnified by the darkness, they towered mysteriously against the silver-washed sky, and vanished, unnervingly into shadow whenever a cloud rushed over the face of the moon. In the daylight the stones had seemed tall, but now they were immense, dominating the headland, and all the dim moonlit valleys that stretched inland.[69]

By vanishing and reappearing, the stones seem to shift between the solid primary world and the ephemeral secondary world. That they are viewed by

30 • Landscape in Children's Literature

inconstant moonlight heightens this effect. Like other sacred spaces, the stone circle has an ethereal and supernatural presence as well as a physical reality. The sacred nature of the stone circle is so well established that when the reader comes to the description of the Greenwitch ceremony—a pagan ritual to ensure a good harvest—Cooper barely mentions the stones at all.[70] During this ceremony, it is the actions of the humans within the stone circle, and not the circle itself, which is the focus of attention.

Figure 1.3 The Nine Maidens, Cornwall. ©Jane Carroll.

Greenwitch

Throughout the *Sequence*, Cooper extrapolates from the physical and symbolic motifs associated with the sanctuary topos, highlighting limits and boundaries of the domestic and sacred spaces as often as she writes about the rooms at their centre. In *Greenwitch* she explicitly draws attention to the threshold between the adjoining cottages the Drews have rented with the Stantons:

> [Will] was prevented from asking more questions by a sudden noise from the wall beside him. A large wooden door swung open, narrowly missing his back, revealing Merriman in the act of closing another identical door behind it.
> 'This is where the two cottages connect,' Merriman said, looking down at Will's surprise with a faint grin. 'They lock both doors if the two are let separately.'[71]

Within this short passage, Cooper refers to the margins of the house—the wall, the door—and explicitly connects them to the limits of the human body: Will's back and Merriman's mouth. The reference to the 'identical door' effectively creates a doubling effect, allowing the threshold to act as the surface of a mirror. This passage serves no narrative purpose; it is simply there to focus the reader's attention on the margins within the houses.

The internal boundaries echo and reflect the solid outer limits of the cottages. Jane Drew stays in a little bedroom at the front of the cottage, overlooking the harbour and the streets of Trewissick:

> The ceiling sloped down so that the wall on one side was only half the height of the wall on the other, and there was space only for a bed, a dressing-table and a chair. But the little room seemed full of sunshine, even though the sky outside the curtains was grey.[72]

The boundaries of the space are quickly established in this brief description which also calls attention to the distinction between the room and the outside world. Here, the contrast between sunshine and gloom influences the reader's perception of the relationship between inside and outside; the interior space is firmly cast as preferred. By placing such emphasis on the windows, thresholds, and walls of the holiday house, Cooper establishes the space as part of the sanctuary topos, indicating that once its borders are intact, it will protect the characters against all harm. The alert reader, aware of the topological value of the space as a sanctuary, knows that even when the Greenwitch and the forces of the Dark fight in the streets of Trewissick, Jane and her brothers will be safe within the cottage. Jane, however, is not so attuned to the symbolic functions of the space and needs Merriman to reassure her that 'no harm can come to [her] here.'[73]

The Grey King

Even though the homes of the Evans and Davies families are mentioned only briefly, they are brought within the paradigms of the sanctuary topos when Will walks, and firmly fixes, the borders of Clwyd Farm where the homes are located. Will's uncle has only 'roughly pencilled'[74] the boundaries in on a map; nevertheless, he finds his way. The act of walking the borders—beating the bounds—'reinforces the limits of the property'[75] and so sanctifies the space. Beating the bounds was traditionally carried out by a priest and the young people of the parish.[76] As an Old One and a twelve-year-old boy, Will conflates both these roles. Other manifestations of the topos in this text include St. Cadfan's church in Tywyn and Cader Idris, a mountain which borders Clwyd Farm.

St. Cadfan's is described in terms of its holy contents, physical boundaries and liminality. In her brief description Cooper emphasises the verticality of the church, writing that, although its porch is 'low-roofed' the building is 'deep as a cave.'[77] Inside it is 'shadowy and cool, with sturdy white painted walls and massive white pillars'[78] and so the brightness of the interior is sharply contrasted to the gloomy entrance. Through the mention of walls and pillars, Cooper draws attention to the physical limits of the space. Whereas the church stands between light and dark, it also stands between the profane world and the sacred, mythic world for at the rear of the church there is 'a strange long grey stone set up on end, incised with marks too ancient for [Will] to decipher.'[79] The stone is St. Cadfan's stone, a grave-marker bearing an inscription in Old Welsh ('The body of Cungen is on the side between where the marks will be [...] beneath a similar mound is extended Cadfan, sad that it should enclose the praise of the earth')[80] and by mentioning it, Cooper draws attention to the idea of the after-life and so allows the church to become a nexus between this world and the next.

The second sacred space in *The Grey King* is Cader Idris, the mountain home of the Brenin Llwyd, the Grey King. Bran warns Will that 'there is a saying that anyone who spends the night alone up on Cader will come down next morning either a poet, or mad.'[81] In addition to this sublime and defamiliarising power, the mountain also seems to be a site of hierophany as the Grey King appears to Will there. Thus, the Cader seems to function as a liminal space between earth and heaven and, as such, could be considered to offer communication between the profane world and the gods. However, as I will discuss in greater detail in Chapter Two, the Grey King is not a god, but a *genius locus* and an emissary of the Dark. The Cader is not, therefore, an axis between earth and heaven, but a meeting point between the primary world and the secondary world.

Silver on the Tree

The fifth book in the *Sequence* uses many familiar aspects of the sanctuary space especially in the scenes set within the Stantons' house, but also introduces new variations on the topos, such as the Tower of Glass in the Lost Land which is protected by a spinning wheel.[82] Throughout Will and Bran's journey through the Lost Land, Cooper draws attention to thresholds and doorways which all bear short, inscribed epigraphs.[83] The Lost Land, as a space entirely set within the secondary world does not play any major role in the topoanalysis of the *Sequence* but serves to reflect and repeat many of the landscape motifs which feature in the other texts. As a geographically and temporally sunken space, the Lost Land will be discussed in greater detail in Chapter Four as an example of the Lapsed Topos. Here I will deal with Cooper's representation of Llyn Barfog, the bearded lake.

Although Llyn Barfog is geographically close to Cader Idris, it offers readers of the *Sequence* a completely different experience of sacred spaces. Whereas the Cader is grim and threatening, Llyn Barfog and the valley it is set within, Cwm Maethlon, the happy valley, are 'real tourist stuff'[84] and beautifully picturesque. The lake is not even desecrated by the fact that it has become a tourist attraction. On the contrary, John Sears observes that tourist sites

> [integrate] the functions [of sacred spaces] in a new form that [yoke] the sacred and the profane, the spiritual and the commercial, the mythic and the trivial, the natural and the artificial, the profound and the superficial, the elite and the popular in a sometimes uneasy combination.[85]

It has been suggested that 'a pilgrim is half a tourist' and that a tourist is 'half a pilgrim,'[86] particularly in the wake of Romanticism which promoted the sublimity of natural landscapes.[87] By deciding to walk through Cwn Maethlon, rather than drive as many of the other tourists do, Bran, Will and the three Drew siblings mark themselves out as pilgrims as well as tourists. The journey on foot, which is considered in greater detail in Chapter Three, puts the traveller in close physical contact with the landscape and enables the children to experience the valley and its attractions in a deeper, slower, more considered way than is possible for those staring out of the windows of a moving car.

Bran, who feels that the Drews, being ordinary humans, are beneath his notice, scornfully aligns Jane and her brothers with the idiotic tourists. On the way up to the lake, he snaps at her: 'You will probably have nothing to do but look at a valley and a lake and say, oh how pretty. What's the fuss?'[88] But Jane's reaction is not that of an ordinary person and 'watching Jane, Will felt suddenly that he was seeing someone he had never met before. Her face was drawn into furious lines of emotion that seemed to belong to someone else.'[89] Jane's apparent transformation is the first indication of the defamiliarisation which will take place at Llyn Barfog and indicates that, unlike the passive, mindless tourist Bran makes her out to be, she is properly attuned to the sacred space she is about to visit. Indeed, Jane's status as a liminal character, first mentioned in *Greenwitch* when she becomes a 'wild thing'[90] at the end of the novel, is now firmly established. Simon apologetically informs Will that his sister is 'going through a *stage*,'[91] suggesting that she has reached puberty, an especially marginal stage of identity. It is, as Maria Nikolajeva observes, 'the threshold of adulthood.'[92] Jane is on the verge of becoming someone else and it is appropriate that her encounter with a sacred space should tip the balance in favour of this new identity. Will sagely observes that they 'should be specially watching'[93] her to see what happens.

Once they reach Llyn Barfog, the sacred nature of the lake is made abundantly clear. The lake is consecrated through mythic events. Here, King Arthur's horse trod and he dragged a monster, the Afanc, out of the lake. Will knows that the lake provides a strong connection to the mythic, secondary world and that, as a result, 'they were in the presence of the High Magic.'[94] The lake's liminal status and its role as a sanctuary are also reiterated through physical signs. Its boundaries are marked by reeds and edged by a 'rock-strewn path,'[95] and the water itself is full of lilies, which blur the division between water and earth. The mist that surrounds the area also blurs the division between the earth and the sky. This lake is a space where the binary aspects of the world not only meet, but merge. At the lakeside, tourists shout out and listen for an echo which rebounds from the nearest mountain. Whereas the echo reinforces the reader's awareness of the limits of the space, it also provides a further connection with the secondary world.

While the other tourists shout obscenities and nonsense, Will, Bran, and the Drews realise that the echo is really a sign of something more and should be treated with respect:

> Jane said, 'If you listen very carefully it's really a double echo, the second very faint.' 'Fat face!' shouted the most raucous of [the tourists] again, delighted with himself. Barney said in a clear precise voice, 'Funny how people can never think of anything intelligent to shout to make an echo [...] You can't shout rude rhymes for an echo [...] Echoes are special. People ought to . . . to sing to them.'[96]

The faint, double echo, the sound of a voice in miniature, indicates that what happens at the lakeside is a microcosmic version of something greater. Barney says that one 'makes' an echo, and thus recalls that the beginning of all creation is sound.[97] To speak, mindful of the true, sacred meaning of words, is to consecrate a space. Once the tourists have left, the children can speak and make their own, sacred echoes. Simon begins by quoting Prospero, '"*Thou earth, thou! Speak!* . . ."' and very faintly indeed, perhaps only an imagining, [Jane] heard the echo: "*. . . speak . . . speak.*"'[98] Here, Cooper indicates that these words and their accompanying echo are beyond the parameters of ordinary language; the italicised words deviate from the usual presentation of language in the text, while the repeated silent spaces between the words imply that there is much left unsaid and that silence, ordinarily an unremarked part of speech, has taken on a new significance. Furthermore, these silences also draw attention to the idea of time that Cooper plays with here. Simon's words, in echoing Shakespeare's, (and Prospero-as-Shakespeare's) bridge that gap between creator and created, between the past and the present and the echo, with the lags and silences of language repeated and intensified, serves to extend and distort the present moment. Thus, the lake provides not only a liminal space, but also a liminal and a mythical time.

Will is the next to make an echo. When he sings, his voice is appropriately 'high and sweet and unearthly'.[99] The sound affects Jane so much that she

> stood without breathing, caught out of movement, feeling every stilled muscle and yet as totally transported as if she had no body at all. [...] The voice soared up on the wind, from behind the hill, distant but clear, in a strange lovely line of melody, and with it and behind it very faint in a following descant came the echo of the song, a ghostly second voice twining with the first.
> It was as if the mountains were singing.[100]

Here, the echo is definitely cast as a sign of the supernatural. It is 'strange' and 'ghostly' and it shakes Jane free of the ordinary, mundane concerns of the primary world. In this new, defamiliarised state, she is prepared to witness the hierophany of the true emissary of the sacred, secondary world of the *Sequence*; the Lady. The Lady entrusts Jane with a message, saying

> 'Some things there are that may be communicated only between like and like,' the sweet soft voice said from the mist. 'It is the pattern of a child's game of dominoes. For you and I are much the same, Jane, Jana, Juno, Jane, in clear ways that separate us from all others concerned with this quest. [...] Remember,' the Lady said. Her white form was beginning to fade, and the glow dying in the rose of the ring. The voice grew softer, softer. 'Remember my daughter. And be brave, Jane. Be brave ... brave.'[101]

In this passage, Cooper uses the motif of the echo to great effect. The Lady's speech, particularly at the end when she fades away, takes the same linguistic and typographic form of the echoes that Simon draws from the mountain. Moreover, Jane herself is figured as an echo of the Lady; a diminutive and less potent reflection. Here, Jane comes to be very much like the landscape, a liminal space which enables the words of a person to be carried on and extended beyond their normal temporal reach. At this point, Cooper vocalises the paradigms of landscape discussion which are present, if often implicit, throughout the *Sequence*; the echoes create a symbiosis between person and space. The earth speaks in the words given to it by the children. And in causing the earth to speak, the children demonstrate a mindful relationship with their environment. Through the interface of the sanctuary topos, the child characters of the *Sequence* come into perfect harmony with the landscape.

Figure 1.4 Llyn Barfog, Cwm Maethlon, Wales. ©Jane Carroll.

The Dark Is Rising

The representations of the sanctuary topos are at their most interesting and most complex in *The Dark Is Rising*. The action of the text is dominated by the strange snowfall that keeps the majority of characters trapped indoors and so the vast majority of the scenes are set indoors, within domestic and sacred spaces. Of the five books in the *Sequence*, *The Dark Is Rising* is the only one in which the boundaries of the sanctuary topos are consistently threatened and breached from without. Some of these irruptions are insidious, some overt and violent, but all are disturbing and lead to the juxtaposition of the primary world with the secondary world. Whereas the burglary in *Over Sea, Under Stone* can be attributed to Mrs. Palk's negligence and malice, the violations of the sacred and domestic space in *The Dark Is Rising* come about as the direct result of the Dark. These intrusions undermine the sanctity and security of the topos and create a great sense of unease within the text. Cooper draws directly on the defence in the doorway trope three times in the novel. With each occurrence, it is clear that the power of the Dark is growing but also, in tandem, Will's power and status as an Old One is growing.

The Hall of the Light

The first—failed—defence comes on the morning of Will's eleventh birthday, December 21, when he tries to defend the Hall of the Light against the encroaching Dark. The Hall of the Light is, in many ways, a very typical example of the sanctuary topos. It provides a point of contact between the primary world and the secondary world and also provides a dialogic space within which these worlds can meet. Here, Will meets Merriman and the Lady. Her 'musical voice'[102] carries connotations of the otherworldly and sacred music of Llyn Barfog and is an indication that this space is beyond the mundane world, just as she is beyond mundane speech while Merriman's 'grim'[103] face suggests something of the dark malice of the Cader. The Hall, as a true sacred space, is welcoming and exclusive, joyful and awesome. It has the same defamiliarising effect as the stone circle and within this space 'the light and the day and the world changed so that he [Will] forgot utterly what they had been,'[104] and finds that 'the world he had inhabited since he was born seemed to whirl and break and come down again in a pattern that was not the same as before.'[105] The sameness of the primary world is shattered by the sublime nature of the sacred space.

Although the Hall provides a connection between two worlds, it is also, in its own right, a tightly enclosed space. Again, Cooper draws attention to the boundaries of the space, to the 'lofty stone walls' with thin windows and the 'enormous fireplace,'[106] but especially to the 'great doors' at the end of the hall. These doors mark the threshold between the ordinary and fantastic worlds and, for Will, the transition between his life as an ordinary eleven-year-old and his new life as an Old One who is outside of time. Once Will crosses the threshold 'the two huge doors swung shut behind him,'[107] and he soon realises that 'the great wooden doors had vanished.'[108] Once Will is safely inside, there is no more need for the threshold or the doorway; the hall's sole function now is to protect those inside it. A great round shield hanging up on the wall reinforces the sense that this is a protected, inviolable space.

But Will is too inexperienced to interpret these topological signifiers correctly and when the Hall is besieged by the forces of the Dark, he is terrified. He does not realise that although the boundaries of the sacred space may be threatened, they cannot be breached under ordinary circumstances. But Will, as a newly awakened Old One, does not fully understand the nature of the Dark, nor does he properly understand the function of the spaces he inhabits. Having been attacked in his own bedroom the night before, he does not trust that the Hall is impenetrable. When he hears the sound of the rising Dark, a 'hideous mixture of moaning and mumbling and strident wailing, like the caged voices of an evil zoo [...] a sound more purely nasty than any he had ever heard',[109] he panics and is tricked into opening the doors, breaching the boundaries of the space and compromising the sanctity of the Hall. Despite the Lady's efforts to re-sanctify the space, Will and Merriman, much like the Drews in *Over Sea, Under Stone*, decide to leave the Hall rather than linger there.[110]

Huntercombe Church

The second defence in the doorway takes place on Christmas morning in the little church where Will sings in the choir. As with St. Cadfan's, the Huntercombe church is established as a sanctuary through the insistent focus on physical and metaphysical limits. Whereas the space is used for Christian worship and is sanctified by the presence of the bible and the cross, Will and the other Old Ones know it to be doubly sanctified by the presence of the Sign of Stone embedded in the church wall.[111] Like other sacred places, this church acts as a nexus between the profane, primary world and the supernatural secondary world. Consequently, when it is besieged by the Dark, Will initially finds it difficult to believe that a sacred place could be vulnerable to such malice:

> But in a church? said Will the Anglican choirboy, incredulous: surely you can't feel it inside a church? Ah, said Will the Old One unhappily, any church of any religion is vulnerable to their attack, for places like this are where men give thought to matters of the Light and the Dark.[112]

This passage not only illustrates the duality of Will's own personality but also allows the reader an insight into the process by which Will is made mature; among the other gifts and powers he possesses, he now has a growing topological awareness. Using this new awareness of the significance of places, Will realises the church is not simply a safe place, but also a liminal space, where people give thought to things beyond the primary world, and, as such, it is a conduit for the supernatural. Although he knows that 'no harm could actually enter its walls'[113] Will realises that danger is 'hovering just outside.'[114] He knows that the sanctity of the church depends on the clearly demarcated distinctions between the sacred interior and the 'raging ill-will,'[115] 'destruction and chaos'[116] which lie beyond its walls. While Will is sensitive to his surroundings and can 'feel his neck prickling, as though with the electricity that hangs strongly oppressive in the air before a giant storm,' the rector, Mr. Beaumont, is perfectly oblivious and 'still chatting, reached out an absent-minded hand and turned off the lights inside the church, leaving it in a cold grey murk, brighter only beside the door where the whiteness of the snow reflected in.'[117] In turning out the lights, Mr. Beaumont plunges the church into darkness and narrows the distinction between the sacred space and the gloom outside. In the absence of light, the snow—which is representative of both the outside world and the secondary world—is able to 'reflect' into and affect the interior of the church. He thus unwittingly undermines the sanctity of the space. He ushers the congregation towards the doors of the church, blithely pushing them towards the danger that lies beyond. It is only when the Dark attacks the Old Ones in the doorway of the church that Mr. Beaumont realises the gravity of the situation:

Mr. Beaumont turned very white. There was a glistening of sweat on his forehead, through the church was very cold again now [...] he stumbled a few paces nearer the church door like a man struggling through waves in the sea, and leaning forward slightly made a sweeping sign of the Cross.[118]

The Cross proves ineffective and Will and the other Old Ones have to use their magic to reinforce the boundaries of the space. Will closes off the minds of his brother and Mr. Beaumont behind magical barriers[119] and creates an 'invisible wall'[120] between the church and the attacking Dark. Through the erection of these boundaries and through the power of the Signs, Will and the Old Ones manage to consecrate the space; reinforcing its borders and re-establishing the difference between it and what lies beyond it.

Greythorne Manor

The third and the most dramatic defence in the doorway takes place two days after Christmas at Greythorne Manor where all the people in Huntercombe village have come for warmth and protection during the storms. Greythorne Manor, the home of the Old One Miss Greythorne, is typical of the domestic and sacred spaces in the *Sequence*. Miss Greythorne is 'a figure of total mystery in Huntercombe'[121] and so she is at once a domestic presence which sanctifies the space through dwelling there and a supernatural presence which consecrates the space through a connection with the secondary world. Through this space, Will is led 'into a different time and a different Christmas,'[122] and so Cooper establishes the Manor as an interface between the ordinary and the fantastic. Yet the Manor is a well-protected and safe place. Even though the heavy snowstorms subvert the borders of the other houses in Huntercombe, sealing them off from the world, leaving their occupants 'restless' and 'enclosed,'[123] imprisoned in their own homes, the Manor, as an old place and 'strengthened by Time'[124] and by being continuously dwelt in comes into its own as a sanctuary. Yet, by inviting the villagers in to the Manor, Miss Greythorne breaches boundaries of etiquette and class, social boundaries which had been in place for centuries and, in so doing, weakens the topological status of the Manor as a safe place.

This breach in etiquette culminates when the Walker, a mere tramp, enters the Manor. His presence effects a dramatic subversion of social boundaries which, in turn, enables him to bring about further destabilisation by disrupting the physical limits of the space by opening the door to the Dark. The Walker overrides the sacred boundaries of the space by inviting the forces of the Dark inside:

> The Walker was standing tall now, his eyes bright, his head flung up, and his back straight. He held one arm high and called out in a strong, clear

voice: 'Come wolf, come hound, come cat, come rat, come Held, come Holda, I call you in! Come Ura, come Tann, come Coll, come Quert, come Morra, come Master, I bring you in!'[125]

The Walker's words take the form of an incantation, a prayer, an appropriate summons for supernatural forces within a sacred space. The forces of the Dark, led by Mitothin, soon come close, threatening the building. Cooper constructs Mitothin's approach to the Manor as a perfect echo of Grendel's approach to Heorot. Just as Grendel is 'bent on the destruction'[126] of the hall, Mitothin is 'coming near, wishing ill to the Manor and all inside it.'[127] Mitothin knocks three times and on the third knock, Will, like Beowulf, the only one left alert, answers the door:

Snow spat in at him, sleet slashed his face, winds whistled through the hall. Out in the darkness, the great black horse reared up high over Will's head, hooves flailing, eyes rolling white, the foam flying from bared teeth. And above it gleamed the blue eyes of the Rider and the flaring red of his hair. In spite of himself Will cried out, and threw up one arm instinctively in self-defence.[128]

Here, Cooper's language evokes the strong alliterative metre of Old English verse which reinforces the clear narrative parallels with medieval literature. Like Grendel and Glám, Mitothin is distinguished by his gleaming eyes in the darkness. Will's reflexive, defensive gesture allows his raised arm to echo the horizontal lines of the threshold and the lintel, effectively barring the doorway against Mitothin. But even though Will can hold the door, he cannot reinforce all of the boundaries of Greythorne Manor, and so the forces of the Dark enter through other weak points. The Dark invades through the chimney, in the form of snow which extinguishes the hearth fire, a sure sign of how the domestic space has been overrun.[129] Once this real, life-giving fire has been extinguished, strange icy flames spring up around the rooms, spreading fear and cold throughout the Manor. It is only through the actions of the assembled Old Ones that the Dark can be expelled and the borders of the space, like those of the church, can be shored up.

The Stantons' Home

Running parallel to these three scenes are the attacks made by the Dark on the Stantons' own home. As this is the only one of the five books of the *Sequence* in which the protagonist is at home, the representations of the Stantons' home are especially significant. Cooper carefully positions this building within the sanctuary topos by drawing attention to its boundaries, its verticality and to the fact that it is sacred to her protagonist. Will Stanton's home is the very centre of his world; the geographic and emotional axis around which his life revolves. From the outset, Cooper draws the reader's attention to the peripheral zones of the Stantons' house. Her opening lines focus on space and the relationship of her characters to their physical and geographical environment:

> 'Too many!' James shouted, and slammed the door behind him. [...] James stood fuming on the landing like a small angry locomotive, then stumped across to the window-seat and stared out at the garden. Will put aside his book and pulled up his legs to make room. [...] They both looked out the window.[130]

Once again, Cooper draws attention to liminal spaces—the door, the landing, the window-seat and the window. In placing her characters indoors but having them focus on the world outside, both through the book and through the window, she creates an uneasy tension between the designations of space, suggesting that throughout this text, the human relationship with space will be challenged.

Cooper reiterates this focus on the limits and boundaries of the Stantons' house many times over the course of the novel, continually reminding the reader that this building, like all of the houses in the *Sequence* and, by extension the identity Will has founded upon it, is fragile. The most explicit of these iterations comes when Will, newly aware of his role in the struggle against the forces of the Dark, places sprigs of holly on all the thresholds, windows, and limits of his home.[131] Although the borders of the home are clear, they are not impermeable and even though Will adds this extra protection to his home, its boundaries are pushed and threatened many times over the course of the novel. The snow which acts as a potent signifier of the secondary world and of the Dark pushes in from all sides, smashes a window in the kitchen,[132] forces open the skylight in Will's bedroom,[133] and, when it finally melts, seeps in through the cracks and gaps under the doors and carries things off. [134]

The Dark also has a human presence in the form of Mitothin, the Rider. On Christmas morning Mitothin, who poses as a jeweller-friend of Roger Stanton, is invited in to meet the family. As with the Walker's invitation to the Dark, Roger Stanton's takes the form of an incantation through the repeated, even perhaps echoed, 'come in, do come in.'[135] Just as the agents of the Dark are permitted to enter Greythorne Manor, the Rider can cross the Stantons' threshold because of this invitation. In so doing, Mitothin enacts a strange kind of hierophany: he is a presence from another world that irrupts into the mundane realm. The Stantons' home thus becomes a hinterland between the primary world, symbolised by the family and their pyjamas and their Christmas presents, and the secondary world, symbolised by the Rider and his dark cloak and strange accent. Even though his family is unaware of the conjunction of the two worlds, or of the significance of their home as an interface between them, Will is an Old One and through footfall knowledge of the landscape gained when he goes walking on the morning of his birthday and through his experiences in the secondary world he becomes more fully aware of the true topological significance of the spaces he inhabits. Accordingly, he is not as blithely accepting of the stranger's intrusion as his father:

> He was instantly a furious Old One, so furious that he did not pause to think what he should do. He could feel every inch of himself, as if he had grown in his rage to three times his own height. He stretched out his right hand with his fingers spread stiff towards his family, and saw them all instantly caught into a stop in time, frozen out of all movement.[136]

As with Jane in *Silver on the Tree*, Will's fury is a sign of something supernatural, beyond the everyday. Whereas Jane is 'caught out of movement'[137] in the sanctuary, Will forces the same stillness upon his family. Jane feels as though she has no body, but Will can feel every inch of his. These differences in perception indicate the distinct roles the characters play within the topos and the dissimilarity in their relationship with the spaces they encounter. Whereas Jane's role in the sanctuary was as a passive echo, Will is very much in control of this space; this is his home and it is sanctified by his presence and his close emotional relationship with it. Nonetheless Will's empathy with his environment and his love for his home cannot prevent it from being invaded and over the course of the book Will's close relationship with his home is challenged and compromised.

By far the most dramatic and unsettling disruption of the domestic space occurs when the Dark attacks Will's attic bedroom on the night before his eleventh birthday.[138] As the attic stands, synecdochally, for the house as a whole, this attic represents the violation of all that Will holds dear. This attack alters his relationship with his world and marks the beginning of his journey towards understanding and topological awareness. At the beginning of *The Dark Is Rising*, Will Stanton is a perfect example of the way in which a character's identity is bound up with the image of the house. He is one of the few protagonists in children's literature who operates within a domestic structure. His life is based around the routines of dinner-time and bed-time, to the point that before one day's routine is properly over, the Stantons are busy planning the next.[139] Casey suggests that 'the sense of self, personal or collective grows out of and reflects the places from which we come and where we have been.'[140] The home is sacred because it becomes synonymous with its inhabitants. It is the 'the centre of meaning,'[141] the 'focus of personal sentiments,'[142] the focus of landscape and the focus of identity. And so the home is not merely the physical centre of Will's universe, but also the ideological centre, the corner-stone of his thinking. For Will, at the start of the novel at least, his home is the ultimate metanarrative, the image which structures and centres his whole life. It is unsurprising that, for Will, the failure of the domestic space to protect him heralds the collapse of the symbol of the home as a metanarrative.

As indicated in the opening lines of the novel, Will is a liminal figure, most often seen on the margins of the home, in doorways, beside windows, or on stairwells. Will's liminality, like Jane Drew's, marks him out as different from the other members of his family. Therefore, it seems appropriate that he is the only one of the Stanton children who does not have to share a bedroom. His bedroom is in the 'slant-roofed attic at the top of the house,'[143] on the very edges of the domestic space. Will treats his attic bedroom as a kind of personal sanctuary and, at first glance, Cooper's first description of the attic seems to add weight to this idea. Once again, there is with great emphasis on the borders of the space: Will sits at the window, watching the snow pile up on the sill and listening to the wind 'whining round the roof close above him, and in all the chimneys.'[144] The central focus of the space is provided by 'a kind of private shrine'[145] on which Will keeps a box of letters and a photograph of his brother Stephen. It appears that this bedroom is sort of inner sanctum: a safe, personalised and highly exclusive sanctuary within a sanctuary. Yet there are indications that Will has badly misconstrued this space.

The acquisition of the attic bedroom places Will at the symbolic head of the household, and quite literally, above his brothers and sisters. The attic bedroom is a symbol of power and status in the hierarchy of children and by having him move into the highest space at the top of the house, Cooper sets Will up as symbolically superior in understanding. Although he is the youngest child, by virtue of being an Old One, he is the oldest of them all within the fantastic paradigm of the novel. But Will's authority is precarious; he inherited the attic from his eldest brother Stephen 'only a few months before'[146] and, even as he hands possession of the bedroom over, Stephen says 'my attic ought to be lived in.'[147] Stephen's language implies that he has not really given up possession of the bedroom. Furthermore, the 'private shrine' in the room is not made up of Will's own things, but of things which remind him of Stephen. Will's hero-worship of his eldest brother leads the space to remain consecrated to Stephen rather than to its current occupant. This badly unbalances the dynamics of the space. The attic is not truly appropriated to Will. Therefore, it is not a space in which his identity can be protected but a space in which his identity may be challenged.

Will constructs his attic as a private sanctuary and ignores the fact that it is at a great remove from the hearth and the true centre of the home. He does not recognise that the attic is a boundary area of the main building and not a safe place in its own right. Nor does he realise that his hold on the space is so tenuous. At this point he has not come into his identity as an Old One and is not topologically attuned so he does not see the attic for what it is: a marginal and extremely vulnerable space. When the Dark attacks he is taken by surprise:

> in a dreadful furious moment, horror seized him like a nightmare made real; there came a wrenching crash, with the howling of the wind suddenly much louder and closer, and a great blast of cold; and the Feeling came hurtling against him with such force of dread that it flung him cowering away. Will shrieked. [148]

Whereas the Dark hovers outside the Hall of the Light and Huntercombe Church, it comes crashing right into Will's space, tearing through the flimsy limits of the attic. The proper reaction to such incursion is defence. But rather than trying to assert his mastery of the space, Will once again defects to Stephen: 'Frightened of the dark he thought: how awful. Just like a baby, Stephen would never have been frightened of the dark, up here.'[149] Stephen may not have been frightened by the dark, but the forces of the Dark—a symbolic, mythic, and moral darkness—are terrifying. But Will, by deferring to his brother, has already lost the battle for his space and the forces of the Dark are able to enforce a complete transformation of the attic. Cooper writes that 'for an appalling pitch-black moment he lay scarcely conscious, lost somewhere out of the world, out in black space.'[150] The attic is transformed into a featureless and empty space and even the borders of the space are violently breached when the attic window is forced open by the snow.

Like the snow that forces its way down the chimney at Greythorne Manor, the snow that forces the window open is not merely meteorological but is a potent sign of the secondary world. Peter Davidson notes that snow is a sign of the north, 'a place of darkness and dearth, the seat of evil'[151] and, as Naomi Wood observes, cold, ice and snow are antithetical to all that is traditional, mundane and routine.[152] Thus, snow becomes an especially apt signifier of secondary and other worlds in children's fantasy. In *The Dark Is Rising*, snow is a malignant, active force, and an agent of the Dark, which has the power not only to disrupt domestic routines but to transform, damage, and annihilate the very spaces that enable such routines to take place. Its chief effect is to displace the topoi of the primary world; that is, to obscure the places and space which characterise the world and endow the people within it with a sense of identity. When the snow, and with it the fantastic, secondary world, invades Will's bedroom, it shatters the boundary between inside and outside, safety and danger, normal and uncanny, and brings about a startling conflation of spaces.

The Dark poses both a physical and a psychological threat and, like many of the irruptions of the secondary world into the primary world it provokes an intense, physical reaction:

> The fear jumped at him for the third time like a great animal that had been waiting to spring. Will lay terrified, shaking, feeling himself shake, and yet, unable to move. He felt he must be going mad.[153]

Here—as when Mitothin invades on Christmas morning—Will experiences the attack physically: he is supremely aware of his body and of the effect of the fear upon his body. As the house is bound up with identity, any attack on the house is also an attack on its occupants and the physical 'pushing'[154] by the snow and the Dark at the boundaries of the house is also effected psychically. The Dark defamiliarises the attic but it also threatens to defamiliarise Will through madness. He feels as though 'some huge weight were pushing at his mind, threatening, trying to take him over, turn him into something he didn't want to be.'[155] Thus, the human body and the domestic space are conflated. So, when the forces of the Dark disrupt the boundaries of the sanctuary and render the attic unfamiliar (*Unheimlich*)[156] they also disrupt Will's relationship with his environment and his sense of Self. Will can no longer feel at home (*Heimlich*) here and when Paul, one of his older brothers, comes to see what the matter is, Will is only too pleased to abandon the attic space which he once loved.[157]

Will's loss of faith in his bedroom, and by extension his home, has far wider implications than we may first expect: this is the first stage of his initiation as an Old One. He learns to distrust the places and to questions their true topological importance. He now realises that apparently safe places can easily become spaces of terror. Displaced by his fears and by Paul's suggestion that they trade bedrooms, Will no longer feels that he is the master of his own space and is forced to accept that he does not truly belong there.[158] He comes to question his role within the family and whether he truly belongs in his home at all. From now on Will itches to be outside. He is uneasy and unhappy within the confines of the house, making constant excuses to get away from the family home:

> He was growing increasingly desperate as the cold tightened and the snow floated down and down; he felt that if he did not get out of the house soon he would find the Dark had boxed him up forever.[159]

The sanctuary has failed to protect him and it can no longer operate as a metaphor for his personal identity, he realises that 'his house no longer seemed quite the unassailable fortress it had always been.'[160] Now the home is a cipher, a dead image which cannot hope to provide a stable basis for Will's identity and so he must leave it behind. Dewan suggests that 'if a home no longer reflects the self, the protagonist often leaves it in search of a new home,'[161] but because Will's persona was so dependent on the domestic space, he does not leave in search of a new home, but of a new identity.

The night before his eleventh birthday, Will abandons his attic bedroom and on the morning of the winter solstice he abandons his house altogether. He wakes to discover that the usual landscape surrounding his home has been replaced by a snowy forest:

> In the first shining moment he saw the whole strange-familiar world, glistening white [...] and when he looked back through the window he saw that his own world had gone [...] there were no roofs, there were no fields. There were only trees. Will was looking over a great white forest: a forest of massive trees, sturdy as towers and ancient as rock.[162]

Here, the landscape undergoes a physical change to reflect the intellectual and emotional change that has taken place within Will. He has been changed by the events in the attic and his perspective on the world has changed too; his outlook is entirely different and he actually looks out on a transformed world. He has come to the solemn realisation that his house can no longer protect him and that he no longer truly belongs there. The sturdiness and ancientness of this new landscape offers him the opportunity to forge a new, secure identity which is supported by a deep sense of time and a wide reaching awareness of space. He abandons the domestic space, and with it the dead meta narratives of childhood, and walks out into a strange-familiar world in which he is about to discover an entirely new identity.

The Dark Is Rising concerns Will Stanton's quest to negotiate a balance between his family life and his new life as an Old One but also to restore the balance between the two worlds and to reconsecrate the boundaries of his own world and prevent the Dark invading again. When Will walks out between the worlds on Midwinter morning, he confirms his liminal status forever. He becomes a *mearcstapa*, a boundary walker, the one who has a foot in the real and the unreal, not just dwelling in the margins but patrolling them and guarding them too. When he visits Clwyd Farm in *The Grey King*, he walks the borders of the farm, reasserting the boundaries of the space through footfall.

When the borders of Will's attic are compromised, the space ceases to perform its role as a sanctuary. Thus, both Will's sense of identity, which is bound up with the domestic space, and the typological function of the space itself, are undermined, confused and contested by the invasion of the Dark. His loss of faith in the sanctuary provides the impetus for him to leave the home behind on his birthday, to meet with the Old Ones and to take the first step towards embracing a new meta-temporal identity, one which is not so rigidly fixed in space or time.[163] This process of self-discovery and the central role of the roadway topos to this process will be examined in Chapter Three.

Figure 2.1 Mountainside at Tal y Llyn, Wales. ©Jane Carroll.

Chapter Two
The Green Topos
Gardens, Farms, Wilderness

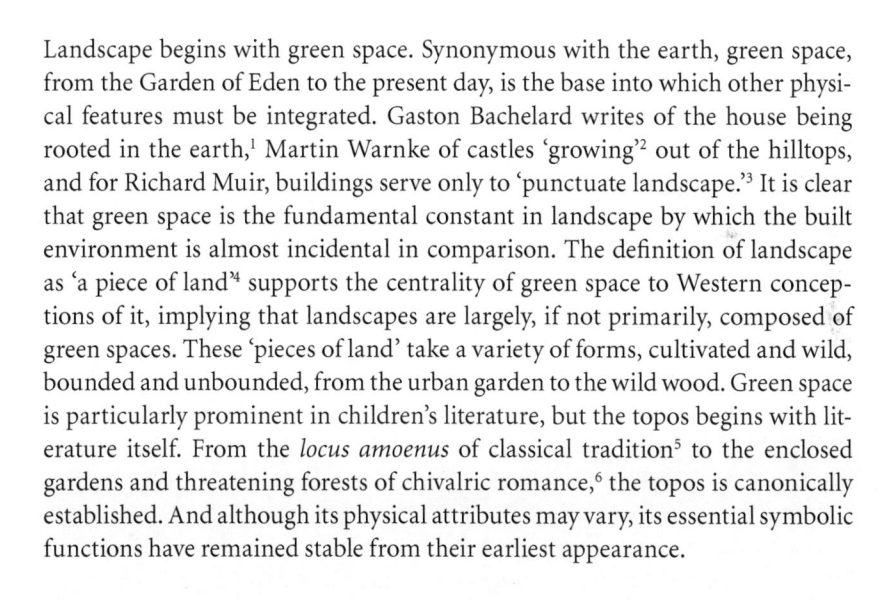

Landscape begins with green space. Synonymous with the earth, green space, from the Garden of Eden to the present day, is the base into which other physical features must be integrated. Gaston Bachelard writes of the house being rooted in the earth,[1] Martin Warnke of castles 'growing'[2] out of the hilltops, and for Richard Muir, buildings serve only to 'punctuate landscape.'[3] It is clear that green space is the fundamental constant in landscape by which the built environment is almost incidental in comparison. The definition of landscape as 'a piece of land'[4] supports the centrality of green space to Western conceptions of it, implying that landscapes are largely, if not primarily, composed of green spaces. These 'pieces of land' take a variety of forms, cultivated and wild, bounded and unbounded, from the urban garden to the wild wood. Green space is particularly prominent in children's literature, but the topos begins with literature itself. From the *locus amoenus* of classical tradition[5] to the enclosed gardens and threatening forests of chivalric romance,[6] the topos is canonically established. And although its physical attributes may vary, its essential symbolic functions have remained stable from their earliest appearance.

The Symbolic Function of the Green Topos

Even in its earliest stages, the green space is a divided topos. Brutality and violence exist within the luxuriant greenery. This dialectic is played out in traditional and post-modern representations of green space where it is a locus both of decay and death as well as renewal and life. Green spaces are immediately associated with life, fertility, and sexuality.[7] The topos is characterized physically by prolific vegetative growth for even in winter plants may still be 'wick,'[8] ultimately capable of renewal in the spring. Because of this apparently miraculous renewal, the green space is a symbol for human renewal and spiritual regeneration through pleasure and relaxation.[9] In comparison to the busy city and its destructive pleasures, the pleasure associated with green space is an *otium*, a drowsy reinvigoration of the spirit, a return to a quieter, more considered lifestyle which repairs the damage of the urban environment.[10]

The green space topos has a long-standing association with life but it has an equally ancient association with death.[11] Although it may be 'perverse to see only [...] decay and death [in green spaces]'[12] it is impossible to overlook the continuity between the vital and lifeless aspects of the topos. What Pagan calls the 'essential ephemerality'[13] of green space is played out again and again in literature. From the fatalistic observations of *The Seafarer* ('the meadows become beautiful, the world hastens on [...] the cuckoo, sad-voiced, Summer's ward sings, bodes sorrow, bitterness in the breast-hoard'[14]) to the rage expressed by Spenser at the 'great enemy [...] wicked Tyme'[15] who ravages the green space and its inhabitants, the topos by its very beauty inspires the fear and knowledge of loss. Able to renew themselves, plants are emblems of immortality, but among them humanity is faced with its inevitable mortality.[16] In literature the contradistinction between cyclical vegetative regeneration and the linear progression of the individual human life throws into relief the transience and impermanence of the human condition.

The green space offers a liminal interstice between life and death. It represents both 'the healing power of the green world [which allows for] the restoration of unity to all the fractures created by civilisation'[17] and a 'nightmare world'[18] where the impermanence of human existence is laid bare. Dusinberre neatly expresses this binary, describing it as a space in which 'the dead survive and withered flowers come to life again.'[19] Drawing together these opposing functions, I will show how pleasure and death are intimately related in both the bounded and domesticated, and in the unbounded, wild forms of the green topos.

A strictly morphological treatment of the topos and its manifestations in medieval and modern literature divides this chapter into two sections. The first discusses garden and farm as bounded green spaces. The second examines pleasance and wilderness as unbounded spaces and Cooper's divergence from the received landscape paradigms, presenting the wilderness not as a background but as an embodied agent. In the *Sequence*, Cooper uses the Brenin Llwyd, Herne the Hunter and the Greenwitch—all associated with Wild Magic—to make the symbolic association of the green space with life, death and renewal unambiguous. The landscape's agency is realised with these figures, and their actions force both readers and other characters to reassess the significance of the natural world. In the representation of pleasance, garden and farm, Cooper writes within a long historical literary tradition, but through her use of the Brenin Llwyd, Herne, and especially through her invention of the Greenwitch, she writes back into the tradition, enriching and developing it for a new age. Cooper engages with, subverts, but ultimately renews and enlarges this, arguably the oldest of all topoi.

Figure 2.2 Cottage garden in Mevagissey, Cornwall. ©Jane Carroll.

The Garden

The Edenic myth embodies the origin of landscape as well as of humankind. The Edenic garden's significance as a 'prototype'[20] is reflected in terrestrial gardens which attempt to recreate or recover something of it. The effects of its loss may be seen to a lesser or greater extent in farmlands and industrial landscapes. Thus, it is a self-replicating virus of a garden, each replication containing a degree of mutation which took it away from or back towards the original, or inverted the values, or revealed something perhaps, a thing which was deeply embedded and hidden in that first garden of significance. [. . .] Eden [is] inescapable.[21]

Even though the garden, literary or literal, may have become a place of fallen pleasures, its original prelapsarian meaning, its innocence and happiness, can never be entirely forgotten. The garden is the site for 'the purest of human pleasures.'[22] Reflecting Eden, 'all gardens exist on the principle of exclusion.'[23] But the garden, bounded, 'unites artifice and nature';[24] it is a deliberately distilled version of the natural world. Like the house, it is kept strictly separate from other less selective, less rarefied spaces. To Sir William Temple's list of garden essentials, 'flowers, fruit, shade, and water,'[25] we must add another characteristic for 'all gardens have a boundary.'[26]

The boundary delimits the garden and also shapes and orders the space within. As Anne Van Erp-Houtepen notes, 'the fence or wall is a basic and characteristic feature of the garden: a garden without a fence is in fact no longer a proper garden.'[27] The fence defines the garden metaphysically as well, turning the garden into an exclusive zone of privilege and concealment, a private pleasance where the emphasis lies, not on wild and unrestricted growth, but on careful cultivation and choice. 'All savage things have been banished'[28] from the garden and only a selection of plants is permitted to grow there. The bounded nature of the garden is reinforced by internal divisions delineating flowerbeds, lawns, and pathways. The rigid demarcations produce an enclosed, cultivated space, one which is in such close proximity to the house and its uses 'as to be like one of the rooms,'[29] and it is often erroneously considered an extension of the domestic space.[30] Although it invites and is vulnerable to many of the same dangers as the house, the garden is not a true domestic space; its boundaries cannot be fully secured and defended like those of the sanctuary topos. The garden's 'foundation is soil';[31] it is open to the earth and also to the sky and so to many kinds of attack which the house, by virtue of its enclosed nature, resists. The garden, in truth, lies between the house and the wider world. It is a liminal space, open but restricted, poised between nature and culture, between private domestic space and public space, and, most importantly, between life and death.

In much of Western literature the garden is an 'anteroom to the netherworld.'[32] Although plants are capable of renewal, the garden's equilibrium is delicate; it is balanced against the weight of the wilderness, against the chaos which threatens to over-run it. Gardening is a constant chore of selection, protection, and exclusion. The vulnerability of the space reminds the audience of the 'essential ephemerality'[33] of human life and human work. From its inception in Eden and the Fall, the social history of the garden topos is associated with mortality and loss.[34] The paradisiacal garden is 'the beginning and end of man's quest for perfection.'[35] Its associations of birth, death, and rebirth are continued in secular literature where the earthly garden is a locus of pleasure and pain, a space where decay and revitalisation meet. In medieval texts and modern children's literature alike, the garden is an appropriate site of both delight and death.

The Garden in Medieval Literature

Western medieval literary gardens are heavily influenced by classical tradition but are transmuted within distinctly Northern European terms.[36] The Anglo-Saxon *Genesis A* offers a peculiarly domestic Eden. It is a 'hope-filled home of joys and pleasures.'[37] After they eat the apple, Adam and Eve are cast out, not into the land of Nod, but into the forest: 'they turned away, the two of them, and walked together, sorrowing, into the green weald and sat apart [...] they covered their bodies with leaves, clothed themselves with greenery, they did not have clothes.'[38] The text presents sin and greenery as intimately linked. Original sin is read as a weed that spreads through the world:

> From that sin,
> sprang forth a seedling, growing
> longer and stronger, a malignant and
> horrible fruit. The tendrils of that crime reached wide
> throughout the tribes of men.
> The branches of sorrow touched hard and sore
> the children of men [...]
> from those broad leaves, each of evils began to sprout.[39]

Although lacking in the set-piece descriptions characteristic of Virgil's *Eclogues*, for instance, this piece, like many Anglo-Saxon texts, demonstrates a sophisticated understanding of the relationship between the green space and death and of the garden as an ordered space set apart, not only from chaos but even from the rest of the unfallen world.

The fourteenth-century *Pearl* clearly relies on the relationship between garden and death. It is a thinly veiled allegory: the speaker has lost his 'pleasant pearl'[40] in a garden, but as the poem continues it becomes clear that the pearl is probably a daughter, now dead and buried. The relationship between the pearl and the lost daughter is intricate; both things are natural, pure, highly valued. The 'pearl' acts as a substitute for the girl's name but also as a substitute for her being: 'the notion that the pearl lost in the ground will eventually rot away combines with the knowledge that bodies likewise rot.'[41] However, the decomposition of the body/pearl also results in 'superlatively fertile soil'[42] which, in turn, gives rise to 'a mound of flowers [...] shadowed full fair and sheen, / with gillyflowers, ginger, and gromwell crowned/ and peonies powdered all between.'[43] The poet acknowledges the relationship between death and renewal: 'each grass must grow from grains that are dead, / no wheat would else to barn be won.'[44] These cycles of renewal are inescapable in the green space.

The Garden in Children's Literature

The complex associations of the garden with death and regeneration seen in the medieval foundation of the topos may similarly be traced in modern children's literature. Whereas some texts such as Mark Haddon's *The Curious Incident of the Dog in the Night-Time* (2003) and Daniel Handler's *The Basic Eight* (1999) use the garden as the location for murders, the garden is most often a ludic space where pleasure is physically and vocally expressed rather than quietly enjoyed. In *The Secret Garden* (1911) Burnett suggests that children need gardens as spaces where they are protected and can play freely without disturbing their elders.[45] In *Tom's Midnight Garden* (1958), Hatty Melbourne initiates play by showing Tom Long around the garden[46] and thus Pearce invokes an unfallen Eden where 'at once, their [Hatty and Tom's] play began again in the garden, and went on as though the garden and their games need never end.'[47] The children's play is inseparable from the garden. Their games can only continue so long as the garden exists. Tellingly, on the night before Hatty's wedding, one of the garden's great trees is struck by lightning and dies, so the damaged garden is indelibly linked to the end of Hatty's childhood, the end of her desire to play, and, one assumes, her initiation into sexual experience.[48]

The Edenic myth establishes the link between green space and death; this link is continuously played out in the canon of children's literature. It is made robustly in Oscar Wilde's *The Happy Prince and Other Stories* (1888). In 'The Young King' Death is explicitly linked to the green space as he owns a garden and wants seeds to plant in it. In 'The Nightingale and the Rose' the garden becomes death's domain. The nightingale is an agent of death and passes 'over the garden like a shadow'[49] but she will sacrifice herself so a withered tree can produce a single red rose.[50] But the student who plucks the rose, spurned by his lover, throws the hard-won rose in the gutter. By discarding it, he ends the chain of renewal and regeneration which should follow a green death.

Deaths that are ultimately futile, such as that of the Nightingale, are a rare occurrence in children's literature especially in texts engaging with the Christian motif of sacrifice and salvation. In Wilde's 'The Selfish Giant' winter/death rules in the Giant's garden where nothing grows and everything is asleep under the snow.[51] The children's arrival heralds the reawakening of the green space. The physical renewal of the space is explicitly linked to the Giant's spiritual regeneration. His picturesque death 'under the tree, all covered with white blossoms'[52] marks, not the end of life but the end of a single stage of life; the blossoms fall at spring's end, promising summer, and then fruition and a rich harvest. With the Giant's death, this cycle is made certain to continue as regeneration is personified by the children who continue to play in his garden. Life after death is, here, both spiritual and metaphoric, and physical and literal.

Though it is not a domestic fantasy, *The Secret Garden,* as perhaps the most celebrated expression of the connection between gardens and renewal, must be discussed here. Natov notes that Burnett juxtaposes images of death and decay with 'prelapsarian'[53] children and greenery which in turn sets up the central philosophy of the text; that physical growth and renewal may initiate spiritual growth and renewal. Although it insists on the 'healing power of the green world,'[54] this healing would be without meaning were it not for the ubiquity of death in the story. Death fills this text; from the cholera epidemic which kills Mary's family, to Colin's mother's death, to Mary's sickliness and the debilitating illness Colin believes he suffers from. The repercussions of these deaths and potential deaths are everywhere; in Mr. Craven's grief which keeps him away from his son, in both Colin and Mary's misery, and, most significantly, in the seeming neglect of the garden. Through Dickon, who acts as a force of nature in the text, Mary begins to restore the garden. The garden and the girl are sympathetic; as she brings it back to life, it has an equal effect on her, indeed, 'the landscape matches her own emotional state.'[55] Mary passes on her newfound sense of health to her cousin Colin, enticing him out of his sick-room with her stories of the beautiful garden. The garden has an immediate effect on Colin.[56] The children transform the garden from a place of death to a place of life, and it continues to transform all who enter into it. The sickness and death which prevailed at the novel's opening are exchanged for general growth and happiness at its end.

One of the purest expressions of the relationship between the garden and death is made by Pullman at the end of *The Amber Spyglass* (2000) as Lyra and Will, who have been able to come together by cutting doorways between worlds, realise they must seal the gap between their worlds and so be parted. It is exceptionally appropriate that their final valediction takes place in the Botanical Garden in Oxford, an intricately liminal space. Built on water meadows beside the Cherwell over the site of a medieval Jewish cemetery[57] and beside Magdalen Tower where songs greet the dawn on May Day because 'sumer is icumen in,'[58] the gardens are deeply imbued with the connotations of death and natural cycles of renewal. This inherent symbolism is enriched because as a 'physic' garden, the plants within are used to cure disease. Thus, the associations of magic and science, of death and healing are all present in the space before a single word of dialogue is spoken. The profound nuances of this space are supported and echoed by the text when Lyra and Will speak about their deaths and separation. Their decision to come to the same place at the same time every year means that, in effect, their relationship will be cyclically renewed, a renewal which is silently present in the annual regeneration of the garden and expressly articulated in the May Day rituals at Magdalen Tower. Pullman's subtle evocations of space, through the sounds of the water-bird and the traffic, the unmentioned but understood flow of the water, and the explicit references to the passing of time, allow the topographical setting to support and lend symbolic weight to the narrative action.[59] Here, the cycles of death and renewal inherent in the green topos and especially in garden space are foregrounded.

The Garden in The Dark Is Rising Sequence

Considering the general importance of landscape in Cooper's *Sequence*, it is noteworthy that the garden sub-topos appears in only one book, *Silver on the Tree*. There are two gardens, the Stantons' and one in the Lost Land. Cooper, demonstrating her awareness of the topos' functions, uses them to provide very different reflections of the garden space.

Silver on the Tree

The Stantons' garden, first glimpsed through the window in the opening scene of *The Dark Is Rising,* is closely associated with house and family. As with all earthly gardens, the family must work hard to maintain it. Cooper presents this maintenance as a physical struggle. Stephen 'fights'[60] with a tangled rose bush and when Will mows the lawn, it is described in terms of battle and victory: 'At a triumphant trot Will mowed the last patch of grass, and collapsed, panting, draped over the lawn-mower handle. Sweat was trickling down the side of his nose, and his bare chest was damp, speckled with tiny cut stems of grass.'[61] Although the garden is full of natural things, none is allowed to take its natural form. But the garden is by no means passive. Cooper shows the plants as dangerous and actively resistant to human control. Stephen is 'embraced by the sprawling branches of a climbing rose,'[62] and when Will and Barbara go to help him they too are assaulted by 'wildly sprawling arms.' The rose bush is anthropomorphized. Their pruning and staking is described in violent, intensely physical terms: they 'drove stakes into the gravelly earth' and 'tied the branches to keep the billowing sprays of roses off the ground'[63] and Barbara is lashed and cut by 'a rebellious rose-branch [that] scored a thin red line across her bare back.'[64]

This garden, like all others, recalls Eden; there are overt references here to the celestial garden and to the Fall. Will is unimpressed by Barbara's complaints about the roses:

> 'Ouch!' said Barbara for the fifth time [...]
> 'Your own fault,' said Will unfeelingly. 'You should have more clothes on.'
> 'It's a sunsuit. For the sunshine, duckie.'
> 'Nekkidness,' said her younger brother solemnly, 'be a shameful condition for a yooman bein'. Tain't roight. 'Tes a disgrace to the neighbour'ood, so 'tes.'[65]

This verbal sparring between Will and his siblings illustrates the garden's function as a ludic space; the children play, not boisterously like Hatty and Tom, but by teasing and joking, initiating a word-play in which whole family can join. But Will's moralistic comments, in their mock-yokel accent, have deeper significance, recalling Eden and the sin that began in that archetypal garden. By suggesting that nakedness is a 'shameful condition' Will alludes to original sin. Nakedness was the prelapsarian condition for a human being. After Adam and Eve eat of the forbidden fruit, they recognise nakedness. Their decision to wear clothing marks a turning point in self-awareness. By making and wearing artificial clothes they set themselves apart from the animals and, most importantly, construct an identity independent of their God. Cooper depicts the earthly garden in terms of original sin's results—labour, pain, mortality, and shame—but also offers a potential sign of redemption in the rose-bush, its thorns, and the blood it draws from Stephen and Barbara which echo Christ's redeeming sacrifice.[66] The garden is, then, a place of renewed awareness of the body and of its relationship with space.

The Lost Land

The garden of the Lost Land offers an alternative to the Stantons' domestic garden, providing a paradigm for a different kind of garden, the formal garden. Formal gardens appeal not so much to the pleasures of the senses but to the mind in the satisfaction of 'leisured aesthetics.'[67] They are 'product[s] of the orderly mind rather than the playground of the unchained senses,'[68] providing a space, not for play, but for subdued reflection and refined pleasures. The garden in the Lost Land is clearly a formal, carefully cultivated garden. Not only is the garden itself enclosed, but the roses are grown in carefully defined beds and the marble balustrades guide the human visitors through the space. Cooper's lengthy description pays particular attention to the contrast between the abundant roses and the 'cool lines' of the architecture:

> The air was heavy with fragrance, and everywhere there were roses. Squares, triangles, circles of bright blossom patched the grass all around, red and yellow and white and all colours between. Before them was the entrance to an enclosed circular garden, a tall arch in a high hedge of tumbling red roses. They walked through, almost giddy with the scent. In the great circle of the garden inside, formal balustrades and seats of white marble were set round a glittering fountain [. . .] And as if to offset the cool lines of the marble, mounds of roses billowed everywhere, enormous bushes growing rampant, tall as trees.[69]

There is nothing wild or uncultivated here. It is as contrived as a green space can possibly be. The garden is laid out in squares, triangles and circles, geometric patterns offering a sense of order and regularity to the space, and it is no accident that the rhythm and form of the conversations there are dictated by the rhythm and form of the landscape. The Black Rider, Mitothin, speaks 'coldly' and 'formally' and uses 'assured, almost affected' gestures mimicking the polite and affected behaviour once expected of visitors to the great formal European gardens.[70] But the cumulative effect of the formal arrangement of space and formal speech is oddly disturbing.

In its stilted formality, the garden of the Lost Land diverges from the other green spaces in the *Sequence*, creating unease within the description of this topos. Cooper writes:

> the Rider bent and broke off one yellow rose and sniffed it. 'Such flowers, now. Roses of all the centuries. *Marechal Niel*, here, never such a scent anywhere . . . or that strange tall rose beside you with the small red flowers, called *moyseii*, that goes its own way, sometimes blooming more heavily than any other rose and then perhaps for years not blooming at all.'[71]

Here, the problems of the Lost Land are laid bare. The Lost Land and its exquisite rose garden are outside of nature. There is 'never such a scent anywhere' as in this garden, which implies that the scent and, by extension, the garden does not properly exist. In addition, the *moyseii* flowers by dropping out of or speeding up the cycle of the years' growth and regrowth defy the patterns of nature. Here, roses 'of all the centuries' bloom together, and all at once; the garden is outside of time, untouched by the cycles of growth and decay. Here, life is not counterbalanced by death. In the Lost Land, time and distance are collapsed and stretched out to bizarre proportions, death is endlessly spun out and deferred. The Lost Land and its metonymic garden are static. The deferral of death is particularly important because, as we know, death ought to be, and is, intrinsic to the ordinary green spaces of *The Dark Is Rising Sequence*.

Figure 2.3 Farmland near St. Austell, Cornwall. ©Jane Carroll.

The Farm

There is a sub-set of the green topos which cannot be described as a pleasurable space. Whereas the garden and the pleasance are spaces for relaxation, recreation and pleasure, the farm is a utilitarian space. Whereas the pleasures of the garden may negate the hardship of the work needed to maintain it, farming is 'the work that's never finished,'[72] a work that is, in English, linguistically and metaphorically indivisible from the space itself. The bounded nature of the farm is indicative of a level of control and contrivance needed to wrest a space from the chaotic and undifferentiated wilderness. However, even though the pleasures of the garden are widely extolled, there is comparatively little literature about the pleasures of the farm. The farm is not 'equally blessed,' suggests J. B. Jackson, 'because classical tradition still assigned [farm labourers] the lowest place in the social order—because, in the words of a medieval prelate, "They are anxious only for this present life, like brute beasts, and care not for God."'[73] Whereas even the meanest garden aspires to the ideals of Eden, operating spiritually and vertically as well as physically and horizontally, the farm is firmly rooted in the earth.[74] Cain, the first farmer, was also the first murderer. On the farm nature is realistic and unidealised, 'known through the need to make a living.'[75]

The earthly and secular nature of the farm impacts on its representations in literature. Virgil's *Georgics* provide the classical exemplar of an ambiguous view of farm life. It is only with the picturesque and Romantic movements that rural life is regularly idealised.[76] As a result, perhaps, of the violent reaction against industrialization and urbanization, the Romantics promoted 'an idealisation of rural life that obscures the realities of labour and hardship.'[77] This romanticism has continued to mark the representations of farms and farming in Western literature so that, as Tuan observes, 'what we have is a vast, largely sentimental literature on farming life written by people with uncallused hands.'[78]

The Farm in Medieval Literature

As in many modern texts, agricultural economy often has only an assumed existence in medieval literature. In *Beowulf*, for instance, there is no mention of agriculture or of the processes by which the great feasts are prepared. But the *Beowulf* poet's intention is not to provide a picture of everyday life but to tell of an exalted life. Where writers have depicted the everyday realities and hardships, the farm's representation is topographically and socially accurate. In medieval literature, the farm is characterised as a space set apart from the wilderness but at some remove from the house, given over either to ploughland or to pasture-land.[79] Without the mechanical and chemical aids which make modern farming easier, medieval farming is characterised by heavy labour and fear. 'There is no guarantee that one good year will be followed by another';[80] all efforts may come to nothing. The farm is a place of constant struggle against vermin, weeds, weather, and disease. It is a space 'threatened by the entire universe.'[81]

The effects of these threats are visible in medieval literature where the struggle between nature and culture is foregrounded. As a bounded space brought under human control, the farm is the antithesis of the barren and hostile wilderness. Farm-work is a struggle to prevent this cultivated land from reverting to its natural, wild state. It is a struggle to impose an artificial order on the landscape and an artificial calendar on the natural year by planting and harvesting, breeding and slaughter. Thus, the same cycles of death and renewal seen in the garden space are writ large in the farm. However, whereas these cycles occur reflexively in the garden, they are rigorously enforced on the farm. Farming, then, exemplifies not only a struggle against the wilderness but a battle for growth and renewal.

In Aelfric's *Colloquy of the Occupations*, a children's schoolbook from the later tenth century,[82] the harsh realities of farm life are explicit. The fifteen characters who speak the dialogue in this dramatic text describe their work and try to ascertain their usefulness to the whole community. Although the *Colloquy* has a playful humour, the hardships of farming life are not softened as in many modern children's texts. The ploughman, occupying the lowest rung of the social ladder, speaks first. He 'goes out in the day-red' and ploughs 'a full acre or more each day.' He 'do[es] not dare to loiter at home for fear of [his] lord's ire.' His remark '*Þerle ic swince*'[83]—'I work hard'—is an almost humorous understatement. Even his companion, a small boy who helps to drive the cattle is 'hoarse from cold and shouting.' The Shepherd, speaking next, describes his 'great hardships.' And, unlike the drowsing shepherds of Virgil's *Eclogues*, he must 'stand over his flock in heat and cold for fear that wolves devour them.'[84]

The grim depiction of farming and farm-life is also evident in medieval texts aimed at an adult audience. In the third branch of the *Mabinogion*, Manawydan's farm is stripped bare by mice. After his year of hard work and his patient waiting for the harvest, he is ready to despair: '"Oh Lord God," he said, "who is trying to destroy me completely? I know this much: whoever began this destruction is now bringing it to an end, and has destroyed the land along with me."'[85] Here, the land is synonymous with the labour invested in it. Even though there is no attempt to equate the farm with the sanctuary topos, it is clear that Manawydan's identity, as much as his fortunes, is bound up in his farm. The intense personal relationship with the agricultural landscape is also expressed in medieval Icelandic literature where 'sagawriting was rooted in a nonclerical and nonaristocratic farm culture.'[86] In a culture where even the most highly regarded members of society were working farmers, farms and the farming calendar were a vital part of the literature. The land is defined by settlement, by farming, and, in turn, the people are identified by the land around them. Lönnroth notes that whenever a character is introduced in *Njal's Saga*, his name is closely, if not immediately, followed by the name of his farm.[87] Compared to the romanticised landscapes of modern literature

> the landscape of the Old Icelandic sagas is [...] compellingly real. A thousand details of hill and harbor and grazing slope, of Icelandic nights and winters, build up an unmistakably authenticity of background. [...] there can be no other national literature where the topographical

pilgrimage is so romantically rewarding. But the romance, let us be clear, is ours, for [. . .] land is described according to its use, not its beauty.[88]

Farms shape lives in the sagas. The steadings are the background and setting for much of the dramatic action of the texts, providing a context against which violent actions seem more heinous,[89] as when Hoskuld is murdered in his cornfield by Njal's sons. Hoskuld dies sword in one hand and seed-basket in the other, an image which demonstrates the unity of the lethal and regenerative aspects of the green topos expressed in the farm in medieval Icelandic literature.[90]

To Hoskuld we may compare Gunnar. Unlike the other men in *Njal's Saga*, Gunnar does not have a proper nickname but is simply called *Gunnar of Hlidarendi*, Gunnar of the Slope's End. He is absolutely synonymous with his farm. Unsurprisingly, when Gunnar is outlawed, he cannot bear to be parted from his steading. As he looks back on his farm he is overcome with desire:

> Then he said, 'Lovely are the slopes, more lovely than I have ever seen them before, pale cornfields and new-mown meadows. I am going back home, and I will not go away.'[91]

Gunnar's words *'og fara hvergi'* 'I will not go away' seem to foreshadow his death, and it is one of the greatest ironies of the saga that Gunnar's death comes about because he feels he cannot live without his farm. Gunnar is an unusual character in that he has a deep awareness of beauty. He knows that the fields are lovely as well as useful commodities, and, as Pearsall and Salter suggest, his 'sense of beauty is a pride in use'.[92] Gunnar does not romanticise Hlidarendi; he does not want to go home in order to relax and enjoy the view but to work the land he has settled. He sees the function of the space as an intrinsic quality. The slopes of Hlidarendi are lovely because they are fair and they are fair because his corn grows there. Gunnar looks at the landscape as a farmer; what he feels when he looks at his home is not mere pleasure but satisfaction.

The Farm in Children's Literature

The same functional aesthetic is rarely seen in modern British children's literature. There are two discernable reasons; first, during the Norman Conquest 'a profound contempt for the unnoble [sic] classes of society, was introduced into our island,'[93] and second, the rise of Romanticism caused a movement towards the picturesque and idealistic aspects of the countryside, particularly farm life.[94] This trend ultimately resulted in representations of the farm as a holiday site and as a place of rest in texts such as Enid Blyton's *The Children of Cherry-Tree Farm* (1940) and *Five Go to Finniston Farm* (1960). Dick King-Smith's *The Sheep Pig* (1983) presents a deeply unrealistic version of farm life where sheep may be herded with polite smiles and where, despite the passing months measured by the pig's growth, the weather only changes once.[95] Steve Augarde's *The Various* (2003) similarly romanticizes the farm. Populated by curiously silent livestock, the farm is contrasted to the city life which Midge shares with her mother, a driven, self-centred musician. Not only is the farm at a remove from urbanization (which is established as distasteful and boring), but the space also takes on many of the elements of the *locus amoenus*, in which there is no possibility of work.[96] Such texts represent a complete break with the 'work that's never finished'[97] or the hardship and labour Adam is condemned to in Genesis.[98]

There is, however, a handful of texts aimed at older readers which resists this trend including Kate Thompson's *Annan Water* (2004) which presents a highly unromantic vision of keeping horses and Meg Rosoff's *How I Live Now* (2004) which treats the farm as a source of food and a place of hard work. I will discuss Rosoff's text in detail in Chapter Five. Other texts which resist this trend may be set in a time before Romanticism or in an alternate world where Romanticism had little impact or never existed. Susan Price's *The Sterkarm Handshake* (1998), set in an alternative sixteenth-century Britain, is one such example. Here, farms are populated by sheep with 'long shaggy coats of wiry hair rather than fleece'[99] and shepherds ride armed with lances and swords for fear of attack.[100] Livestock are precious and jealously guarded. Another example of this anti-romantic portrayal of farming may be found in Terry Pratchett's *The Wee Free Men* (2003) where the farm is big and busy and Tiffany Aching, at nine years old, is made responsible for the dairy.[101] Pratchett resists idealizing the farm and its livestock. Sheep are described as 'just bags of bones, eyeballs and teeth, lookin' for new ways to die.'[102] The contrast between the realistic and idealized versions of farm life is sharpest when Tiffany brings a china shepherdess home from a fair as a gift to her Granny Aching:

> The china shepherdess has an old-fashioned long dress with the bulgy bits in the side that made it look as though she had saddlebags in her knickers. [. . .] This wasn't a shepherdess who'd ever worn big boots stuffed with wool, and tramped the hills in the howling wind with the sleet being driven along like nails. She'd never tried in that dress to pull out a ram who'd got his horns tangled in a thorn patch. This wasn't a shepherdess who'd kept up with the champion shearer for seven hours, sheep for sheep, until the air was hazy with grease and wool and blue with cussing [. . .] It was a lovely thing but it was a joke of a shepherdess made by someone who'd probably never seen a sheep up close.[103]

Pratchett's description of the two versions of shepherding plainly condemns the idealization of farm life as being inauthentic because it is so far removed from the animals and the landscape which make farming possible and difficult. Like the 'sentimental literature on farming life written by people with uncallused hands'[104] the china shepherdess represents an impossible and idyllic version of rural life starkly at odds with the realities of farming. The ornament is an offensive joke because it undermines the sense that a 'pride in use' might be more important than a love of aesthetics. Pratchett, like Price, does not just resist the romantic trend so common in children's literature but actively writes against it; presenting an alternative which is rooted in topography and in a practical awareness of farming as a constant struggle which can, nevertheless, impart a deep and authentic sense of satisfaction.

The Farm in The Dark Is Rising Sequence

This same satisfaction is reflected by Cooper's farmers who share the attitudes of their counterparts in the Norse sagas and are unsentimental, practical, and even blunt in their treatment of land and livestock. In *The Grey King*, Will's cousin Rhys Evans tersely remarks that he had been 'out since six with only an old cup of tea inside.'[105] Cooper's descriptions of their farms are suitably spare. In *The Dark Is Rising*, she describes the farm as a 'great earthen square enclosed by buildings on three sides [...] The cowshed must have been mucked out that day; Old George, the toothless cattleman, was piling dung across the yard.'[106] The farm is neither beautiful nor romantic and the work that takes place there is far from glamorous. In this way Cooper breaks away from the romanticizing trend of children's literature and in doing so, connects the farms in the *Sequence* to an older literary tradition, a tradition which arises from and is deeply embedded in the landscape.

Silver on the Tree

Although death is omnipresent in the green topos there are few incidents which directly confront the reader with the realities of mortality. In *Silver on the Tree* a mink enters the Stantons' garden and attacks their chickens, killing six of them. The account of the scene is fractured, unfolding in half-light, and it takes some time for Will, and the reader, to understand properly what is taking place. The garden is 'full of colliding bodies' and 'the cackling of frightened birds.'[107] Death fills the space, takes it over, pushing out all of the pleasurable elements of the topos. Death here is not peaceful as in 'The Selfish Giant' or noble and selfless as in 'The Nightingale and the Rose', but rather overwhelmingly brutal.[108] 'Will could feel the sense of malevolence, of immanent undiluted ill-wishing, so strong all around him that he could scarcely move.'[109] This evil is, for Will, a lack of causality. The mink's actions are unjustifiable; it does not kill for food, or because it is frightened but for malice and 'for the love of it'[110] and so, in Will's mind, the chickens' deaths are shocking and futile.

Mrs. Stanton, however, finds a way to turn a symbolic loss into a very practical gain. She 'picked up a pair of dangling dead chickens. "Well," she said with brisk resignation, "bring them in. We'll just have to make the best of it and hope the wretched animal didn't choose the best layers."'[111] If the mink won't eat the chickens, she suggests, the family will. She transforms the context and the nature of the deaths, endowing them with a new purpose. Her actions and her attitude do not fit with the expected mood of the garden topos but have more in keeping with the attitude of the farm. Cooper here reminds us of Mrs. Stanton's farming background and, acknowledging a sympathy between land and occupier, notes that 'their house had once been a vicarage, never a farm, but the chickens and rabbits that their farm-bred mother kept were enough to change its mood.'[112] Mrs. Stanton's actions overhaul the orientation of the garden space, blurring the distinctions between two different aspects of the topos. Although she cannot change the physical aspects of the garden, she succeeds in changing the figurative positioning of the space. Thus, Cooper implies that spaces are directly affected by the attitudes and behaviour of the people within them.

Mrs. Stanton's practical outlook fits well with that of the farming community she comes from. Whereas the connection between the garden and death is largely symbolic, the connection between death and the farm is borne out in realism. Death on the farm is systematic, professional, and coldly accepted. Here, death is a practical end function to lives brought about specifically for the purpose of utility, not a sign or an index of some greater level of significance. It is surprising then, that the connection between death and the farm topos is one which is so often denied in children's literature. Virgil notes in the *Georgics* how the 'world forces all things to be bad, to founder and to fall'[113] at certain times and that a field must sometimes be allowed to lie fallow before it can be replanted. Fallow periods, like winter, are periods of death and decay which must be scheduled into the farming calendar,[114] and are often preceded by rituals which instigate, celebrate and pre-empt these periodic and symbolic deaths.[115]

On a practical level, there is the idea of the food chain in which death is necessary for the continuation of life. The cycles of harvest and slaughter are associated specifically with the farm as opposed to any other aspect of the green space. At the very beginning of *The Dark Is Rising*, Will and his brother James pay a visit to a nearby farm to collect some hay to feed their pet rabbits. Farmer Dawson gives Will a message to pass on to Mrs. Stanton:

> 'Tell your mum I'll have ten birds off her tomorrow. And four rabbits. Don't look like that, young Will. If it's not their happy Christmas, it's one for the folks as'll have them.'[116]

Will is sad that his pets will be killed and eaten, but Farmer Dawson makes it clear that such an attitude is unacceptable, reminding Will that the rabbits and hens exist as part of a food chain, a natural, ecological cycle. On the farm, death is an expected and accepted part of life. Whereas death may be implicit in the garden, the farm makes the association of death and the green space explicit.

The Grey King

On Clwyd Farm, death is built into the routines of work and is brought about with brusque efficiency. When Will first walks about the farm he meets John Rowlands, the farmhand who is busy cutting back the hedgerows:

> [Rowlands] moved gradually along the hedge, first chopping carefully here and there with a murderous tool like a cross between an axe and a pirate's cutlass [. . .] before him, the hedge grew wild and high, great arms groping out uncontrolled in all directions as the hazel and hawthorn did their best to grow into full-fledged trees, Behind him, [. . .] he left instead a neat fence: scores of beheaded branches bristling waist-high like spears, with every fifth branch bent mercilessly down at right angles.[117]

Rowlands cuts the hedge back 'like a butcher jointing a sheep';[118] he is efficient but brutal in his actions. Whereas his actions may be seen as a mere extension of the weeding which helps to maintain order in the garden, the analogy of the butcher and the sheep turns the hedge into a living thing which Rowlands has killed, an idea which is carefully extrapolated through the mention of its 'arms' and 'heads' and 'limbs.' The hedge is treated as something animate, fleshly and, most disturbingly, sentient. Through Will's eyes, the trees are seen to 'do their best to grow' and so their unrestricted growth is cast as positive, Rowlands's actions are, by implication, negative, and perhaps even evil. Here, the narrative voice strongly reflects Will's discomfort with Rowlands's actions. Will's distaste for killing and pain add to the sensitivity and likeable nature of his character. As the youngest of the Old Ones he stands in contradistinction to the others who see death as something inevitable and are largely indifferent to it. Will displays the same disquiet at the apparent butchery of the hedge as he did at the anticipated butchery of the rabbits and the hens in *The Dark Is Rising*.

It is not long before Rowlands reiterates the lesson Will learned from Farmer Dawson; death is natural and sometimes essential. He says 'Well, let me tell you now, if we were to leave this lovely wild hedge the way it is now, it would take over half the field before this time next year. [. . .] Like life it is, Will—sometimes you must seem to hurt something in order to do good for it'.[119] For Rowlands the butchery of the hedge is merely a stage in a long and bitter territorial war. The hedge threatens to 'take over' and he must cut it back in order to preserve the function of space and retain possession of the farmland. The existence of the farm is maintained through the agency of death. Some things must die to ensure the survival of others.

Yet this knowledge sits uneasily with Will. As an Old One, he is 'outside time'[120] and cannot die, yet he must accept that everyone and everything around him is mortal. The impending deaths of his family and friends weigh heavily on him. Towards the end of *The Grey King* he tries to explain some of this to Rowlands, saying 'in this sort of a war, it is not possible to pause, to smooth the way for one human being, because even that one small thing could mean an end of the world for all the rest.'[121] Will tries, somewhat unsuccessfully, to justify what he feels to be a 'cold absolute good'[122] but it is clear that although he has grown and changed over the course of the *Sequence*, there is still some part of him that feels that death is wrong: he sees it as the antithesis to life rather than as part of life.

Even though the Clwyd farmers acknowledge the importance of death as a means to preserve life, not all deaths are acceptable. When Cafall is shot by Caradog Pritchard for worrying sheep, the farmers, Owen Davies among them, concur that when a dog goes 'bad in the head' it has to be disposed of. Davies tries to console Bran, saying:

> 'Cafall was going for the sheep, there is no question. We all saw. He was a lovely dog, a beauty'—his voice shook, and he cleared his throat—'but he must have gone bad in the head. I cannot say that I would not have shot him myself, in Caradog's place. That is the right of it. Once a dog turns killer, it is the only thing to do.'[123]

Like the other deaths on the farms, Cafall's death serves a purpose; it is a means of preserving life, in this case the life of the sheep. But Owen Davies later admits that sometimes a sheep-killer can be spared and re-homed, moved somewhere away from sheep so death is by no means 'the only thing to do.' There is a strong suggestion that Cafall's death does not sit properly with the other farm deaths. Farm deaths should be timely as well as useful; Cafall's untimely and violent death serves no real purpose other than Caradog Pritchard's desire to hurt Bran and his father. Cafall's death cannot be made useful in the way that Mrs. Stanton makes use of the dead chickens, nor can it be seen as a relief, as Hawkin's death, which I will discuss shortly, can. But in two ways it is exactly like all of the other deaths in the *Sequence* and can be seen to fit in with the pattern which Cooper has laid down in her texts. First, like all the others, it is very physical. In the *Sequence*, death is a bodily thing rather than a metaphysical symbol. Second, it takes place outside, in a green space. By making these deaths physical and in rooting them in green spaces, Cooper reinforces the idea that death is not simply part of the natural cycle, but part of the landscape itself. Moving beyond the bounded spaces under human control and into the wild green spaces, it becomes clear that landscape supports and embraces death just as readily as it supports and embraces life. Nowhere is death, as a threat to human life and its works, more evident than in the representations of the wilderness.

Figure 2.4 View from Dynsynni Valley, Wales. ©Jane Carroll.

Unbounded Green Spaces

Beyond the fragile gardens and strictly ordered farms lie the pleasance and the wilderness, 'the most potent construction[s] of nature available.'[124] Both the pleasance, with its unrestricted growth, and the wilderness, with its barren wastes, resist human habitation and human interference. These unbounded spaces 'confront and confound [human] design.'[125] Nash defines wild spaces as areas 'untrammeled by man, where man himself is a visitor who does not remain.'[126] Although these spaces lie beyond human divisions and appropriations of landscape, they are not beyond the cultural imagination which popularly divides wild spaces into two categories. Simon Schama suggests 'there have always been two kinds of arcadia: shaggy and smooth; dark and light; a place of bucolic pleasure and a place of primitive panic.'[127] Thus, the unpopulated, unbounded green spaces beyond the reach of the city and of civilisation may be either positive or negative. They are either pleasures or wildernesses. But, even though they appear to offer an alternative to the bounded spaces already discussed, they subscribe to the same tensions and symbolic functions of all green spaces.

Figure 2.5 Riverbank at Pentewan, Cornwall. ©Jane Carroll.

The Pleasance

All gardens attempt to reflect the original, Edenic space but, ironically, the manual labour needed to maintain such spaces emanates from the Fall. Paradoxically, the harder one works in the garden, the further one diverges from the true value of the original, archetypal paradise. It is, however, possible to attain that relaxing, pleasurable space without any effort at all. As a sub-topos, the pleasance is almost defined by the lack of work that occurs there. Even though it may be associated with shepherding, it is not truly a part of the farm but is 'given over less to usefulness and a rich harvest than to pleasure.'[128] The pleasance is a wild space; it is set apart from civilisation, from buildings and development and, consequently, removed from the idea of work.

Although the garden is indisputably the first topos, the pleasance too has a long provenance and is closely related to the *locus amoenus*, the 'lovely place' of classical literature. Curtius identifies six physical attributes of the topos—grass, trees, shade, flowing water, wild flowers, and a gentle breeze—which are invariably present.[129] These features are well combined; the tree provides shade, the breeze makes its presence felt by stirring the leaves of the tree and the grass and flowers around it. Water flows through the scene, provides fertility, and relieves the thirst brought on by the hot sun. The attributes of the *locus amoenus* allow us to recognise a temporal as well as geographical setting. A gentle breeze is redundant on a bitterly cold day, shade is unremarkable at night, and wild flowers are not common in winter, so the *locus amoenus* is not only a physical topos, but a temporal topos too. It belongs to hot summer afternoons—a lovely time as well as a lovely place. The pleasures associated with this space are, then, sensual and physical rather than intellectual or spiritual, and they have dictated its literary function. In *The Experience of Landscape* (1996) Appleton posits a sociological explanation as to why the charms of the pleasance are so difficult to resist, suggesting that human enjoyment of spaces and landscapes are deeply ingrained and are linked to evolutionary desires. Humans, Appleton observes, feel most comfortable in a space where there are 'prospects,' or vantage points and 'refuges' in which one may hide in case of an attack.[130] Viewed in terms of Appleton's theory, the *locus amoenus* is nothing short of the ideal space; prospects and refuges are provided by the trees and food is in ample and obvious supply. In some versions of this topos—as in the medieval romance *Sir Orfeo*—the tree is a fruit tree and it provides both prospect and refuge, both food and shelter.[131] The pleasance is ideally suited to human habitation and the struggles and hardships presented by rough or inhospitable terrain are conspicuously absent here. The combination of prospect and refuge means that within the pleasance, one relaxes and enjoys doing nothing and, very often, falls asleep.

Yet sleep is 'death's brother'[132] and the pleasance, although it seems unlikely, is easily transmuted into a wilderness, an environment for death and suffering. Schama's description of the 'two arcadias' shows an awareness of the dichotomous, even duplicitous, nature of the unbounded space, but still presents the two aspects as completely separate. It is Natov's term 'dark pastoral' which perhaps best unites the oxymoronic aspects of the wild spaces.[133] Natov argues that '[the] relationship between the light and the dark sides of the green world is not simply dichotomous: it is not a matter of good and evil [...] both are part of the imagination and function.'[134] The integration of light and dark, life and death, reconfigures the pleasance as a liminal space where the wild abandon and murderous impulses of the Bacchanal can coexist with the drowsing shepherd and his lover.

The Pleasance in Medieval Literature

The *locus amoenus* is not only one of the first topoi identified, but among the most common in literature. Although 'the possibility of a literary pastoral tradition in the early English vernacular has received little critical attention, and has often been explicitly denied [...] it seems that Old English poetry can reflect knowledge and exploitation of the literary *locus amoenus*.'[135] Indeed, within English medieval literature, the topos has been 're-made within the poetic idioms of the vernacular,'[136] and it is transposed in terms of the vernacular landscape; in the cooler Northern European summers, the gentle breeze may be redundant, for instance. The most striking correspondence between the classical and Northern European use of the topos is that in both cases, the topos serves three main functions. First, it is a site for physical indulgence, from the wild Bacchic orgies described in classical literature to the early modern depictions of the land of Cockaigne where work was illegal and food was supplied in grotesque abundance.[137] Second, the *locus amoenus* allows for the loosening, and even the abandonment, of social restrictions. Third, and perhaps most significantly, it provides a space for dreaming. In *Sir Orfeo*, the topos takes the form of an orchard where the Queen falls 'a slepe opon the grene. / The maidens durst hir nought awake, / Bot lete hir ligge and rest take. / So she slepe till afternone / that undertide was all y-done.'[138] Like much of the sleep which takes place in the *locus amoenus*, the Queen's sleep has an unnatural, even a supernatural quality; she sleeps through the day, rather than at night, and once she wakes she is distressed and uneasy, finding that she cannot sleep except in the orchard. As an idealized prospect/refuge, the orchard is already a dream-landscape, and hence it becomes a proper locus for dreaming.

The opening scene of William Langland's fourteenth-century text, *Piers the Ploughman*, illustrates the three functions of the pleasance. The poet/protagonist lies down on a sunny riverbank—an obvious, if sparsely described version of the topos—and dreams a long and complicated dream with prophetic and allegorical significance. Langland writes:

> In a summer season, when soft was the sun/ I shaped myself in shrouds, as if I were a shepherd/ in the habit of a hermit of unholy works/ I went out into the world to hear of wonders./ But on a May morning, in the Malvern

Hills,/ a strange thing befell me, of fairy magic, I thought; / I was weary from my wanderings and went to rest/ under a broad bank beside a brook/ and as I lay, I leaned down and looked into the waters/ they swayed so prettily I slumbered into sleep./ Then I had a marvelous dream.[139]

Here, Langland touches on many of the aspects of the *locus amoenus*. It is summer-time, the poet seeks rest and shade by a riverbank and has stepped outside of his usual social role in order to do so; he dresses 'as if' he were a shepherd. The topos allows social norms and restrictions to be put aside. Langland definitively invokes the pleasance by allowing his speaker to have 'a marvellous dream', which is magically induced. *Piers the Ploughman* is a strong indicator of how the *locus amoenus* has been assimilated into the English literary tradition and when we come to depictions of the *locus amoenus* in *The Dark Is Rising Sequence*, it is clear that Cooper consciously follows in this tradition.

The Pleasance in Children's Literature

The pleasance occurs regularly in children's literature. As John David Moore notes, childhood and the pleasance are inseparable; 'Arcadia of the Golden Age is the mytho-historical childhood of the race.'[140] Thus, the pleasance is an appropriately common topos, and, in children's literature, it comes with all the associations of drowsing and dreaming that it has had since its earliest inception. In children's literature, as in medieval texts, the pleasance is generally situated at the beginning of a text, enabling the onset of a dream-world, or the establishment of an idyllic calm which is to be somehow shattered or intruded upon over the course of the narrative. For example, Carroll's *Alice's Adventures in Wonderland* (1865) opens and closes with a 'golden afternoon'[141] on a riverbank, a true incarnation of the pleasance; indeed, it is the only realistic piece of landscape in the text, for everything else is part of the dream Alice slips into while drowsing in the sun. By bookending his text with images of the pleasance and drawing upon the typical, even stereotypical physical elements of the sub-topos, Carroll deftly places his text within the greater tradition of dream-narratives, lending canonical weight to a text which deliberately presents itself as nonsensical.

The pleasance also makes an appearance, albeit one which is reduced in significance, in Kipling's *Puck of Pook's Hill* (1906). Unlike Carroll's pleasance, this is not a site for dreaming, but a peaceful place away from the bustle of the farm and a safe place where Puck and the other spirits of the land might come and visit Dan and Una. Perhaps the most iconic and enduring pleasances are the ones created by Grahame in *The Wind in the Willows* (1908). Manlove suggests Grahame's text contains 'the purest idyll'[142] and Carpenter goes even further, claiming that 'of all the Victorians and Edwardians who tried to create Arcadia in print, only Grahame really managed it.'[143] On Mole and Ratty's first excursion together on the river they find a picnic site:

> Leaving the main stream, they now passed into what seemed at first sight like a little land-locked lake. Green turf sloped down to either edge, brown snaky tree-roots gleamed below the surface of the quiet water, while ahead of them [lay] the silvery shoulder and foamy tumble of a weir, [...] The Mole begged as a favour to be allowed to unpack [the picnic basket] all by himself; and the Rat was very pleased to indulge him, and to sprawl at full length on the grass and rest.[144]

As with Carroll and Kipling, Grahame introduces recognisable elements of the traditional pleasance in order to persuade the reader of the beauty and genuine peacefulness of this spot.

The Pleasance in The Dark Is Rising Sequence
In her depictions of the pleasance, Cooper demonstrates her awareness of traditional canonical representations of the topos. There are two pleasances in the *Sequence*, one in *Silver on the Tree* and one in *The Dark Is Rising*. Here, I deliberately invert the chronological order of the discussion because the pleasance which appears in *Silver on the Tree* upholds the established conventions of the topos whereas the other inverts some of the expected characteristics of the space. The pleasance which appears in *The Dark Is Rising* is perfect in every aspect except that the scene is set in winter, and is thus more closely associated with the dark pastoral and has more robust connotations of death. This innovative twist is illustrative of Cooper's ability to engage with and transform the landscapes of canonical literature for a new audience.

Silver on the Tree
This text opens with an image of a pleasance where Will and two of his brothers, Stephen and James, are idling away a summer afternoon in a meadow beside a stream. Cooper follows the tradition carefully. The only significant change she makes is by setting the topos in June whereas the pleasance is normally associated with April or May. Cooper could not have set this topos in April or May simply because Will and his brothers would not be on their school holidays. In order for them to fully indulge in the pleasures of the topos, there must be a sense of freedom from social obligations and absolutely no possibility of work. This meadow has all the physical indicators of the pleasance: there are flowers, trees, grass, a stream, a breeze, and plenty of shade. Indeed, the boys need shade for it is a hot summer day and James wipes 'a mist of sweat from his plump pink face.'[145] Stephen nibbles at stems of grass and later picks a scarlet pimpernel for his buttonhole. The whole atmosphere is one of sleepy indulgence and idyllic peace, where

> grasshoppers skirled unseen from the grass, chirruping their solos over the deep summer insect hum: it was a sleepy, lulling sound. [Will] sighed with happiness. Sunshine and high summer [...] The world smiled on him; nothing could possibly be improved.[146]

While his brothers fish in the slow-moving river, Will lies down to read at the edge of a copse. In reading, Will participates in literary tradition, and Cooper thus indicates that Will is in the lineage of the poets of the medieval and classical pleasances. The long history of the topos dictates that Will, as the poet-figure, should fall asleep and have a dream of some considerable importance which will affect the formation of the narrative. Our expectations are rewarded here, for Will soon feels the irresistible, almost magical pull of sleep which affects the Queen in *Sir Orfeo*, the poet in *Piers the Ploughman* and indeed Carroll's Alice.[147] Cooper writes:

> He felt his eyelids droop; he jerked them apart again. Again they closed in sleepy content; again he forced them open. For a flicker of a moment he wondered why he would not let himself fall harmlessly asleep [...] And Will knew, with dread and delight, that a part of his life which had been sleeping was broad awake once more.[148]

Although Will tries to resist the temptations of sleep, the topological setting means that sleep is inevitable. Although sleep ordinarily closes the dreamer off from the world, it is through sleep that Will, like Piers Plowman, can be alerted to the dangers which threaten his world.[149] Piers dreams of 'a tower, high up against the sun, and splendidly built on top of a hill; and far beneath it was a great gulf, with a dungeon in it, surrounded by deep, dark pits, dreadful to see.'[150] Piers's dreams warn against the disintegration and corruption of the political system and Will's dreams warn against 'the threat [that] was once more rising, roaring down,'[151] the forthcoming onslaught of the Dark.

Through Will's disturbing dreams, the dark pastoral is fully integrated within Cooper's representation of the pleasance. Whereas the sleep of the shepherds and the lovers is normally light, refreshing, and born of idleness, the sleep which claims Will Stanton is nightmarish and difficult to awake from. In his dream he sees a small, frightened group of people running away from 'heathen devils' and feels 'a wave of fear so intense that it turn[s] his stomach.'[152] The terror and violence which accompany this dream are incompatible with the beauty of the landscape. Through his dreams, Will knows:

> as vividly as these fugitives, the animal terror of cruel violent death: of pain, of hurting, of hate. Or of something worse than hate: a dreadful remote blankness, that took joy only from destruction and tormenting and others' fear.[153]

Although Will himself is in no immediate danger, he dreams of people who are. The fugitives' horrified accounts of dismemberment and torture at the hands of the 'heathen devils' bring an awareness of death to the foreground of this lovely place. Here, the dark and light elements of the landscape combine, resulting in a 'strange double landscape'[154] in which disparate elements coexist and subtly overlap. Here, both aspects of the *locus amoenus*—the dark and the light, the beautiful and the violent—are seen at once, not side-by-side but with one aspect layered on top of the other 'ghostly as an image reflected in a window-pane.'[155] This ghostly quality is, perhaps, the essence of the dark pastoral, and the blurring of the living into and alongside the dead is a sure reminder of human mortality. Will comes to understand the layering of death with life through his vision of the dead fugitives, and the knowledgeable reader comes to understand the layering of text and intertext and the embedded layers of reference and intertext in Cooper's narrative.

The Dark Is Rising

This 'strange double landscape' is not the first dark pastoral in the *Sequence*. At the end of *The Dark Is Rising*, a transient, subverted kind of pleasure briefly appears in the form of a little island in the centre of the swollen river Thames. This island challenges the expected criteria of the topos. First, it appears in winter, even though we expect to encounter the *locus amoenus* only in summer. Second, there are no green things visible, for they are buried under the snow. Nevertheless, other expected topological elements—the breeze, the tree, the shade, and the moving water—are present and, moreover, Cooper preserves the function of the topos. Here, Hawkin's attempt to usurp Will as the Seeker hints at the social upheavals associated with the topos. Having failed, Hakwin is thrown from a horse and lies dying, 'twisted at a terrible angle,'[156] and his death allows Cooper to explore the association of the topos with sleep and with dreams in a new way.

Given the grateful relief from suffering that it brings, Hawkin's death is an extension of the dreaming which so often takes place in the *locus amoenus*.[157] For Arthur and his seven sleepers beneath the Welsh hills in *The Grey King*, sleep is a sort of suspended death but for Hawkin, death is sleep perfected, unbroken by dreams or intervals or the possibility of waking. Like sleep, death brings about the negation of external stimuli; however, whereas sleep dampens our awareness of the world, death cancels it altogether. Cooper presents Hawkin's death as a gradual negation; as his life ebbs away his stock of signs—his social position, his body, and his voice—is gradually cancelled. He says that his body is 'not there,' suggesting that he has already begun to pass out of the world.[158] Hawkin is ready for death but he is posed like one ready for sleep, lying flat on his back—the earth providing both bed and grave—covered by a 'blanket' of snow.[159] Here, snow is not only a blanket, but also a blankness; it not only covers, but completely conceals what lies beneath. As I discussed in Chapter One, the blanketing snow negates all topological, symbolic, and semiotic signs, resulting in blankness of both landscape and identity; in its ability to negate, the snow is expressly connected with death.

Wilderness

Whereas the social perception and literary representation of the pleasance have been consistent, wild spaces receive far more ambiguous treatment. Over the years, attitudes towards wilderness have changed dramatically. To the modern, eco-friendly mind, wildness is attractive. For ecocritics such as Garrard, wild spaces present 'nature in a state uncontaminated by civilization.'[160] Here, the purity of the natural world is set up against the corruptibility of humanity, and so wilderness becomes 'a place for the reinvigoration of those tired of the moral and material pollution of the city [. . .] [having] an almost sacramental value.'[161] However, human attitudes to wilderness were not always so positive. Indeed, up until the eighteenth century or so, wilderness was considered awesome, terrifying and sublime.[162] Garrard observes that 'the very earliest documents of Western Eurasian civilisation, such as *The Epic of Gilgamesh*, depict wilderness as a threat.'[163] Thomas Burnet's *Sacred Theory of the Earth* (1684) 'explained mountain ranges as being the physical outcome of God's displeasure with mankind, scars inflicted upon the previously unwrinkled globe.'[164] To the medieval mind, wilderness was 'a potent symbol [of] moral chaos of the unregenerate or to the godly man's conception of life on earth.'[165] The wilderness is not just unpopulated; it is hostile and resistant to human occupation.

Andrén observes that the strict 'spatial hierarchy' of medieval civilisation puts church and domestic spaces at the top and rigorously divided the green spaces in order of worth: 'it was the farm, the fields and the meadows that were important, but not the pastures and above all not the forest.'[166] The forest, like the mountain and the desert, was synonymous with wilderness in the middle ages.[167] It was a dangerous place, 'the haunt of evil-minded spirits.'[168] Nor is this view completely dead for, as Bechmann notes, 'there remains in our subconscious an attraction mixed with fear'[169] for wild spaces, and Schama observes that even in at the end of the twentieth century the sublime could be found in 'shadow and darkness and dread and trembling, in cave and chasms, at the edge of the precipice, in the shroud of cloud, in the fissures of the earth.'[170] These views affect the treatment of wilderness in many modern children's texts where it is antithetical to home and safety. In texts which centre on a quest for a new home, the wilderness is an obstacle to be overcome.[171] In these texts, as in many medieval texts, wilderness is characterised by its utter hostility and awesome power. An overview of the role of the wilderness in medieval literature will help to explain how this view developed.

Wilderness in Medieval Literature

Whereas many aspects of the green topos may be traced to biblical and even classical literature, the wilderness—in the sense identified by Garrard, Schama, and Nash—has its roots in Northern European literary traditions. The Teutonic etymological roots of wilderness are widely acknowledged. A compound of *wild* (which ultimately shares a root with *willed* and *wilful*) and *déor* meaning an animal, an untamed beast, *wilderness* is a chaotic place populated by wild animals or a place that embodies something of the unruly, uncontrollable qualities of a wild animal.[172] As might be expected, wilderness features prominently in northern medieval literature. Nash notes that 'one of the earliest uses [of the topos] was in the eighth-century epic *Beowulf* where *wildéor* appeared in reference to savage and fantastic beasts inhabiting a dismal region of forests, crags, and cliffs.'[173] The Old English *Maxims II* assert that these wild places are the proper dwelling places for monsters; '*þyrs sceal on fenne gewunian, /ana innan lande*', 'a monster must live in the fens, / alone in the land'.[174] Those who violate human order through murder or sin must be pushed outside the boundaries of civilisation. Grendel is one such monster, a *mearcstapa*,[175] a boundary-stepper, who lives beyond the bounded spaces. But whereas Will patrols the boundaries of the sanctuary from the inside, securing them and reinforcing them, Grendel prowls along the outside of these boundaries, looking for a way in. His attack on Heorot makes it clear that he is on the side of the wild things and all that opposes the safety and sanctity of the hall.

> He came in the colourless night
> The wandering shadow-stepper, a swift warrior
> To the horn-gabled hall [...]
> He came off the moor, under the mist-slopes,
> Grendel going, bearing God's ire[176]

'The great set-piece symbolic landscape of Old English poetry'[177] is the description of Grendel's home in the wilderness. The poet says 'they a secret land / inhabit, wolf-slopes, windy headlands, / terrible fen-paths where mountain streams/ under dark slopes fall downward, / A flood beneath the earth.'[178] The mention of wolves marks this place firmly as a realm of *wildéor*. The poet constructs this awesome landscape as a kind of anti–*locus amoenus*, where the characteristics of the pleasance—water, shade, trees, grass, and a breeze—are distorted, resulting in a horrible, frightening landscape. Pearsall and Salter note that 'the intention [...] is to arouse horror, and every detail is charged with symbolic power [...] for the real associations of the passage are with the hell landscapes of Christian homilists.'[179] The scene bears some resemblance to the hell in *Genesis B*.[180] Any doubts that this place and the monsters that live there are antithetical to the civilisation exemplified by Heorot are soon dispelled. The poet says that:

> Even if a heath-stepper [deer] is trapped by hounds,
> A hart with strong horns, hunted from the woods
> From afar put to flight, he will sell his life,
> His body on the bank before he will go in [to the mere][181]

At first glance this passage seems only to involve animals, but considering the word *Heorot* is both the word for a stag and the name of Hrothgár's hall, the passage has a deeper significance. As Heorot is the absolute antithesis of this wild place the two can never occupy the same space and the hart (and by extension Hrothgár and his retinue) would rather die than come into contact with the mere.

The civilisation/wilderness dialectic is also displayed in *Sir Gawain and the Green Knight*, where wilderness is not simply a geographical space but also a state of being personified by the Green Knight. Rudd remarks that 'it is surely impossible to conceive of a greener person than this knight who so suddenly rides into Arthur's court'[182] and, as such, the Knight is the purest expression of nature and the very essence of wilderness. He carries an axe and a holly-branch, symbols of the destruction and the renewal of vegetation, and his richly embroidered robe with its animal and insect designs aligns him very clearly with the *wildéor* of the forest. Rudd notes that 'the timing of his entry into Arthur's court also suggests connections with the folkloric Green Man who embodies the principles of new life returning after the dead of winter.'[183] However, the Green Knight's rudeness and hostile manner indicate that he is uninterested in the rituals of the hall; he refuses to give his name when Gawain asks and also, very unchivalrously, refuses to die when his head has been cut off. Rudd writes:

> The Green Knight's refusal to identify himself is a significant evasion of the usual courtly exchange of names that precedes combat [. . .] it is clear than in this Green Knight we have a laughing and indestructible figure who flaunts his knowledge of human rules and also his ability to flout them.[184]

So, even though this incarnation of the Green Man is a knight, he is not a courtly knight and he is the perfect antithesis to all the court stands for.

The Green Knight's presence 'hints at the distance humans [both Arthur's court and the reader] have put between themselves and the rest of the natural world, to the extent that the simple processes of nature have become imbued with an air of the supernatural.'[185] The Green Knight's challenge, then, is not simply a parlour-game, but a demand that some human be brave enough to give up the courtly life and come out into the wild spaces of the world and to take a proper part in the cycle of death and renewal. Significantly, it is Gawain, the youngest and most inexperienced of Arthur's knights, who accepts the challenge: as the youngest, he is possibly less entrenched in the rituals of courtly life than the others. Even still, Gawain has no idea what he is getting himself in for and wastes the first part of his journey 'seeking a Chapel, some kind of building, rather than considering the phrase 'green chapel' as a whole and admitting the possibility that his destination is some kind of natural landscape, not an artifact.'[186] Journeying through

> the wilderness of Wirral [...]
> The knight took strange ways
> by many a dreary bank,
> his view full oft did change
> before that chapel he could see.[187]

When Gawain arrives at the green chapel he finds

> a worn barrow in a brae by the bank, with brimming water beside
> by the fall of a flood that was flowing down [...]
> It had at hole at the end and at either side,
> and overgrown with grass in green patches all over,
> and was all hollow within: nought but an old cave,
> or a crevice of an old crag.[188]

The poet effectively provides an inverted pleasance, hostile to human interference and absolutely adverse to pleasure and relaxation. This is a true wilderness and an appropriate locus for the Green Knight.

Sir Gawain and the Green Knight exemplifies 'the great contrast [...] between nature and culture'[189] but the poet suggests that there can be negotiations between these two environmental extremes. Before Gawain can complete his quest, he must forge a connection between himself and his environment. Arthur's court and the Green Knight are at opposite ends of the civilisation/wilderness divide, and Gawain has to find a middle way; he must become a cultured, courteous knight with a profound awareness of and respect for the natural world. This balance is among the Gawain poet's great innovations, but his primary achievement is that in this poem, as in no other medieval text, the wilderness is not just somewhere the young knight has to go. It is some*one* he must encounter and fight with too. The manifestation of the wilderness as a person, a *genius locus*, has largely died out in adult fiction but it has survived in canonical children's fantasy.

Wilderness in Children's Literature

In twentieth- and twenty-first-century children's literature, wilderness is often manifested through a figure or a person. In many texts, this figure is a *genius locus*, a spirit of the topos, and is closely linked with a feature of the landscape. Bramwell notes that 'the Green Man currently appears to be becoming the pre-eminent literary Pagan god, a role occupied by Pan a century ago.'[190] Manifestations of Pan appear in *The Wind in the Willows* (1908), *The Secret Garden* (1911), *The Little White Horse* (1946), and, through Mr. Tumnus, *The Lion, The Witch and the Wardrobe* (1950). In Grahame's *The Wind in the Willows*, Pan appears as 'a mixture of the beneficent and the fearful sides of nature.'[191] Bramwell notes that in *The Secret Garden* 'the close-to-nature, pipe-playing Dickon' is a version of Pan.[192]

80 • Landscape in Children's Literature

Other kinds of *genius locus* appear in twentieth-century children's literature; Kipling presents Puck of Pook's Hill (1906) as 'the oldest Old Thing in England'[193] and a force of nature. Puck looks after plants and animals and acts as a mentor for the children, inculcating a sense of England's landscape and history in them. In Briggs's *Hobberdy Dick* (1955), the hobgoblin Dick is tied to a manor house and its surrounding fields until he is released through the gift of clothes, a motif borrowed by Rowling in her depiction of the house elves.[194] Apart from Grahame's vision of the 'august Presence'[195] of Pan, these natural spirits are friendly and relatively powerless. However, late twentieth- and twenty-first-century wild spirits tend to be more brutal and violent.

In Pratchett's *The Wee Free Men*, (2003) the *genius locus* is Jenny Greenteeth, a child-snatching fairy that lives in a slow-moving stream.[196] One of the most interesting depictions of the embodied wilderness is *The Savage* (2008) by Almond and McKean. The Savage is a human boy exiled from society and subsumed by the natural world, he moves between unbounded and civic spaces and lives 'in a cave under the rooined [sic] chapel.'[197] The ruined chapel in the woods echoes the Green Chapel where the Green Knight lives. Like the Green Knight, the Savage is also often shown as being green. McKean's roughcast, violent illustrations wash the figure in green or dark blue, aligning him with the natural world and emphasizing his wildness. The spirit of the Savage enters into Blue, the story's narrator, who comes to feel 'like the savage was living right inside me.'[198] Like Gawain, who goes into the wilderness to fight with nature, Blue goes to the ruined chapel in order to purge himself of the Savage.[199] In presenting the wilderness as something which is not only embodied but has agency within the narrative, Almond and McKean connect with canonical representations of wildness which originate in medieval literature. The traces of this tradition may be clearly seen in Cooper's *Sequence*.

Wilderness in The Dark Is Rising Sequence

Landscape is not a passive background to Cooper's *Sequence* but has its own role within the events of the narrative and, at times, its own agency. This agency is partly implicit—in *Over Sea, Under Stone*, the landscape keeps the Arthurian grail safely hidden, and in *The Dark Is Rising*, the power of the Dark is manifested through the landscape before it is manifested through Mitothin—and partly explicit, at times becoming a powerful, vital, and embodied thing. Drawing on the medieval attitude towards wilderness as something actively opposed to human life, Cooper uses the device of 'wild magic' and allows wilderness to be embodied in four distinct forms: Herne the Hunter, the Brenin Llwyd, Tethys, and the Greenwitch.[200] As a sea-spirit, and a kind of goddess, Tethys does not concern me here, but will be discussed in greater detail in Chapter Four. The remaining figures are variations of the *genius locus* and are tied to specific parts of the landscape; the Brenin Llwyd is the spirit of the Welsh mountains, Herne the Hunter is expressly linked with the Thames Valley, particularly with Herne's Oak in Windsor Park, and the Greenwitch is associated with the Cornish town, Trewissick. Each is a physical manifestation of an ethereal force and embodies the wild forces of Cooper's landscapes.

Figure 2.6 Mist at Cader Idris, Wales. ©Jane Carroll.

The Brenin Llwyd (The Grey King)

The Brenin Llwyd is a spectre of death explicitly connected with the landscape of North Wales. He stays in his 'fastnesses among the Cader Idris peaks,'[201] and, it is implied, a great deal of his power comes from this symbiosis with the landscape. He draws out the power inherent in the landscape and brings it to bear upon the human characters, breathing fog, starting fire on the mountainside, and causing the earth to 'shrug' and dislodge people from his mountain:

> [Will] could never explain, afterwards, how he came to stumble. He could only have said, very simply, that the mountain shrugged. [. . .] Nevertheless, the mountain did shrug, through the malice of its master the Brenin Llwyd, so that a piece of the path beneath Will's feet jumped perceptibly to one side and back again, like a cat humping its back and Will saw it with sick horror only in the moment that he lost his balance and went rolling down.[202]

Even though his actions stem from a petty malevolence which seems at odds with his ancient and massive stature, the consequences of his actions are very real. The Brenin Llwyd threatens Will and the other characters with death.

That death is part of the natural cycle and therefore part of the landscape is reiterated throughout the *Sequence*, but it is in the figure of the Brenin Llwyd, the Grey King, that this association is made absolutely clear. Like the Mari Llwyd, the skeletal horse that Bran and Will encounter in the Lost Land,[203] the Brenin Llwyd is a spectre of death. His breath is a chilling mist and he is associated with the colour grey, an association which echoes many literary depictions of death. The Brenin Llwyd has existed since the beginnings of time, and it is this association with time that cements his association with death. Here, Cooper describes Will's meeting with the Brenin Llwyd:

> The figure was so huge that at first he could not realize it was there. [. . .] Will could see its outline from the corner of his eye, but when he looked directly at any part of it, there was nothing there. Yet there the figure loomed before him, immense and terrible, and he knew that this was a being of greater power than anything he had ever encountered in his life before. Of all the Great Lords of the Dark, none was singly more powerful and dangerous than the Grey King. But because he had remained always from the beginnings of time in his fastnesses among the Cader Idris peaks, never descending to the valleys or lower slopes, none of the Old Ones had ever encountered him.[204]

Death is the only thing that none of the Old Ones has ever encountered. Being immortal and outside of the natural cycle of time, death is alien to them. The Brenin Llwyd is 'of greater power than anything he had ever encountered in his life before' because death can only be encountered once, and Cooper makes it clear that Will only survives the meeting because he is 'of the Light'[205]

Figure 2.7 Green man in St. Cadfan's Church, Tywyn, Wales. ©Jane Carroll.

and cannot be killed. Here, Cooper describes death as something separate to the physical actions of dying, figuring death as a kind of ultimate negation. When Will looks directly at the figure of the Grey King, there is nothing there. The Brenin Llwyd is not a symbol of death but a manifestation of that vague and chilling power, something that can only be perceived obliquely.[206]

Herne the Hunter

The mountainous landscape inhabited by the Brenin Llwyd is one kind of wilderness. Another, more common depiction of wilderness is the forest. Bechmann notes that the forest wilderness is a place of 'mythical and often ambiguous creatures'[207] and 'mixed divinities'.[208] Among the most physically ambiguous of these creatures is Herne the Hunter; a man with a stag's antlers (and sometimes a stag's head) who is at once predator and prey, a self-consuming figure which epitomises the cycles of death and renewal inherent in the green topos. Herne the Hunter is Cernunnos, a horned chthonic deity. 'The cult of Cernunnos was concerned with fecundity and he was also a god of the underworld, two good reasons why [...] the image of the horned god may have been taken over by Christian artists to represent the Devil.'[209] Nigel Pennick notes that Cernunnos later became synonymous with Herne, patron of hunters. The similarity in appearance may account for the conflation of the two figures.[210] Herne is also closely related to Arawn, the lord of the underworld who appears in the First Branch of the *Mabinogion*. Cooper's Herne has red-eared hounds exactly like those Pwyll encounters on his hunt with shining white coats and red ears.[211] Even though Cooper localises Herne to Windsor Park, the story of a ghostly hunter and the wild hunt is widespread. Bechmann notes that

> among the myths linked to the forest, the ghost hunter was one of the most widely disseminated in Europe [...] In the legends of the Pyrenees and of Southern France, it is King Arthur, who left mass upon seeing a magnificent wild boar go by. [...] The merry wives of Shakespeare evoke the hunter Herne, who rides in the forest of Windsor. His name must be compared to the one he has in other regions: *Hellequin* or *Hennequin* (that gave *Arlequin*), a deformation of Erl-King, the *Roi des Aulnes* (Roi des *Elfes* or des *Erles*).[212]

So, even though Cooper situates Herne in Windsor Park, he is also a universal figure;[213] he is at once a *genius locus* and a manifestation of the awesome power of the green space.

In *The Dark Is Rising*, Herne, along with his pack of red-eared yell-hounds, commands the winter wind to chase the agents of the Dark from the Thames Valley. His actions are deliberate and carry a mythic weight which befits his otherworldly appearance:

> At the peak of the power now, in full cry, [the Wild Hunt] came roaring out of the great dark thundercloud, through streaking lightning and grey-purple clouds, riding on the storm. The yellow-eyed antlered man rode laughing dreadfully, crying out the avaunt that rallies hounds on the full chase [and] the magnificence of the Dark flinched and swayed and seemed to tremble.[214]

A potent mixture of cultured, human elements and natural, bestial elements, Herne embodies the dichotomies that lie at the heart of the green topos. His antlered head appears as an organic thing, but the reader knows it is really a carnival mask from the Caribbean that Will received as a present from his brother. The carnival, as I will show in my next chapter, is an urban genre, yet Herne is a hunter stalking through the forest. Of all the contradictions bound up in Herne, the most telling is his dreadful laugh which unites the pleasure and death which are so intrinsic to the green topos.[215]

In spite of his universal significance, Herne's power is limited because he can only ride out on a particular night, the Twelfth Night of Christmas. Like the Brenin Llwyd, his apparently immense power is subject to restrictions. The Greenwitch, on the other hand, is not subject to these same kinds of limitations. She is made on land and is moved out to sea so, although she is associated with Trewissick, she is not tied there and she can call upon the power of both land and sea to defeat her opponents. The Greenwitch's power is not limited to a particular place, like the Brenin Llwyd, or to a particular time, like Herne, but represents the landscape in its entirety. Although she can be petty, even childish, she is, for Cooper, the ultimate symbol of Wild Magic and therefore, the perfect embodiment of the green topos. Nowhere is the agency of the landscape more evident than in the figure of the Greenwitch.

Figure 2.8 The 'Mud Maid,' by Sue and Pete Hill, at the Lost Gardens of Heligan, Cornwall.

The Greenwitch

The making of the Greenwitch is 'just a sort of spring thing [...] an old custom'[216] but one about which the Drew children, like the reader, know nothing. The Greenwitch is 'a figure surrounded by total and complete silence';[217] the secrecy surrounding the making and Mrs. Penhallow's refusal to speak of the subject in front of foreigners endows the custom with a sense of mystery and excitement. When Jane, as Merriman's only female guest, is invited to attend the making, her brothers are suitably jealous. But even when Jane is out on the headland with the village women, she still has little idea of what is about to take place:

> Yet still she had been given no idea of what was to happen. Nobody had told her what the thing called the Greenwitch would be like, or how it would be made, or what would happen to it. She only knew that the business would occupy the whole night, and end when the fishermen came home. Jane shivered again. Night was falling, and she was not over-fond of the nights in Cornwall; they held too much of the unknown.[218]

In this short passage, Cooper provides subtle clues as to the nature of what is to follow. Jane's nervous anticipation suggests something frightening or dangerous will occur. Trewissick is an apt setting for such events, having been established as an ancient and mythic place in *Over Sea, Under Stone*. Indeed, the headland where the making ceremony is to take place is directly above the spot where the Drews found the Arthurian grail. The ancient and sacred overtones of this spot, coupled with the night-time setting, suggest that the making is something occult and possibly illicit. But the real mystery lies in Jane's uncertainty as to 'what the thing called the Greenwitch would be like.' Some clues are provided by the Greenwitch's name: the 'green' aspect sets up an immediate and indisputable association with the green topos and the suffix 'witch' brings definite connotations of power and traditional magic with specifically feminine overtones. These connotations are, indeed, borne out and made definite in the making ceremony. But it is the clause 'what would happen to it' which is most suggestive. Cooper implies that the Greenwitch will be a passive entity; it is not the subject, but rather the object of the making.

Although Cooper claims that the making ceremony in *Greenwitch* is a complete fabrication,[219] there are many significant parallels between Cooper's fictional ritual and authentic rituals which are traditional across northern and western Europe. These rituals may be encompassed under Frazer's term 'the killing of the tree-spirit' for each of them involves some sort of green effigy or totem.[220] Some of these rituals—such as those surrounding Jack in the Green associated with May Day in Hastings, England or *Le Loup Vert,* the Green Wolf that is made and destroyed each year in Picardy in France—continue even today.[221] Each of these ceremonies requires the totemic tree-spirit to be violently killed, usually through drowning or burning, but sometimes through hanging or dismemberment.[222] The death of the tree-spirit is then welcomed with shouts of joy and celebration because the death of greenery is temporary and always results in a renewal of life. Frazer notes that 'the killing of the tree-spirit is always associated with a revival or resurrection of him in a more youthful and vigorous form.'[223] Whitlock notes that the building and sacrifice of the Greenman or the Corn Doll, like many traditional festivals, marks a special time in the yearly calendar; a time significant in terms of the natural cycle of birth, death, and renewal of planting, ripening, and harvesting and suggests that such rituals serve to remind participants of the power of nature and of the need for humans to submit to the natural calendar. Through the sacrifice of the totemic tree-spirit, the fertility and renewable power of nature is reasserted.[224]

The making ceremony described in *Greenwitch* has many of the elements common to the ceremonies described in *The Golden Bough,* and it is clear that the Greenwitch is a version of the tree-spirit, a totem invested with power and meaning through a repeated series of ceremonies and rituals. The making ceremony is described almost entirely by Jane Drew who watches, 'half-invisible [...] unnoticed.'[225] Because Jane is an outsider, distanced physically and symbolically from the processes involved in the making, Cooper is able to borrow something of the detached prose style associated with anthropological texts, and the making is described with a kind of disinterested observation. The village women 'set to working, in a curiously ordered way in small groups [making] what began very slowly to emerge as a kind of frame.'[226] The frame becomes the basis for the Greenwitch—a huge totem made of 'hazel [...], rowan [...], hawthorn boughs, and hawthorn blossoms. With the stones within, for the sinking.'[227] One woman tells Jane something of the function of the Greenwitch, saying 'and those who are crossed, or barren, or who would make any wish, must touch the Greenwitch then before she be put to cliff.'[228] There is a subtle suggestion of rhyme in her words, in the assonance between 'wish' and 'cliff' and 'witch' and even 'touch,' and so Cooper suggests that the line is a kind of maxim which carries an ancient and traditional wisdom. As in the authentic ceremonies described by Frazer and Whitlock, physical contact with the totem is important, and it is considered lucky to touch the Greenwitch just as it is lucky to touch Jack of the Green or to bear away one of the leaves from his costume.[229] The Greenwitch promises fertility, not just 'good fishing and a good harvest,'[230] but is also credited with curing infertility in people and with helping young women to secure a good marriage.[231]

As with other fertility totems, the Corn Dolly[232] or the Scottish Cailleach[233] or the Garland King,[234] the Greenwitch must be newly made and sacrificed each year. The Greenwitch ritual is, then, a microcosmic actualisation of a macrocosmic phenomenon. Her making and sacrifice over the course of a single day represents the cycles of life and death which take place over the course of a whole year. Like the other totems, the Greenwitch 'dies' violently—she is pushed off the cliffs above Trewissick bay into the sea to drown—but because she is made of earth, made by firelight, tossed into the air and then drowned in the sea, her death may be said to unite each of the elements. Her death is greeted with 'cheers and shouts'[235] and a cheerfulness which, for Jane, belies the violence and savagery inherent in the ceremony. To the reader, aware of the anthropological history behind the fictional event, the 'cheers and shouts' take on a different meaning; the death of the old year is not to be mourned because it heralds in a new harvest which is to be celebrated.

The fact that the Greenwitch ceremony has so many authentic counterparts suggests that the ritual is far more than 'a sort of spring thing.' Nigel Pennick notes that 'the tree of life is a symbol present in every human culture. It symbolizes [...] the nurturer of growth who carries and sustains all life.'[236] The power of the tree-spirit is not confined to trees and forests but is credited with the power of making the rain fall, the sun shine, flocks and herds multiply, and women bear healthy children.[237] Thus the Greenwitch is representative of the power of the green space as a whole:

> As Jane looked at the huge image they [the village women] had made out of leaves and branches she could not understand their lightness. For she knew suddenly, out there in the cold dawn, that this silent image somehow held within it more power than she had ever sensed before in any creature or thing. Thunder and storms and earthquakes were there, and all the force of the earth and sea. It was outside Time, boundless, ageless, beyond any line drawn between good and evil. Jane stared at it, horrified, and from its sightless head the Greenwitch stared back.[238]

This passage represents a shift in the Greenwitch's status and role within the making. At the beginning of the passage, she is an inanimate object, an image which 'they had made' but by the end, she becomes a sentient subject, staring out at Jane Drew. It is Jane's recognition of the Greenwitch's true significance that actuates this shift in status. Whereas it is tempting to see the various elements of nature as ranging 'from the benevolent to the malign,'[239] the Greenwitch is neither good nor malign but exists beyond any such classification. She represents the wild forces of nature before which human life and human categorisation are insignificant. When Jane recognises this, and freely acknowledges that the Greenwitch holds 'more power than [...] any creature or thing,' she unconsciously re-invests the making ceremony with its true and original significance, allowing the inanimate totem to become a powerful living embodiment of the landscape.

As an agent of the landscape, the Greenwitch has full control over the faculties of the landscape and is capable of bringing these forces to bear on Trewissick. When an agent of the Dark defies her and contravenes a natural law by invoking taboo spells, the spells of Mana, Reck and Lir,[240] the Greenwitch unleashes all of her power:

> And suddenly the whole world was luminous with green light, as for one terrible moment the Greenwitch in all its wild power loomed out of the sky, every live detail clear with a brilliance they [the Drews] never afterwards mentioned even to one another. [...] and the Greenwitch, crying rage from a great mouth, spread terrible arms wide as if to engulf the whole village.[241]

Her possession of the village is an extended version of the agency manifested through the malign snowfall in *The Dark Is Rising*, or the shifting earth in *The Grey King*.

Whereas the snow acts on behalf of the Dark and the ground acts on behalf of the Brenin Llwyd, the Greenwitch acts of her own accord. Before this moment, the landscape in the *Sequence* is open to use by the forces of good or evil but here the landscape has a will and an objective of its own, and, for the first time, is given a voice of its own. The Greenwitch's voice becomes doubly significant when contrasted with the abject silence of the Drews. In this passage, Cooper strips the human characters of their free agency and empowers the Greenwitch. The children are speechless, but, Cooper implies, they are not merely unwilling but unable to speak of this moment, the moment when the landscape itself becomes articulate. She says: 'I have no friend. It matters nothing to me what happens between the Light and the Dark.'[242] By uttering the words 'I' and 'me,' the Greenwitch declares herself as Self, as an entity with her own consciousness and self-awareness. This kind of self-awareness endows her with a personhood which seems at odds with her status as a wild thing 'without discipline or pattern'[243] yet it is in this dichotomy that the Greenwitch acquires her liminal status. She is neither completely wild nor completely civilised, neither inanimate nor properly human, but a complicated synthesis of both. Although the Greenwitch claims to stand apart from the world of humans, Will argues:

'Men have everything to do with you. Without them, you would not exist. They make you, each year. Each year, they throw you to the sea. Without men, the Greenwitch would never have been born.'[244]

Even though she is composed of natural things—branches, leaves, stones—she is also a human construction, depending on humans for form, meaning, and significance. Her form is humanoid, albeit distorted and strange with 'a huge head, long, squarish, without features.'[245] What Cooper suggests but leaves unspoken is that without the Greenwitch and the power she represents, humans would not exist either. Humankind and the landscape are, at least in the *Sequence*, locked in unbreakable symbiosis. The Greenwitch is built and sacrificed annually in order to ensure 'good fishing and a good harvest,' and this ritual acknowledges the dependence of the people of Trewissick upon nature's bounty and serves as a reminder of how some human activity is dictated by the cycles of nature. The Greenwitch represents the connection between the opposing forces of nature and civilisation and provides a sort of liminal space in which these dichotomous elements may be tentatively connected.

Conclusion

If we accept the Greenwitch as an metonymic figure—as a sort of substitute for the landscape as a whole—it must follow that the entire landscape of the *Sequence* is of this dichotomous sort, a space where 'human memory and natural form rebound endlessly upon each other'.[246] Within the *Sequence* certain characters acknowledge this symbiosis and accept that nature has, at times, greater power than human will. Often this acceptance comes in the form of a resignation to the natural cycles of death and rebirth. Mrs. Stanton's stoic acceptance of the chickens' deaths and John Rowlands's submission to the demands of the plant and animal life on the farm are two such examples. Thus, a rise in the agency of the landscape is accompanied by an equivalent fall in the agency of the human characters. Rowlands cuts the hedgerows back not out of choice but out of necessity and it is the growth of the plants and trees that dictates when he must perform the hedging. Fundamental to this attitude is the acceptance of the cycles of life and death and the realisation that these cycles are intimately bound together, expressed, and focalised through the medium of the green space.

Whereas the Greenwitch ceremony eloquently expresses the intersection of natural cycles with human culture, such ritual expressions are not confined to the green topos. Chapter Three will investigate the roadway topos and its relationship with exclusively human life cycles. This chapter will specifically examine the role of the civic street in the ritual, carnivalesque expression of human life cycles, and the function of the open road in the formation of individual identity.

Figure 3.1 Track near Tintagel, Cornwall. ©Jane Carroll.

Chapter Three
The Roadway Topos

Although some of the books in Cooper's *Sequence* can be described as adventure stories and others as domestic fantasies, each of the five books follows the same home-away-home narrative pattern identified by Perry Nodelman.[1] This narrative pattern has two prerequisites; that there is an established, stable domestic space which is the start and end point of the text and, second, that there is an environment beyond the domestic space to which, and through which, protagonists must move. This 'centrifugal movement away from a home base'[2] generates narrative action. However, this analysis of the pattern of domestic fantasies is based upon a static and inflexible binary, a binary that establishes tensions between the home and the away sections of a narrative.[3] It is my contention that the narrative structure of domestic fantasies is better described as 'home–going away–returning home' and that the standard domestic fantasy narrative is more about the landscape's agency in the processes of moving from one place to another than about the static sites at either end of the story. Thus, even the 'small, intimate journeys from small personal homes'[4] may show how the roadway topos is invested with great significance. Focusing on scenes of movement in literature, this chapter will examine the importance, even the centrality, of roadways, railways, and streets—the means of movement—in children's literature.

The Appearance of the Roadway

Like the green topos, the roadway topos is readily identifiable; it has clear physical characteristics and a definite function within literature. Like many other topoi, the function of the roadway is linked to its appearance. Physically, roadways are remarkable in that they always take the same form. Roadways are flat fillets of ground, clear of vegetative growth or obstacles, which stretch over the surface of the landscape. Some roadways follow the natural curvature and elevation of the landscape, winding around large obstacles such as mountains, whereas others cut through the landscape and across obstacles like rivers and forests. They are narrow in relation to the ground they cover. The function of the roadway is, then, to cover ground, avoiding or routing around obstacles and facilitating movement between one fixed site and another. Accordingly, the roadway is seldom treated as a topos in its own right; it is not a destination but a means of travelling from one place to another. The roadway facilitates movement while at the same time remaining immobile.

However homogenous they might be in appearance and function, the various aspects of the topos differ greatly in terms of character. This diversity is reflected in the wide range of words and terms we have to describe them; roads, ways, tracks, trails, lanes, paths, streets, leys, alleys, and railways are all aspects of this single topos and each word carries its own unique set of connotations and images. In *Topophilia*, Yi-Fu Tuan notes the ambiguity of topos, saying that whereas a roadway

> would seem to be a fairly specific type of physical environment [...] in fact its character and use can vary enormously. At one extreme, it is a narrow crooked lane, unpaved or paved with cobble, packed with jostling people and carts, a place that assaults the senses with noise, odor, and color. At the other, it is a wide straight avenue, bordered by trees or blank walls, an imposing space that is almost devoid of life.[5]

Tuan's analysis reveals that the roadway has little or no distinct characteristics of its own; rather, it takes on, and is imprinted by, the characteristics of the landscape around it. The roadway takes on 'extreme' forms; it can be either a noisy, cramped, crowded lane or a quiet, broad, empty avenue. At each extremity, the character of the space is defined by the traffic that passes upon it. Furthermore, Tuan's language hints at additional ambiguities as shown by his hesitation between the terms 'space' and 'place,' clearly unsure of how to categorise the topos. Tuan uses the word 'avenue,' 'a means of approach or arrival,' thus binding the roadway to the idea of movement, of transition. The roadway is always the approach, never the destination. It is always in a state of lack, of incompletion. Because the roadway is not a destination within its own right, but a thread that links two otherwise disconnected places, it may be described as a liminal space.

The Time-Scale of the Roadway

The liminality of the roadway, the paradoxical placelessness of the topos, leads to confusion about the function of the topos in relation to time. Having identified the cyclical time-scale of the natural world in *Topophilia*, Tuan then attempts to set the roadway as a part of the built environment in contradistinction to this natural cycle. He writes:

> The ancients believed that the movement in nature was disposed towards the circular path. The circle symbolised perfection [...] Time is

commonly modelled on the recurrent phases of nature, those of the stars or of the earth in rotation and revolution. Modern man recognizes these recurrent phases but for him they are little more than waves in the directional time stream. Time for him has direction, change is progressive.[6]

Tuan's argument connects cyclical time to the natural environment and thus implies that linear time is indivisible from the built environment. He goes on to suggest that travel and, in particular, long-distance travel cements the bond between linear movement and linear temporality. For Tuan, the roadway is synonymous with modernity and with industrialization. He writes that 'long-distance travel and migrations may in themselves have had an effect in breaking up cyclical time and the vertical cosmos, substituting them for linear time and horizontal space.'[7] The built environment and the roadway topos entail an unnatural timescale and an unnatural, direct, kind of movement; the interconnectivity of destinations can only be achieved at the expense of natural movement and a natural timescale.

Tuan's argument relies heavily upon a rigid binary division between the organic and the synthetic. Whereas the green space topos, with its cycles of life, death, and rebirth, entails a cyclical cosmology, it does not follow that the roadway topos is always unnatural. Although the roadway is usually part of the built rather than spontaneous environment, it does not always move against or counter to nature. Many roadways follow the curves and gradients of the natural environment and furthermore, insects, animals, rivers, and glaciers—undeniably part of the natural environment—are all in the habit of carving out pathways and track ways for themselves. And even though the roadway is flat and narrow, its linear appearance should not be assumed to imply only a linear timescale.

Time is indelibly associated with the roadway. Edward Casey points out that the most common indicator of this association is the habit of judging distance in terms of the time it takes to travel a certain distance.[8] Hence, a town may be 'half an hour's drive away' or a shop may be 'five minutes down the road.' Indeed, the word 'journey' connotes both a period of time and a measure of distance, meaning the amount of travel that can be achieved in a single day.[9] Time and distance are conflated in the roadway topos. Benjamin writes of the *Zeitraum* or 'time–space' of the street,[10] and Bakhtin uses the word 'chronotope' or 'time-place' to describe the integration of time and space.[11] The chronotope is 'the intrinsic interconnectedness of temporal and spatial relationships that are artistically expressed in literature [...] the chronotope expresses the inseparability of space and time.'[12] Every literary topos has an implicit time-scale which involves both time within the narrative and the time in which the reader experiences the narrative action. Whereas time is merely a conditional, even peripheral factor in some topoi, it is absolutely inseparable from the spatial dimensions of the roadway topos.

The roadway is not flatly superficial but is worn into the surface of the landscape in the same way as a glacier or a river. The landscape is comprised of palimpsestic layers and the roadway is worn down into those layers, sometimes through the constant repetition and reiteration of a route. Thus, roadways are made over generations of constant treading. If one looks at a track or footway through a field or green area which is used as a shortcut—such as the ones made by children during school-terms—this process becomes very clear. The roadway, like the grave, which will be discussed in the next chapter, is deliberately cut into the surface of the landscape and so exposes some of these palimpsestic layers. There are, however, important differences between the two: the grave is starkly recessed into the earth, exposing deep layers of history, but is thus at a great remove from anyone standing on the surface of the ground. The roadway is much shallower, and so places the exposed layers of history at one's feet. The grave highlights the separation of past and present, of living and dead, and presents a solid dichotomy between the two, but the roadway represents the simultaneity of past and present. So, rather than viewing the roadway as a thin fillet on the surface of the landscape, it is better to see it as a vast tunnel in time, stretching forward and backward, but also above and below, both paradigmatic and syntagmatic in its meaning. The chronotope of the roadway topos provides both narratological and ideological structure within a text and exposes an interaction between the synchronic and diachronic functions of a narrative.[13] Far from being flat, and superficial, the roadway is deep and inheres a diachronic rather than a linear time-scale.

The Symbolic Function of the Roadway Topos

As a liminal space, a 'space in-between the designations of identity,'[14] the roadway topos 'becomes the process of symbolic interaction [...] the temporal movement and passage that it allows prevents identities at either end of it from settling into primordial polarities [providing] interstitial passage between fixed identifications.'[15] Bhabha suggests that as fixed places are associated with fixed personal identities, the roadway provides connections, not just between places, but also between identifications. It challenges the desire to divide the landscape up into neat, clearly separated places and compromises the rigid, polar, and binary divisions between the places that it connects. In providing an interstitial space between fixed places, the roadway opens up a degree of fluidity within the landscape and, as a result, brings about fluidity within personal identity.

Identity is affected by environment and so, travellers on the roadway, sympathetic to and affected by environmental tensions, and displaced by their journeys, must come to question their own identity. In his discussion of personal and collective identity Shepard notes that

> Individual and tribal identity are built up in connection with widely separated places and the paths connecting them. Different places are successfully assimilated or internalized. They become distinct, though unconscious elements of the self, enhanced by mythology and ceremony, generating a network of deep emotional attachments that cements the

personality. Throughout life those places have a role in the evocation of the self and group consciousness.[16]

Even though Shepard notes the importance of places to the development and internalization of identity, he stresses that the 'paths connecting' these places are of equal importance. The placelessness of the roadway topos undoubtedly generates questions about identity. In providing a means of displacement, by removing the traveller from home and, by extension, from a fixed sense

Figure 3.2 Street at Mevagissey, Cornwall. ©Jane Carroll.

of place and identity, the roadway enforces a kind of defamiliarisation. By alienating the traveller from home, the roadway topos supports a new attitude towards home and causes the traveller to consider, and perhaps even to revise, a sense of self. This chapter addresses the ways in which roadways affect identity. Collective identity will be investigated in relation to the civic street and individual identity in relation to the open road.

The Street

Enclosed by the parameters and delimited by the shape of the urban space, the street becomes something very different from the open road. Whereas the road is a space for a solitary wanderer, Benjamin suggests that the street is 'the dwelling place of the collective.'[17] By comparing, even conflating, the house and the street, Benjamin blurs the division between the normal sense of public and private areas and threatens the distinctions between topoi, saying that

> for this collective, glossy enamelled shop signs are a wall decoration as good as, if not better than, an oil painting in the drawing room of a bourgeois; walls with their 'Post No Bills' are its writing desk, newspaper stands its libraries, mailboxes its bronze busts, benches its bedroom furniture.[18]

But the street lacks the comfort and privacy of the domestic space. The street is noisy, busy, and crowded with people who rub shoulders together without ever properly interacting with one another. As a variant of the roadway, the street does not have a fixed identity and is, therefore, only tentatively domestic, only provisionally safe. Lefebvre notes 'the city's contexture or fabric—its streets, its underground levels, its frontiers—unravel, and generate not concord but violence.'[19] The collective is not a stable unit, but a roiling mass of disparate and dissipating identities thrust together in the street. The street is antithetical to the sanctuary topos. Virginia Woolf observes that on the street 'we shed the self our friends know us by and become part of the vast republican army of anonymous trampers.'[20] Without a fixed identity of its own, the street cannot support or instil a sense of fixed identity in the people who traverse it. Bakhtin claims that any journey leads to the problematisation of identity.[21] Over the course of a long journey, travellers come to question their own sense of self and, in doing so, to purge an old identity and create a new one. In the street, where journeys are shorter and where people are unnaturally forced together in great numbers, the deterioration of self identity and the potential creation of a new collective identity is catalysed. As a result, the collective Benjamin speaks of can never be a stable, content, or secure entity. If each individual that has been subsumed into the collective mass comes to question that mass identity, the result is a violent purging of old identities and a turbulent, aggressive creation of new identities. The collective is 'eternally unquiet, eternally agitated,'[22] restless and dangerous. Whereas the home is usually the centre of fixed identifications in children's literature, the street is often a space of provisional, rootless and unformed identifications. In the street, the security of the domestic space is regularly subverted.

The Street and Carnival

The subversive qualities of the street are never more obvious than in the carnival. Carnivalesque literature, through images of cannibalism, death, and violence, makes the familiar grotesque and frightening. In parodying that which is comforting, domestic, and familiar, the carnival encourages participants to let go of rigidly defined individual identities and become part of a great, celebratory, subversive mass. The carnival is a civic event and it is bound up with the image of the civic street. Carnival is born of the marketplace and of the community.[23] If the street is the 'dwelling place of the collective,'[24] then carnival is the parlour-game of that restless, disquieting, and aggressive collective. In *Rabelais and His World*, Mikhail Bakhtin discusses the close relationship between the collective, civic body, and carnival. He writes that 'carnival is not a spectacle seen by the people; they live in it, and everyone participates because its very idea embraces all the people. While carnival lasts there is no life outside it.'[25] The carnival is all-encompassing and perhaps even all-consuming. The individual is absorbed into the crowd and, as a result, individual identity is absorbed and overpowered by a group identity.[26]

This analysis of the carnival as something grasping, consuming, and dangerous may initially seem very bleak and even though Bakhtin argues that the principle aspect of the carnival is laughter, the darker undercurrents of the carnival cannot be ignored. He catalogues the main aspects of the carnival as: suspension of hierarchies;[27] subversive laughter;[28] exaggerated bodies;[29] human/animal/vegetable interchange;[30] images of eating and particularly of cannibalism;[31] and references to death and rebirth.[32] It is this last aspect, the references to death and rebirth, which is particularly interesting in relation to the roadway topos. Bakhtin writes:

> The feast is always essentially related to time, either to the recurrence of an event in the natural (cosmic) cycle, or to biological or historic timelessness. Moreover, through all the stages of historic development feasts were linked to moments of crisis, of breaking points in the cycle of nature or in the life of society and man. Moments of death and revival, of change and renewal always led to a festive perception of the world.[33]

The imagery of death, revival and renewal draws attention to the cyclical, labyrinthine nature of the civic street. Within the confines of urban limits, the civic street is a closed system. With the exception perhaps of the main street that traverses the urban space, providing the entrance and exit to the closed urban system, the street does not cross the landscape but is forced inwards and even doubles back upon itself.[34]

In an urban echo of the green motif, the symbolic death of the individual is followed by a symbolic rebirth in the carnivalesque crowd. In subsuming the identity of the individual, the carnival gives birth to a new identity; that of the collective. In Louis Althusser's terms, the individual ceases to be interpellated as subject and, newly freed from such ideological constraints, is able to be constructed as part of a unified social identity.[35] It is this symbolic death that is the most disturbing aspect of the carnival; in threatening the integrity of the self, carnival threatens the individual with utter negation. It is frightening because it draws attention to the individual's mortality and to the minor role each person plays within society as a whole. Only in letting go of these identity fixations can the individual enjoy the carnival properly.

The Street in Children's Literature
Ordinarily, my discussion of a topos in children's literature would be preceded by a discussion of the topos in medieval literature. However, as David Wallace points out, 'there is no idea of a city' in medieval literature.[36] Catherine Clarke also observes that 'the "absent city" of later medieval literature is now a critical commonplace' and that the city only becomes 'a key symbolic space or landscape' in the Anglo-Latin tradition.[37] Therefore, I must move directly to a discussion of the role of the civic street and the carnival in children's literature.

The carnivalesque trope loses none of its subversive and frightening power in children's literature. If anything, the destabilisation of identity and the threat of self-negation are even more pronounced in carnivalesque texts aimed at children. In many children's texts, the carnivalesque is portrayed as an incursion into, and a disruption of, domestic routine. In some cases, this incursion is welcomed and allows for a festive shaking-off of normative rules and routines which are, in turn, reinstated at the end of the narrative. In other texts, the carnivalesque element is violent and dangerous rather than playful, and the normative social order, once shattered, is seldom fully repaired. A large number of picture books aimed at very young readers can be read in these terms and most fall very clearly into either the positive and playful category or the subversive and disturbing category. Judith Kerr's *The Tiger Who Came to Tea* (1968) and Raymond Briggs's *The Snowman* (1968) are examples of the former. Examples of the latter include Dave McKee's *Not Now Bernard* (1980) in which the carnivalesque is manifested as a monster who disrupts and subverts the familiar routines of home. Drawing on images of violence, of eating, of death and rebirth (the monster, having consumed Bernard, is symbolically reborn as his victim when he is put to bed by Bernard's parents), this relatively simple story encompasses the fear of annihilation of identity brought about by the carnival. In Maurice Sendak's *Where the Wild Things Are* (1963), a text equally concerned with the ideas of identity, eating, and negation, Max is not eaten up precisely because he is willing to join the carnivalesque forces and to celebrate rather than deny the disruption of normative order.[38] Max's own subversion of domestic order by being naughty and, indeed, by threatening his mother with the very phrase 'I'll eat you up!' leads to further disruption of routine when he is sent to bed without supper. Max's naughtiness stems from his decision to wear a wolf-suit which opens him up to human/animal interchange, allowing him to embrace the carnival and become a 'wild thing'. A similar episode of animal/human interchange takes place in Travers's *Mary Poppins* (1934) where everything is turned upside down in the zoo; animals converse politely and people are put on display in cages. Appropriately, this carnivalesque event takes place on Mary's birthday, and on the night of the full moon, itself a symbol of cyclical change and rebirth.[39] The Banks children participate in the carnival by wearing strange clothes—Jane wears her brother's jacket and Michael a sailor hat and a pair of gloves—and by subverting their normal routines by leaving the house at night.[40] Travers suggests that by freeing oneself from rigid identifications and by embracing strange events, one can paradoxically preserve one's own identity in the wake of the carnival.

These texts are concerned with effects of carnival on the life of an individual or small family groups but Bakhtin argues that true carnival 'embraces all the people.'[41] Matthew Skelton's *Endymion Spring* (2006) and Neil Gaiman's *The Graveyard Book* (2008) are among the few examples of true collective carnival in children's literature. Skelton's and Gaiman's visions of carnival are closely related to the *danse macabre*, a popular motif in medieval art which makes the subversive, deathly, and identity-threatening undercurrents of carnival abundantly clear. Gaiman's young protagonist Bod (already outside of subjectivity because he is called Nobody) watches as the dead walk down from the graveyard to begin the dance:

> The dead walked on, row on row, until they reached the square. Josiah Worthington walked up the steps until he reached Mrs. Caraway, the Lady Mayoress. He extended his arm and said, loud enough that the whole square could hear him, 'Gracious lady, this I pray: join me in the Macabray.'[42]

As with the song in Sendak's *In The Night Kitchen* (1971), the rhyming couplet spoken by Worthington heralds a departure from the normative order by departing from normal speech patterns. As an epitaph, it also has connotations of the cycles of life and death implicit in the ritual celebration. In disrupting the normative order in this way, the carnival opens the way for further disruptions of hierarchy and distinction. Everyone joins in the carnival and everyone becomes part of it.[43] Gaiman's carnival demonstrates many of the qualities Bakhtin identifies as important to the carnivalesque genre.

This carnival takes place on the street, is all-inclusive, and breaks down rigid hierarchies and fixed identifications. Perhaps most importantly, Gaiman pays close attention to carnivalesque time, emphasising the relationship between the carnival and the cycles of life, death, and rebirth. The *danse macabre* is described as being 'ancient a thousand years before' and Bod feels as though he had known the steps to the dance 'forever.' At the end of the dance, 'a clock somewhere began to strike the hour, and Bod counted along with it. Twelve chimes. He wondered if they had been dancing for twelve hours or twenty-four or for no time at all.'[44] Through participating in the carnival, Gaiman's characters come to a fresh awareness of the significance of the street as a synchronic space, a space where 'always' and 'now' are fused together.

Both the joyful and the violent aspects of carnival are brought to the fore in children's literature, and although many of the texts end with a comforting return to normality, it is clear that the cycles of violence, self-negation and subversion associated with the carnivalesque are never far away. In each of these texts—and in countless others—the central concern of the carnivalesque trope is that of identity. Many children's books are based around the *bildungsroman*, the growing-up narrative in which the individual is interpellated as subject and in which a sense of complete and finalised identity is instated. The carnivalesque represents a joyful holiday from these fixed identifications and offers young protagonists and readers an opportunity to explore, rehearse, and discard multiple identities. McKee and Sendak both suggest that resistance to carnival brings the individual under threat and that it is better, and safer, to embrace the carnival. Gaiman's representation of the 'fierce joy' of the *danse macabre* brings this idea to fruition. In order for the cyclical and diachronic aspects of the carnival to work properly, one must learn to let go in order to safely return.

The Street in The Dark Is Rising Sequence

Within the *Sequence*, there are few civic spaces. Despite its small size, the fishing village of Trewissick is the biggest, and busiest, settlement in the series and fulfils the criteria of a civic space; it is a centre of industry (it has a fishing harbour), of culture (it plays host to parades and to the Greenwitch ceremony), of religion (there are both Christian and pagan monuments in the area), and of history (the town was once the seat of King Mark). As the only civic space within the *Sequence*, Trewissick represents the only space in which it is credible for Cooper to include the street as a sub-section of the roadway topos. Nevertheless, Trewissick's small size, and its proximity to wilderness, intensifies and focuses the civic aspects of the village, making it an apt location for two very different scenes which make clear the collective, subversive, and carnivalesque qualities inherent in the street: the Lammas-tide carnival and the hallowing of the town by the Greenwitch ritual.[45] In the first of these scenes, Barney Drew gets drawn into the carnival and has a very positive experience of the street. In the second scene, Jane Drew witnesses the subversive and dangerous power of the street but she is frightened and disturbed by her experience. Each scene presents a very different aspect of the street as sub-topos to the reader and so Cooper demonstrates both the joyful and frightening aspects of the carnival.

Over Sea, Under Stone

During the Lammas-tide carnival, the cyclical and enclosed nature of the civic streets is enhanced and exaggerated because the roads in and out of the town are closed off to allow the carnival passage. In shutting off the roads, the horizontal movements associated with the open road are curtailed and forced inwards. When the carnival is in progress, Barney gets lost and tries to find Simon and Jane by taking short-cuts through the town. Cooper writes:

> He wandered from one winding lane to another, down narrow passages where the slate roofs almost touched overhead, past neat front doors with their brass knockers gleaming golden in the sun, through cobbled alleys where front doors opened not on to a pavement but straight on to the street.[46]

Cooper demonstrates her awareness of the street as a kind of dwelling space, describing the ways in which the buildings on either side of the street almost touch one another, almost becoming an indoor space, a corridor that channels Barney through areas where he does not want to go. This blurring of spatial and topological distinction leads, inevitably, to confusion. Barney's confusion is also signalled semantically; in this section a number of different synonyms for 'roads' are used, and it becomes plain that Barney does not know what to call the spaces. Without any clear definitions, without any proper names, the spaces he moves through lack distinction and soon blur into a homogenous mess. Barney unwittingly moves the wrong way through the town. It is not that he moves in the wrong direction, but that his movement is of the wrong quality for the civic space. In trying to find Jane and Simon, he attempts a linear progression from one point in the town to another but is continually hampered by the circuitous layout of the streets, eventually becoming entangled in 'an extraordinary endless maze of winding little roads.'[47] Through the word 'maze' Cooper conjures up images of the labyrinth and also recalls the 'monotonous wandering' which Benjamin claims is unique to the civic space.[48]

Barney's anxious wanderings are sharply contrasted with the joyful movements of the carnival. He is alone, but the carnival is noisy and busy, and the participants move along the streets of Trewissick together, rather than as individuals. Barney's wanderings are monotonous and reflect an everyday, mundane kind of movement, whereas the cyclical movements of the carnival are extraordinary. The carnival is a holiday, a fantastic departure from the routines of everyday life:

> Edged by delighted, pushing throngs of visitors, came a dancing file of the fantastic figures [...] the monstrous heads lurching and hopping in a slow parody of dance, and others, masked and disguised, weaving in and out of the crowds. Here and there they swooped on the bystanders, taking pretty girls by the hand, pretending to strike squealing old ladies with a ribboned wand, guiding visitors and villagers to join hands and dance with them in rows across the width of the street.[49]

The 'fantastic figures' are an obvious departure from the everyday and the conventional, a departure which the participants further enforce by dancing rather than walking and by moving across rather than along the street. The rules and manners of normal life are ignored; old ladies are symbolically beaten with ribboned wands, and pretty girls are symbolically abducted by being taken into the dancing crowd.

The carnival blurs other boundaries. The costumes used in the parade bring about the fantastic interchange of human, animal and vegetable forms, suggesting death and reincarnation.[50] On his arrival at the broad street where the procession is passing, Barney

> gazed fascinated round him at the bobbing giant heads, the bodies beneath them fantastic and gay in doublets and red, yellow, blue hose. Everywhere he saw costumed figures: a man dancing stiff as a tree, a solid flapping mass of green leaves, pirates, sailors, a hussar in bright red with a tall cap. Slave-girls, jesters, a man in a long blue silk gown made up as a pantomime dame; a girl all in black, twirling sinuous as a cat, with a cat's bewhiskered head.[51]

Here, the divisions between plant, animal and human are collapsed through the images of man-as-tree and girl-as-cat. Here forms are 'interwoven as if giving birth to each other. The borderlines that divide the kingdoms of nature in the usual picture of the world [are] boldly infringed.'[52] Other borderlines are also infringed by the carnivalesque; social hierarchies are flattened by the slave-girls, and even gender roles are playfully deconstructed through the image of the pantomime dame. The carnivalesque blurs and even dismisses social boundaries. Perhaps the most significant blurring of all is that of the distinction between the native and the strange. In *Over Sea, Under Stone* and *Greenwitch*, Cooper stresses that the inhabitants of Trewissick are generally suspicious of outsiders, particularly of foreigners. The Greenwitch ceremony, for example is 'very much a private village affair [...] no visitors are normally allowed near.'[53] But during the Lammas carnival a 'free and familiar contact reign[s] among people who are usually divided by the barriers of caste, property, profession, and age'[54] and the villagers join hands with the visitors, drawing them into the dance. Here, the familiar and the unfamiliar are inverted; the villagers dress in fabulous costumes, rendering the familiar strange and the visitors, who are normally excluded and treated as Other, are welcomed into the dance where they, lacking costumes, take on the roles of ordinary people. The way in which the crowds mingle together is representative of a greater, metaphorical mixing of the strange and the familiar that is a true sign of the carnivalesque.

This mingling of the strange and the familiar, and the ultimate inclusiveness of the carnival, may be seen when Barney is drawn into the parade. He feels 'someone' catch his hand, but he does not know who, and so Cooper draws attention to the anonymity of the crowd while demonstrating how Barney can be caught up within it. The dancers move as one through the streets and, when he is drawn into the crowd, Barney falls into step with the rest. He becomes part of the collective:

> The dancers whirled in and out of the crowd on the edge of the street where he stood; and then suddenly, before Barney knew what was happening they were dancing round him. He felt someone catch his hand and he was drawn out into the centre of the dancing crowd, among the ribbons and the feathers and bright bobbing heads, so that his feet fell into step with the rest. [. . .] People glanced down at him and smiled as he passed, and Barney, giddy with the music and the speed and the twisting black limbs of the cat before his eyes, flung himself laughing where it swung him.[55]

Here, the edge of the street becomes, as a result of the movement of the dancers, frayed and inconstant. As the edge is worn out, Barney is drawn into the very centre of the crowd and becomes a participant in the carnival. The arrival of his carnivalesque mood is heralded by a collapse in linguistic order; Cooper deliberately confuses prepositions as Barney moves 'out into' the crowd. This departure from normal linguistic order is confirmed by Barney's laughter. This laughter is the central and most important aspect of the carnivalesque and with it Barney is drawn from the edge of the crowd to its very centre. This movement is further enforced linguistically, as he moves from being a free subject to a passive object. At the beginning of this passage, he is clearly instated as subject; Cooper uses active verbs, and his name is used as the subject of the sentences. At the end of the passage, Barney has become passive; he is the object rather than the subject of the sentence and his movements are dictated by those of the crowd. His 'feet fall into step with the rest' and he becomes a part of the carnivalesque collective rather than an individual.

Greenwitch

In *Greenwitch*, the third book of the *Sequence*, Cooper presents another carnivalesque scene. Whereas Barney became part of the carnivalesque collective in *Over Sea, Under Stone*, the carnival section in *Greenwitch* is only witnessed by Jane. By this point, the reader is familiar with the subversive, magical, and supernatural aspects of Trewissick and is, perhaps, unsurprised that the quiet little fishing village could erupt into violence so suddenly. In spite of this, and the Greenwitch's rage which pre-empts these events, the carnivalesque section in *Greenwitch* is still startling in its violence and ferocity. Merriman says that 'all the power of the Wild Magic, which is without discipline or pattern, is let loose tonight in this place [...] Trewissick is under possession, this night. It will not be an easy place.'[56] Before the 'possession' takes effect, Merriman and the three Drew siblings have to pass through 'winding zigzag alleys and stairs'[57] to reach their cottage. This comparatively slight reference to the maze-like, entropic, civic streets brings heavy connotations of the carnivalesque section in *Over Sea, Under Stone*. This sense of anticipation is heightened when Jane shivers and remarks 'someone walked over my grave,'[58] subtly recalling the death of personal identity which invariably accompanies the onset of the carnival.

What follows is, in some ways, more properly carnivalesque than the section in *Over Sea, Under Stone* for it begins as a heightened juxtaposition of the familiar and the comforting with the supernatural and the disturbing. Cooper writes:

> Here and there were pools of yellow light from the lamp-posts: two on the quayside, three across the harbour, up on the road past the Grey House; others, more distant, at points within the village. But the pools of light were small. All else was darkness. And in the darkness, wherever she looked, Jane could see things moving.[59]

This movement recalls the restlessness of the carnival and is also suggestive of the dangerous undercurrents of the civic space. Within reach of the light, all appears to be normal and safe. In children's literature, street lights are a sign of civic order and control.[60] In J. K. Rowling's *Harry Potter and the Philosopher's Stone* (1997), Dumbledore turns out all of the street-lights on Privet Drive before he will talk about magic to Professor McGonagle. This signals the switch from the mundane to the magical. But streetlights are also artificial and, at night-time, represent a kind of repression of, or resistance to, the natural order of things. Richard Lehan notes that 'urban order is tenuous; chaos always lies just beneath the surface.'[61] Cooper writes that the pools of light, and therefore the civic resistance, are 'small' and, by implication, weak. Inevitably, the repressed forces of nature and darkness, the Wild Magic, must break through and subvert the polite, civic order of Trewissick.

The outbreak of Wild Magic comes in the form of a carnival. It is a sudden, violent incursion on the order and safety of the town. This is 'a cathartic release of repressed discontent'[62] from the Greenwitch's perspective, but it may be more properly regarded as the cathartic release of repressed disorder, in the sense that the forces of nature—the Wild Magic—breaks through the thin veil of civic order and wreaks havoc on the town. Throughout the

Sequence, as I discussed in Chapter Two, Wild Magic is synonymous with a kind of natural, amoral, and violent power. This power is inherent in the landscape and is released at certain times of year, particularly at solstitial and equinoctial points, and is responsible for the Wild Hunt, the Brenin Llwyd, and the Greenwitch herself. It is probable that the Wild Magic is also the force responsible for the carnival. The Wild Magic is a variation on the 'eternally unquiet, eternally agitated'[63] collective that haunts the civic space.

During the Greenwitch's carnival, the spirits of the dead relive three terrible events in Trewissick's history: the wrecking of ships, the sack of the town by red-haired oarsmen, and the capture of *The Lottery* by revenuers and the subsequent hanging of Roger Toms, a local pirate and hero. The 'horror [that] seemed to take hold of the crowd'[64] here is a far cry from the laughter and gaiety of the Lammas-tide carnival. Yet the horror .only 'seems' to affect the crowd and, furthermore, the crowd itself is only an illusion; no-one can come to any real harm. The horrors that Jane witnesses are really only the ritualised re-enactments of past events. They are a macabre pantomime of terror and destruction. But Jane cannot understand this because she is removed from the civic streets and from the true origin of the carnival. Unable to participate and unable to find any meaning in the events she witnesses, she is left 'cold, frightened'[65] and with an overwhelming sense of fear; 'a dreadful horror of the unknown, of whatever force was sweeping through land and sea, out there. She wanted only to cower into her own corner animal-like, away from it, safe.'[66] It is ironic that Cooper describes Jane's fear for the preservation of her identity as 'animal-like'[67] for this animal-like quality could threaten to destabilise her identity, leaving her open to the human/animal/vegetable interchange Bakhtin describes, if she were outside and closer to the carnival. So, whereas Barney is enticed into the carnival and becomes one with the crowd, able to laugh and to accept freely the blurring of human forms and the dissolution of personal identity, Jane tries to hide from the wild, chaotic forces that give rise to the carnival.

Her identity and sanity are preserved because she remains within the cottage. Although she witnesses the carnival, she cannot be forced to participate because she does not set foot on the street. Those out on the streets are far more vulnerable to the destructive and regenerative forces of the carnival. In particular, one of the agents of the Dark, a painter, who tries to control the Greenwitch, makes himself vulnerable. Cooper writes:

> The command in the voice of the man of the Dark now was like ice; it was the cold absolute arrogance that through centuries had brought men down to terror and grovelling obedience. [...] Will clenched his fists so that the nails cut into his palms; even an Old One could feel the force of such a command bite into his mind. He watched without a breath, wondering; he did not know how such a challenge would touch Wild Magic, a force neither of the Light nor of the Dark nor of men.[68]

Will recognises that the Greenwitch and the forces she embodies are part of the Wild Magic, and pre-empts the carnivalesque outbreak which ensues. By watching 'without a breath' Will symbolically dies, allowing the forces of Wild Magic to pass over him as if he did not exist. The painter's 'absolute arrogance,' on the other hand, shows his determination to assert himself before the Greenwitch. His arrogance is precisely the kind of egotism that goes against everything the carnival represents.

Any attempt to assert one's own personal identity in the face of carnival leads, inevitably, to conflict. Whereas Jane's attempt to assert her self goes unnoticed by the Wild Magic because she is off the street, safe within the cottage, secure inside the sanctuary, the painter stands out on the street, in the space that belongs to the carnival and belongs to the wild, uncontrollable collective and is, therefore, within its power. As the carnival is 'of all the people,' it is obviously more powerful than any individual, and at this point Cooper begins the build-up to the painter's death. The Wild Magic asserts its power by creating a resurgence of the carnival in the area:

> And shadows came flocking into the harbour, from all sides, all the shades and spirits and hauntings of that one haunted night: the past folk of Trewissick from all the centuries that little sea-town had ever seen, focused into one black point of time. [...] They were all around [the painter] crying and calling, pointing, just as villagers of the present had crowded and called and pushed the Greenwitch, as it was taken newly made to tumble headlong from the cliff.[69]

By referencing the Greenwitch's symbolic death, Cooper suggests what is about to happen to the painter. The three Old Ones who witness the death only escape the 'unreasoning rage' of the dead villagers by 'silently, unobtrusively [drawing] their hoods over their heads and [moving] together to one side of the harbour, in the shade of the wall, to stand there unseen.'[70] By sheltering against the wall—a suggestion of an interface with the sanctuary topos—and by covering their faces and so becoming anonymous, faceless and, therefore, part of the deindividualized carnivalesque collective, Will, Merriman, and Captain Toms escape unscathed.

The painter however, continues to assert his separation from the crowd 'pushing feebly at the air' and, in response to the crowd's assertion that he is 'Roger Toms' the painter shouts 'I am not he! You mistake me!'[71] His reiteration of 'I' is a clear attempt to assert his sense of fixed individual identity, but by this time, he is already being deconstructed as subject and being reconfigured as passive object. Cooper writes that the crowds fall 'upon him, making him into [the past's] long shame'[72] and, at the climax of the carnival and at the height of the Wild Magic's powers, the dead crowd onto a ghostly ship and pull the painter to his death: 'and with a glad shriek all the great crowd

Figure 3.3 Pathway through Cwm Maethion, Wales. ©Jane Carroll.

of shades rushed onto the ship, dragging with them the struggling painter.'[73] Here, Cooper conflates many carnivalesque images. The 'glad shriek' is a sure sign of the carnival, a kind of violent laugh connotative of both joy and horror; the 'great crowd' moves as a single unit and the painter who once tried to assert himself as individual subject, has become a helpless object in the grasp of the collective. The cycles of carnival, which reach back into the past and forward into the future, and which are composed of the collective, are more powerful than any single individual. Here, by having a figure from the present borne away by the past, Cooper shows linear historic time as being superseded by cyclical, carnivalesque time.

Through these incidents, Cooper shows how the carnivalesque cycles of deconstruction and reconstruction can be joyful and happy or frightening and traumatic, depending on the attitude of the individual towards the carnivalesque crowd. The more willing the individual is to participate communally and to let go of rigid identification, the more successful the experience of carnival will be. Thus, the nature of the space is defined by the attitude of the human presence within it. However, the impact of the environment upon the human cannot be ignored and I will now examine the ways in which the environment, specifically roads and the journeys which take place upon them, can prove instrumental in the formation and interpellation of the individual as subject.

The Road

Whereas the street is limited to the civic environment, the road, the second aspect of the topos, connects distant places, often crossing vast tracts of land in order to do so. The street entails a cyclical movement, wherein events are repeated, a fact highlighted through cyclically recurring urban carnivals, but the road entails a diachronic, historical motion, where events are sequential and unique. Whereas the street brings about a deterioration of personal identity and initiates the creation of a collective, social identity, the road and the journeys which take place on it are the 'primary narrative structure to depict the formation of identity.'[74] Journeying beyond civic spaces, travellers gain knowledge of the landscape as a whole[75] and build a sense of individual identity which is separate from, but not necessarily antithetical to, that of the community. By removing characters from their home and from their fixed, stable, and therefore static identities, the roadway brings characters through unfamiliar territory.[76] This process of estrangement (of making the character a stranger in these new spaces) encourages the development of a more complex and sophisticated kind of identity by forcing characters to question the values and ideologies they have brought from home. The return home unites these fixed and fluctuating identities and creates a new synthesis of character and space. As Reimer suggests, journeys 'concatenate the knowledge of self with territory'[77] and so, whereas the stability of the sanctuary topos implies fixity of identity, the 'dynamic'[78] roadway topos enables the expansion of identity through experience and movement.

Anomalous Ways

At this stage it is necessary to deal with the one version of the roadway topos which does not conform to the chronotopes identified by Bakhtin. The railway is, in many ways, like other roadways—it lies on the surface of the landscape and enables travel and communication between distant points—but in other ways it is anomalous. Whereas the roadway topos centres on a series of chronotopes whereby space is directly related to time, the railway disrupts these chronotopic correspondences by changing the nature of the relationship between these two factors. Trains move at such high speeds that it is difficult for the passenger to judge spatial relationships accurately. Thus, the railway eats away at human perceptions of landscape. Schivelbusch notes that the noise and smell of the steam-engine overpowered the smells and sounds of the surrounding environment and that even 'visual perception is diminished by velocity.'[79] Enclosed within the carriage, passengers are unable to look directly ahead at the horizon or at the railway beneath the train and have only partial views of the landscape they pass through. Whereas other roads allow travellers to gain a greater experience and understanding of landscape as a whole, the disorientating effects of the railway lead to the 'loss of landscape.'[80] Schivelbusch observes two main factors in this sense of loss; first that the railroad destroyed 'the space between points'[81] and second that

> Compared to the eotechnical space-time relationship, the one created by the railroad appears abstract and disorientating because the railroad—in realising Newton's mechanics—negated all that characterised eotechnical traffic; the railroad did not appear embedded in the space of the landscape the way coach and highway are, but seemed to strike its way through it.[82]

The railway annihilates the relationship with landscape. Thus, as Alice Jenkins suggests, the railway is not a proper topos but a heterotope, 'a miniature world that is both part of and distinct from the larger world surrounding it,'[83] which is capable of 'juxtaposing in a real place several spaces, several sites that are in themselves incompatible.'[84]

The train's heterotopic nature and its ability to cross vast distances quickly means that it is often used at 'initiatory or climactic moments'[85] in children's literature. The railway is especially useful in conveying the idea that the place where the protagonists' adventures will occur is a long way—both geographically and metaphorically—from the world of home. Besides being an almost obligatory opening to any Blyton school story, this distancing technique is seen in Lewis's *Prince Caspian* (1951), Garner's *The Weirdstone of Brisingamen* (1960),

Aiken's *The Wolves of Willoughby Chase* (1963), Bawden's *Carrie's War* (1973), and Rowling's *Harry Potter and the Philosopher's Stone* (1997). In these cases, the quest which draws the character away from home and leads to the formation of a new and independent identity takes place almost instantly and renders the landscape between the two end points of the journey insignificant.

Cooper uses trains and railway imagery quite often. Both *Over Sea, Under Stone* and *The Grey King* open with train journeys and in the opening scene of *The Dark Is Rising*, James Stanton is described as being 'like a small angry locomotive.'[86] However, it is not until the end of *Silver on the Tree* that Cooper exploits the heterotopic nature of the railway journey by having the Light travel towards the site of the last battle with the Dark on a steam train.[87] She uses the train to unite the distant settings of the *Sequence*, allowing the Drews' guest-house in Aberdyfi to be connected with the Chiltern Hills near the Stantons' house without the need for a long and detailed journey. By describing it first as a solid thing, 'screeching and whimpering on the track'[88] but then with increasing vagueness, Cooper heightens the sense of the train as heterotopia. When the Drews first enter the train, the description is grounded in the physical:

> Merriman swung the door shut with a solid crash; they heard the clang of the signal again as its arm went down, and then the locomotive began to stir, a slow heavy chuffing rising in speed and sound, with the dunes slipping past outside, faster and faster, swaying rocking, clickety-clacking, the wheels beginning to sing.[89]

By the end of the section, Cooper creates an image whereby the nature of the vehicle has become vague and insubstantial. She writes: 'in clouds and swirls the mist came swooping round the platform and the dim arch, as if all were dissolving into emptiness'[90] and the train soon becomes a 'great formless vehicle,'[91] thus differentiating clearly between the solid landscapes of the *Sequence* and the liminality of the heterotopic space.

In the *Sequence*, as in the majority of children's texts, journeys on foot are prioritised as they enable a greater degree of interaction with the landscape. The closed railway carriage separates human characters from their environment and, for instance, makes weather something to be observed rather than experienced. Also, the railway restricts narrative action to the fixed sites at the beginning and end of the journey or to the physically confined spaces of the train. The railway strictly prescribes the route of the journey and does not allow for diversions and spontaneous changes of direction like the road. Unlike the bicycle or the motor-car, the train does not allow passengers to look ahead at the horizon. The mode of travel which enables the greatest level of connection between human and landscape is the journey on foot.

The walked road allows the journey to develop organically, at a pace set by the human not dictated by a machine. Pedestrians experience the environment directly, rain falls on them, the sun warms them, and they feel the incline of hills and slopes in their muscles; the journey makes them tired. The environment has a direct effect upon them. Furthermore, pedestrians make their own way across and within the landscape; their imprints and tracks mark their footfall passage through the world. By making their mark on the environment and simultaneously allowing the environment to impact upon them, travellers forge an identity that is a perfect synthesis of experience, personality, memory, and place.

The Road in Medieval Literature
The journey-based narrative is the 'master story of Western civilization,'[92] and it structures stories and folktales wherever there is a culture of travel. Whereas 'most [medieval] people travelled far less than they do today [...] the notion of a peasant spending the whole of his or her life in one place is not necessarily correct'[93] and roads, and the journeys upon them, were an intrinsic part of medieval culture. A variety of travellers, from wanderers, pilgrims, tradespeople, and merchants to kings, made use of the vast network of roads that traversed Europe.[94] Accordingly, the journey is a common literary motif, and pilgrimages and quests regularly structure the narratives of medieval texts. It is, perhaps, surprising that the roads these journeys take place upon are seldom mentioned. In *The Canterbury Tales*, for instance, although the end point of the journey is firmly fixed in the minds of character and reader alike, there are few references to the road itself.[95] There are similarly few references to roads in *The Mabinogion*, although many of Arthur's knights undertake dangerous quests into unfamiliar territory. Moreover, the knights generally return unscathed and largely unaffected by their travels.[96] But in such cases, it may be argued, it is not the actual journey but what the journey represents that is important. The pilgrimage to Canterbury is a metaphorical journey of the soul to a higher place in the world as well as a physical expedition. Similarly, Arthur's knights' quests act as metaphors for their growing maturity and independence from the court as well as an opportunity to showcase their physical prowess and courtly manners. These journeys are symbolic and allegorical, rather than realistic and mundane. As a result, the descriptions of the journeys are highly stylised and, as Hourihan observes, the narrative structure is 'always the same.'[97] Both pilgrimage and quest 'follow an invariable pattern [...] [The hero] leaves the civilized order of home to venture into the wilderness in pursuit of his goal [...] encounters a series of difficulties and is threatened by dangerous opponents. [...] He returns home, perhaps overcoming other threats on the way, and is gratefully welcomed.'[98]

That is not to say, however, that the journeys and the roads upon which they take place have no impact on the traveller. In many medieval texts, the start and end points of the journey, the places which the roadway topos connects, are the focus of the narrative, and many texts establish a binary opposition between departure and arrival scenes. These scenes set up a comparison between the naïve, departing hero and the wise, returning hero. In *Sir Gawain and the Green Knight*, for instance, during Gawain's arming scene before his departure, he is described as 'unsullied' and 'ever faithful.'[99] Even though he laughs and smiles at the Green Man in the comfort of the court, he finds that life beyond the bounds of the sanctuary is 'no game.'[100] The journey has a major effect on the young knight. Travelling alone through Logres and the Wirral, he is 'companionless and alone.'[101] Separated from the court and the company of his fellows, Gawain drifts through the wilderness, taking 'strange ways' through 'countries unknown.'[102] Thus his journey brings him footfall knowledge of a wide and varied landscape. As Casey suggests, 'journeys [...] not only take us to places, but embroil us in them.'[103] As I discussed in Chapter Two, Gawain forges a profound connection with his environment through his journey away from Arthur's court. As the roadway is chronotopic, in that time and space are intimately connected within the topos, Gawain advances both geographically and temporally and matures over the course of his journey. His cheerful arrogance is soon replaced by a more considered outlook on the world. He returns, groaning 'for grief and rue'[104] and when he addresses the court, his words are those of a penitent, rather than a brave warrior:

> 'Lo! Lord,' he said at last, and the lace handled,
> 'This is the band of the blame I bear on my neck!
> This is the grief and loss I have got
> for myself for the cowardice the covetousness and that caught me there!'[105]

Rather than wearing the pentangle, a sign 'to betoken true Troth'[106] he returns wearing 'the token of the perfidy that [he is] taken in.'[107] The change in his armour is an outward and visible sign of a profound change in his personality, a change which has been effected by the road.

The Road in Children's Literature

The journey-based narrative is 'a central, vital element of children's literature'[108] and perhaps 'the most important of the defining characteristics of children's literature as a genre.'[109] Whereas some texts, such as Edith Nesbit's *The Phoenix and the Carpet* (1904) and Enid Blyton's *Adventures of the Wishing Chair* (1937), are constructed as a series of short, generally inconsequential and magical daytrips, the vast majority of journey-based narratives involve long and exhaustive treks across vast areas of landscape. The journey there or 'there and back again'[110] takes up almost the whole of the text, and the destination is usually reached only in the final stages of the novel. The quest may be for a true homecoming as in Anne Holm's *I Am David* (1972), Richard Adams's *Watership Down* (1972) and Siobhan Dowd's *Solace of the Road* (2009). In each of these cases, the protagonists leave a damaged or inadequate home in search of a new and better place to live. Other journeys are driven by the quest for significant objects, as in J. R. R. Tolkien's *The Hobbit* (1937) and

Rosemary Sutcliff's *The Eagle of the Ninth* (1954), or for spiritual rewards, as in Kevin Crossley-Holland's *Gatty's Tale* (2006). These journeys are never simply geographical but represent a transitional period in characters' lives as they move from innocence to experience, from youth to maturity and towards independence. The road enables travellers to move into new parts of the landscape, literally broadening their horizons. Indeed, the open road is synonymous with growth and change. Bakhtin notes that the journey-based narrative 'fuses the course of an individual's life (at its major turning points) with his actual spatial course or road.'[111] The roadway and the journey-based narrative with which it is synonymous represent 'the spatial and temporal growth of a man'[112] and offer a direct correspondence between space and time.

The effects of such a journey are most obvious when the traveller returns home. In Tolkien's *The Hobbit*, Bilbo Baggins is 'not the hobbit that [he was]'[113] when he returns to Hobbiton and in Neil Gaiman's *Stardust* (1987), Tristran Thorn has changed so much that he is unrecognisable to his neighbours in Wall. Robert Westall makes devastating use of the impact of the journey in *The Kingdom by the Sea* (1990) when Harry's great pilgrimage away from his bombed-out house and his dead family is 'undone.'[114] But having forged a new identity, one that suits him and his environment, he can no longer adapt to the quiet sociability of the family. Even though the geographical journey can be reversed, the effects of the journey upon Harry cannot be so easily erased.

The Road in The Dark Is Rising Sequence

Whereas each of the texts in Cooper's quintet is presented as a quest for a significant object or objects—the grail, the six signs, the scroll, the harp, and the crystal sword—the texts are not structured by long journeys as *The Hobbit* and *The Eagle of the Ninth* are. On the contrary, the home-away-home narrative patterning is rather implicit in many of the texts: in *Over Sea, Under Stone*, *Greenwitch* and *Silver on the Tree*, the Drews' journeys to and from home take place outside the parameters of the texts. Even though *The Grey King* opens before Will travels to Wales, the details of his journey are largely absent, and the narrative resumes only when his cousin Rhys collects him from the train station. In these cases, the journeys away from home are short holidays, undertaken in distant, but nevertheless familiar, parts of the country. These journeys are of a fixed duration and although the Drews' experiences in Cornwall and North Wales undoubtedly affect them their trips cannot be considered quests as the roadway topos itself plays little part in their development. Here, I will focus on spontaneous journeys into the unknown, where the protagonist leaves the safety of home for uncertain gains, and in which the roadway topos has a marked impact on characters' emotional and social development. The three journeys I will examine here, two in *The Dark Is Rising* and one in *Silver on the Tree*, are exemplars of the topos. These journeys create a complex interrelation of space and time and have a direct, observable impact on the character, endowing them with a new, mature awareness of self and, through footfall exploration, a renewed awareness of landscape.

The road enables this renewed sense of awareness by drawing the character away from the sanctuary topos and out through the wider territory. In *Over Sea, Under Stone*, Cooper describes the road as a 'threading road,'[115] implying that in connecting diverse places, it somehow stitches the landscape together. The phrase also carries the connotations of the homophonous 'treading' which consolidates the central importance of walking and of footfall. Thus Cooper promotes a profound connection between the human traveller and the physical topos; the road impacts upon the traveller by enabling footfall, but also, reflexively, allows the traveller's footfall to imprint upon it. In this way, the road not only binds places together but also concatenates territory with human identity.

The Dark Is Rising

Will Stanton makes several short journeys over the course of the novel, including a trip to the Dawsons' farm to collect hay and going carolling with his brothers and sisters around the village on Christmas Eve. Some of these journeys, such as his shopping trip to Slough, are significant within their own right (it is the first such trip he makes alone), but they are otherwise of little narrative importance and, because they take place entirely within the bounds of the primary world, only affect that aspect of Will which is still only a small boy. There are two home-away-home journeys which take Will out of the primary world and into the synchronic world of the Old Ones where 'all times co-exist'[116] and which impact on his identity as an Old One too. These journeys are delicately paralleled: both centre on Huntercombe Lane and cross the same geographical territory, the first marks Will's initiation into the world of the Old Ones, the second confirms and consolidates his position within that world. The first journey opens his quest to find the Six Signs and the second brings about the end of this quest and his triumph over the Dark.

On the morning of his eleventh birthday, Will leaves his house and steps into the world of the Old Ones. His journey away from and back towards his home is instrumental in the formation of his identity as the Sign Seeker and the youngest of the Old Ones. In the 'strange familiar world,'[117] the landscape is covered and concealed by snow so that only the house and 'a narrow path leading away'[118] are visible. At this moment, Will faces two polarised choices: either he stays at home and retains his childhood identity or he moves away from the house and all the things it represents and begins to forge a new, independent identity. In many ways, Will has already made his choice clear the moment he pulls on his boots and coat, signalling his desire to depart. When he leaves he closes the door behind him, deliberately shutting himself off from the domestic space and his family, and putting himself beyond the threshold of the sanctuary topos, beyond the limits of the home.[119] His decision to leave is prompted partly by curiosity and partly by the recognition that 'his home no longer seemed quite the unassailable fortress it had always been.'[120] In acknowledging that the boundaries of the sanctuary are not inviolable, Will demonstrates a burgeoning understanding of landscape, an understanding which will be developed, matured, and accentuated through the footfall knowledge he will gain over the course of his journey.

Over the course of this journey through Huntercombe, Will forges an identity which is independent of home and family:

> Turning to the right, he walked up the narrow road that in his own time was called Huntercombe Lane. It was the way that he and James had taken to Dawsons' Farm, the same road that he had trodden almost every day of his life, but it was very different now. Now, it was no more than a track through a forest, great snow-burdened trees enclosing it on both sides.[121]

Here, Cooper connects Will's life to the road and suggests that once the road changes, Will's life will change too. The sense of burgeoning identity is conveyed by the image of the road as 'no more than a track': like Will, the road is nascent but has the potential for development. As in her representations of the civic street, Cooper plays with time here. Huntercombe Lane appears to have gone back in time, but Will, conscious of the fact that it is his birthday, still believes time to be moving forward historically. In truth it is doing neither. Cooper uses Huntercombe Lane to demonstrate the perfect synthesis of time and space in the world of the Old Ones, a world where all times co-exist. Merriman explains Will's new complex relationship with time:

> 'You see, Will,' he said, 'we of the circle are planted only loosely within Time. The doors are a way through it, in any direction we may choose. For all times co-exist, and the future can sometimes affect the past, even though the past is a road that leads to the future.'[122]

Through the road—both physical and metaphorical—Will enters into a chronotope that is both cyclical and linear; he is newly reborn on the morning of his birthday and traces over an old and familiar route, but he also moves forward, away from the static identity of the home and out into the world. The apparently straight road combines with the cyclicality of the year to describe a path for Will that is geographically linear but emotionally and socially spiral.

The journey has a major impact on Will's identity and he soon realises just how much geographical and emotional distance separates him from the small boy he was the day before. Over the course of his journey, Will is interpellated as subject; as he moves away from his home and the twentieth century, he grows into a new identity, one deeply connected with the landscape and with the past, independent of his family. Through this journey, Will becomes an Old One. Merriman tells him:

You were born to inherit it [the power of the Old Ones], Will, when you came to the end of your tenth year. On the night before your birthday, it was beginning to wake, and now on the day of your birth it is free, flowering, fully grown. But it is still confused and unchannelled because you are not in proper control of it yet.'[123]

Here, the word 'unchannelled' suggests that the road is a conduit that has brought Will into new knowledge and that his development is intimately connected with the roadways. He must be channelled by the roads because he is not yet ready to make his own way through the landscape and all that it represents.

Will's journey on Huntercombe Lane is only the beginning of his quest, however. Although he feels 'stronger, taller, more relaxed,'[124] his new identity is not fully fixed until his task is complete. It is especially fitting, then, that Will completes his quest on the same road that initiated it. His journey on the morning of his birthday is paralleled with another journey he makes along Huntercombe Lane towards the end of the text. Although they take place less than three weeks apart, these journeys are almost perfect opposites: the first taking place at dawn, the second at twilight. In the first instance, Will leaves the house alone. The second time he is initially accompanied by his brother Paul. Over the course of each journey, he is rescued by a horse; the first a magical white mare of the Light, the second an ancient shire horse from the Dawsons' farm. The two horses are a clear indication of the difference between the two journeys: the majority of the first journey takes place in a magical, secondary world, outside of time and it is appropriate that the horse is ethereal, but the second takes place largely in the primary world and the physical solidity of the farm horse indicates the increased practicality of this trip. This second journey is not a dreamy wandering but a journey of practicality and necessity. Will must rescue his sister and find the last of the six signs before the night is out. The first time Will acts unconsciously and 'accept[s] everything that came into his mind, without thought or question, as if he were moving through a dream.'[125] In the second journey, Will moves deliberately with the self-awareness and self-confidence of an Old One. This second journey is also concerned with identity but instead of instigating the formation of a new identity, this journey, over the same geographical space, consolidates, confirms, and finalises his identity as an Old One.

This second journey is figured as a voyage into the unknown where the world 'became strange all over again, as the rain carved the snow into new lanes and hillocks.'[126] But Will has acquired footfall knowledge of the territory around Huntercombe and he 'knew very well where they were.'[127] Even though the flood has turned Huntercombe Lane into a 'running stream'[128] Will knows the foundations of the roadway to be old and unchanging, beyond the effects of normal time. Although the lane becomes a 'road-river'[129] and later a 'river-road'[130] with greatly increased power and agency, Will trusts it, allowing it to channel him towards his destination. Moreover, Will now knows what to do and what to say. He knows the proper words in the Old Speech to make the signs glow and light a path for him. Now he speaks and acts deliberately and consciously rather than unconsciously and carelessly as before (when he speaks accidentally in the Old Tongue to John Wayland Smith). Will has become an Old One.

As on the morning of his birthday, he returns home with Merriman by his side. Whereas before Will was very much in awe of Merriman; by the end of the text he has become Merriman's equal and 'they walked as old friends walk, without speaking, sharing the kind of silence that is not so much silence as a kind of still communication.'[131] Merriman acknowledges this shift by saying, 'Come, Old One [...] you are no longer a small boy.'[132] Will is interpellated as subject through his journeys. His decision to move away from his home and the stability of identity that it promotes opened his personality and identity up to fluctuating and changing values. He grows, not simply by progressing through linear time as before, but by forging a synchronic identity. His identity has not so much changed as deepened. He is still the youngest, but whereas he was once simply the youngest in his family, he is now the youngest of the circle of Old Ones. Whereas his identity was once wholly bound up with the domestic space and its routines, through a geographic and historic footfall experience of the landscape around his home, it is now informed and affected by a wider and deeper range of spaces and so secured beyond the limits of the sanctuary topos.

Silver on the Tree
Bran is similarly interpellated through his journey with Will into the Lost Land. His journey is explicitly connected with his coming into his identity as the Pendragon and the heir of Arthur. Bran's journey takes him from innocence to experience, self-awareness, and confidence. He begins his journey as a passive object. The rainbow road that brings the two boys to the Lost Land has, like Huntercombe Lane, an energy and an agency of its own which dictates their movements:

> Down through the bright haze the strange road brought them, arching like a rainbow. Will and Bran found that they made no move of their own. Once they had stepped on to its surface, the road took them up, took them through space and time with a motion they could not afterwards describe.[133]

Bran and Will are the passive objects of the road's actions, but Will has already come into self-awareness and into his full identity. He fulfils for Bran the role Merriman once fulfilled for him, being now a helper and a guide rather than a fellow traveller into self-awareness. Bran is nervous and confused in the Lost Land; his characteristic arrogance is shattered before his personality can be rebuilt. In the first moments, the reader is shown how Bran's old personality is disturbed by the place; when he speaks there is 'a small shake in his voice beneath the bravado.'[134] At first, Bran follows Will without question but where Will was content to accept everything that happened to him, Bran is not so trusting. He declares with sudden helpless force,

> 'This place doesn't mean anything.'
> 'It will, when we arrive,' Will said.
> 'Arrive at what?'
> 'Well—at the meaning! At the crystal sword.'[135]

Will knows to seek meaning from the function of places; his symbiosis with the landscape has made him aware that the road means nothing without the journey and the journey is always eschatological, its purpose being fulfilled and understood only upon its completion. Here, the ideas of destiny and of destination are conflated: the end of the quest is both an object and a state of being.

Before Bran can become the Pendragon he must gain Eirias, the crystal sword but first he must put aside those aspects of his identity which are incompatible with such a role. Like Will, Bran has two distinct sides to his personality; part of him is absolutely rooted in the twentieth century but another, partially buried aspect of his identity is timeless and mythic. Climbing into a magical carriage he jokes: 'First horses, then a coach-and-four. What'll they offer us next, then? Think they'll have a Rolls-Royce?'[136] Here, mixing highly incongruous elements, Bran shows that he is poised between the mythic and the mundane. However, over the course of his journey, as a result of the trials he endures and obstacles he overcomes, the mythic side of his personality emerges fully and he becomes the Pendragon. This metamorphosis has an outward and visible effect; when he receives Eirias he becomes 'somehow a little more erect, more commanding'[137] and when Jane Drew—whom Bran calls 'Jenny-oh' and thus evokes Guinevere[138]—meets him later, she notices that he seems 'full of new life, vibrant as a taut wire.'[139]

This shift in Bran's identity is accompanied by an increased understanding of the landscape and of his cultural heritage. For example, Gwion, his guide through the Lost Land, tells him that birch trees once grew plentifully in Wales[140] and, throughout the journey, Bran and Will encounter elements of Welsh folklore and mythology. For instance, one of the major obstacles to be overcome is the Mari Llwyd, a mythical dancing horse skeleton which has terrified Bran since he was a boy.[141] Similarly, Gwion is an incarnation of Taliesin, a character in the *Mabinogion*, but this incarnation also has a semi-historical basis in Gwion, son of Llanfair a poet from Caereinion who called himself Taliesin 'as an ambitious Hellenistic Greek poet might have taken the name of Homer.'[142] Moreover, by walking through the Lost Land, Bran gains footfall knowledge of the landscape—both its geographical and historical elements. Cooper intensifies the sense that this is a cultural journey as much as a physical one by drawing on motifs associated with quest-narratives of the *Mabinogion* and Middle English romances such as the magical fountain which appears in *The Lady of the Well*.[143]

Furthermore, by providing intricate descriptions of the details and textures of objects, particularly those things made from precious metals or expensive materials, Cooper borrows some of the stylistic elements of these older texts. She also borrows the structure of the quest narrative, and the journey through the Lost Land is tripartite as Will and Bran have to cross through the City, the Country and the Castle before they can win Eirias.[144] The quest narrative also structures the language of these episodes. Using long syntagmatic sentences which follow on from one another with 'and' and 'then' but without any apparent causality or narrative intervention, Cooper recalls the language of traditional quest romances and endows the unfolding action with a sense of dream-like unreality, renacting linguistically the synchronic geography of the journey.

Many of these references are culturally and geographically specific but Cooper also uses motifs which have universal, allegorical significance. For instance, the sequential epigraphs inscribed on the doors and thresholds throughout the Lost Land recall the folk-story "Mr Fox" which in turn recalls the episode in Edmund Spenser's *The Faerie Queene* in which Britomart enters the castle of the wizard Busyrane and is greeted by a series of warnings inscribed over the inner doors.[145] The maze of mirrors Bran passes through may be read as an allegory for doing away with old, partial identities and learning to trust in a single identity and the episode with the Mari Llwyd may show how Bran must overcome his childish fears before he can achieve his new, mature identity. Most importantly in terms of universal significance, Cooper presents the King of the Lost Land as a version of the Fisher King of the Grail legends whose depression and lethargy is reflected in the stagnation of the landscape.[146] Like Perceval/Peredur, Bran's quest is to 'break the spell which retains the Grail King in a semblance of life'[147] and, in doing so, complete his quest and confirm his own identity. By drawing on these established motifs, Cooper posits Bran's journey as a magical, heroic quest and invests the seemingly meaningless tasks and obstacles with a new significance.

Wandering and Exile

The journeys considered thus far are eschatological and derive meaning from their endings. However, some journeys have no apparent end and are undertaken not by heroes but by exiles who travel without purpose and without destination. Wanderers, outlaws, and exiles move not 'from one towne to another or from place to place out of the towne, parishe or village where such a person will dwell'[148] like a pedlar, but beyond the civic space through 'pathless woods, fens and solitudes.'[149] The wandering exile has a place in Western literature that can be traced back to Cain. This tradition has been assimilated into Northern European literature through the Old English Genesis and the treatment of Cain therein.

Wandering and Exile in Medieval Literature

Cain is the first wanderer, and his treatment in *Genesis A* is the exemplar for all others in Old English literature. He is described as 'miserable of mood' and a 'friendless exile,'[150] and these characteristics may be seen in many other exiles in the period. God's words to Cain make the conditions of his exile plain:

> For this murder
> you shall receive punishment and wander in exile,
> accursed eternally. The earth shall not yield you
> fair fruit for your worldly need, for she has swallowed up holy blood,
> from your hands; therefore she withdraws her pleasures from you,
> the brightness of the green earth. You shall be cast out in misery,
> disgraced from your home so you shall go, because you became Abel's
> murderer. Therefore you shall be an exile,
> follow far-flung paths, hated by your dear kin.[151]

Here, wandering is a punishment not a choice. Cain's murderous act is so appalling that he can no longer be accepted within a community. As the ground will not 'yield' crops for him, there is no possibility that Cain can simply establish a new home for himself somewhere else. He is not just cast out of a community, but denied the right to establish a home or a farm of any kind. Cain is cut off from the earth. Most importantly, the early medieval imagination saw Cain's exile as explicitly connected to 'far-flung paths.' Although he must wander aimlessly, his route is already prescribed for him. Cain's attitude to his exile also provides an important source for later depictions of wanderers.

The most obvious and literal descendent of Cain is *Beowulf*'s Grendel. However, whereas Cain enjoys God's protection,[152] Grendel bears 'god's ire'[153] and whereas Cain moves away from civilisation altogether, Grendel is a *mearcstapa*,[154] a boundary-walker, and is inexorably drawn to the world of men, prowling the boundaries of their territory. These differences are, however, outnumbered by the similarities between the two. Like Cain, Grendel is *dreamum bedæled*,[155] 'deprived of joy,' and excluded from the pleasures of society. He is infuriated by the sounds of rejoicing coming from Heorot; his murderous attacks, like Cain's, seem primarily motivated by jealousy. Grendel's status as an outsider is confirmed by these attacks; the hall and all the security and sociability it represents are anathema to him. He is denied the stability of place and of identity that comes with the hall and so even though he is associated with the wild spaces beyond civilisation, the windy-headlands, and the dark mere, he is most often seen in the act of walking. In the twenty-two lines leading up to Grendel's attack on Heorot, the poet uses nine words to express the act of walking, characterising the monster more by movement than by any attribute of his appearance.[156] In his exiled state, Grendel is restless and uneasy. His constant movements provide a stark contrast with the 'warriors who lie down to sleep'[157] in Heorot. Although he is associated with the mere and the wilderness Grendel is never seen in place, never fixed or still.

Another restless exile of Anglo-Saxon poetry is the speaker in *The Wanderer*.[158] Estranged from human society, he has, like the Wandering Jew, outlived the span of his years and has witnessed the collapse of the society he once belonged to. Like Cain he is 'deprived' of the comforts of home. He cannot settle down and, it seems, cannot rest either, but moves almost ceaselessly, 'over the edges of the waves,' and along the *wraeclastis*, 'the paths of exile.'[159] However, the focus of the poem is not on the physical nature of his wandering, but on its emotional effects. The following lines express the intensity of his suffering and summarise the causes of this pain:

> A weary spirit may not withstand the workings of fate,
> Nor may the troubled think about help. Therefore,
> those who yearn for glory often bind despair tightly
> In the coffins of their breasts. So should I bind my spirit.
> I, often wretched and troubled, deprived of a homeland,
> Far from noble kinsmen, have fastened it with fetters
> ever since, very long ago, my gold-lord was covered
> in the darkness of the earth and I, wretched, went thence,
> desolate as Winter, over the edges of the waves.[160]

Despair is both the cause and the ultimate effect of his exile. The speaker is 'weary' but never clarifies whether he is emotionally or physically exhausted and so it is implied that the intensity of the emotion has a direct relationship with the distance travelled. The conditions of his exile are more complex than Grendel's or Cain's, and like the similarly elegiac *Seafarer*[161] he alternately 'drifts'[162] through the world and 'drives his weary spirit on.'[163] His journeys are, therefore, at least partially self-determined.

Wandering and Exile in The Dark Is Rising Sequence

Cooper draws on the literary tradition of wanderers to provide a complex set of intertexts for Hawkin, the dualistic, repugnant, medieval wanderer in *The Dark Is Rising*. While recalling a character of the same name in Langland's *Piers Plowman*, Hawkin is also 'a child of the thirteenth century'[164] and, as something more than human but less than an Old One, he does not fit comfortably into any social grouping. Perfectly poised between the human and the inhuman, between the Light and the Dark, between the linear diachrony of a single human life-span and the complex synchronic time of the Old Ones, Hawkin is the lynchpin for the 'strange-familiar world' of the *Sequence*. This liminality is, at first glance, reflected in Hawkin's double name. Old George and John Smith refer to Hawkin as 'The Walker.' Ordinarily, dual signifiers are symptomatic of di-psychism and are associated with characters with two distinct personalities.[165] However, both of Hawkin's names point to the same purpose in his character. 'The Walker' is a name of deep and unshifting significance as it is directly descriptive of an action carried out. His second name 'Hawkin' has connotations of 'hawking' and spitting but also has its etymological root in the Middle English word 'Hawker' which denotes a tramp or a vagrant. Hawkin's name is, therefore, a tautological double and so his function is redoubled and reinforced. Hawkin is a tramp twice over. His dual names are not the indicators or the symptoms of a dual personality.

Cooper calls attention to Hawkin's medieval origins by highlighting those aspects of his character which make him socially unacceptable: his 'contorted'[166] and 'ugly'[167] features, his unwashed body, his dirty hair and beard and his rough behaviour. When Will meets Hawkin on the morning of his birthday, Cooper places direct emphasis on his physicality rather than on his speech:

> He sniffed, squinting sideways at Will, and rubbed his nose on one greasy sleeve. [. . .] He sniffed again violently, and mumbled to himself; then his eyes narrowed and he came close to Will, peering into his face and giving off a strong repellent smell of ancient sweat and unwashed skin.[168]

Hawkin's medieval origin may explain some of his behaviour. Bakhtin observes that 'the medieval body [is] coarse, hawking, farting, yawning, spitting, hiccupping, noisily nose-blowing, endlessly chewing and drinking.'[169] So even though a certain level of physicality and even an exaggerated or heightened physicality is acceptable in the pre-Enlightenment body, Hawkin's behaviour means that he cannot, indeed does not, fit into the twentieth-century society of the *Sequence*. Everything that comes out of his body is disgusting. He not only excretes a 'repellent smell' and a steady stream of mucus which he smears over his clothes, but he also excretes foul words, constantly mumbling and cursing. These curses are significant. They represent what Bakhtin calls 'unofficial'[170] language and indicate that the speaker is at a remove from normative social orders. In the *Sequence* only three characters swear: Bill, Hawkin, and Caradog Pritchard. Each of these characters is morally deviant, and their curses act as signifiers of this deviance. Whereas Bill and Caradog both participate within their respective communities and have families, as an orphan and an outcast Hawkin is at a further remove from the normative social orders than the others. He also deviates literally from social centres, moving beyond and between settlements.

Hawkin's existence outside of normative society places him into the medieval literary tradition of the wanderer and the exile which I have already discussed. *The Wanderer* is, perhaps, the most important source for Hawkin as it provides the intretextually informed reader with an emotional touchstone.

Although Hawkin's language never meets the elegant and elegiac quality of *The Wanderer*, his sentiments of bitterness and self-pity are the same. Like the Wanderer, he is 'absolutely lonely'[171] and has 'longed for death.'[172] But whereas the Wanderer is nostalgic, Hawkin's resentment develops into a savage hatred for anyone who has what he desires. In this, he resembles Grendel. Like Grendel he is joy-deprived. He stands 'in the doorway'[173] outside of the circle of villagers in Greythorne Manor, and at the Christmas party is admits that he does 'not dance.'[174] His inability to participate in these celebrations leads him to resent other people and their pleasures. Even though he is obsessed with earthly rewards, he does not know how to enjoy earthly pleasures. Like Grendel, Hawkin is restless and associated with fast, scuttling movements, and also with shadows; all but two of his appearances in the text are at twilight or at night-time. Like Cain who, having murdered his brother, becomes 'a fugitive and a wanderer on the earth'[175] and the Wandering Jew who is cursed to wander the earth until the apocalypse,[176] Hawkin has been condemned 'to walk the earth for as long as the Light required it.'[177] Like these mythic wanderers Hawkin moves beyond the limits of normal society and the natural world.

The connection between Hawkin and these archetypal exiles is most clearly established not, as one might expect, on the roadways, but within the Stantons' house. Having found Hawkin half-dead on Christmas morning, Will and Paul bring him home. When Will and Mary bring him a tray of food, he refuses to eat and, in doing so, reveals his typological identity:

> Will held out the tray towards him.
> 'Faugh!' the Walker croaked. It was a noise like spitting.
> Mary said, 'Well!'
> 'D'you want something else instead, then?' said Will. 'Or are you just not hungry?'
> 'Honey,' the Walker said.
> 'Honey?'
> 'Honey and bread. Honey and bread. Honey and–'
> 'All right,' Will said. They took the tray away.[178]

Here, Cooper reiterates Hawkin's medieval physicality and his use of 'unofficial,' non-linguistic speech through the 'noise like spitting' but his insistence upon 'honey and bread' indicates an intertextual connection with notion of the Promised Land of the Old Testament. Honey and bread (in the form of manna) preserved the Old Testament nation of Israel in the wilderness and so are signifiers of salvation. By calling for them, Hawkin aligns himself with other wandering people and expresses a desire to be saved or redeemed as they were.[179]

Hawkin's paths are specific and are grounded in the Huntercombe region. His ambit is limited to a very close geographical space and within that area he is further limited to the roadways that traverse that area.

Although Hawkin does enter the Stantons' house and later, Greythorne Manor, it must be noted that in each case he is physically carried inside by an Old One. Without this external aid, it is seems unlikely that Hawkin could leave the roadways. Hawkin first appears on a narrow roadway that 'ran between Rooks' Wood and the churchyard to the tiny local church and then on to the River Thames',[180] and of his eight subsequent appearances in the novel, six take place on or beside a roadway. Even after he is dug out of the snow and brought indoors, the connection between Hawkin and the roadway topos remains unchanging. When Will sings 'a melancholy little song'[181] at an impromptu concert in Greythorne Manor, Hawkin seems disproportionately affected by the lyrics:

> 'White in the moon the long road lies,
> The moon stands blank above;
> White in the moon the long road lies
> That leads me from my love.
> Still hangs the hedge without a gust,
> Still, still the shadows stay:
> My feet upon the moonlit dust
> Pursue the ceaseless way.'

[...] From the corner of one eye he saw, with a shock, the figure of the Walker; with a blanket wrapped round him like a cloak, the old man was standing in the doorway of the sickroom, listening. For an instant Will saw his face, and was astonished. All guile and terror were gone from that lined triangle; there was only sadness on it, and hopeless longing. There was even a glint of tears in the eyes.[182]

The 'melancholy little song' is poem XXXVI, from A. E. Housman's 1896 collection, *A Shropshire Lad*.[183] Considering Cooper's great interest in geography, it seems unusual that she should select a poem that does not fit with the topology of the *Sequence*. However, the poem expresses the integration of the physical journey with an emotional journey and encompasses both the linear and cyclical qualities of the roadway topos. The poem also expresses the symbiotic relationship between the traveller and the roadway; on the one hand, the road 'leads' the traveller, but on the other, the traveller 'pursues' the road. In this manner, both the road and the traveller shape the journey and each other; the road has agency and prescribes the traveller's movements, but the traveller, impatiently chasing the road, also forces it to move ahead of him. The dualism of the road in the poem lends it special significance for Hawkin. The restless, 'ceaseless' movement of the road echoes his characteristic movements but, more importantly, the poem allows him to express cathartically something of the 'hopeless longing' he feels and to approach the emotional state of the Wanderer or the Seafarer. It is tempting to read this as Cooper reflecting generically on the palimpsestic nature of literature and landscape, a moment of implicit acknowledgement of the transferability of her own methodology, carried to the threshold of understanding by intertextuality.

Hawkin's emotional relationship with the road is coupled by a close physical association with the topos. When Will enters the 'strange-familiar world' on the morning of his eleventh birthday, he meets Hawkin in the doorway of a little hut:

> In the doorway, paused, irresolute with one hand on the rickety door, stood the shambling old tramp of the day before. The long grey hair was the same, and so were the clothes and the wizened, crafty face. [...] He looked at the wretched hut; the lane ended here, but there was scarcely even a proper clearing. The trees stood close all round them, shutting out much of the sun.[184]

Hawkin's role as wanderer and *mearcstapa* seems to be compromised by his hut which, as a part of the sanctuary topos, implies a fixity of place and of identity which seems at odds with Hawkin's character. However, a close reading of the passage reveals that it does not destabilise Hawkin's character but reinforces it. Even though Hawkin is not walking in this passage he is still described in terms of movement; he is 'shambling' and 'irresolute' implying that his actions lack any obvious purpose. Coupled with the fact that he stands poised in the doorway of the little hut, this supports his status as a liminal figure. As an outward and visible sign of Hawkin's personality, the hut strengthens Hawkin's intertextual origins. Like him, the hut is 'wretched' and this wretchedness recalls the Wanderer who 'wretched, went thence over the edges of the waves'[185] and furthers the idea that Hawkin, as an exile and an outcast, is unable to find comfort or joy in the world. The trees that grow nearby shut out much of the sun, a detail that recalls Grendel's home in the shadowy slopes beyond the civilised world. Finally, the hut does not stand apart from the roadway; it may be more correct to say that the laneway ends in the hut itself. Hawkin rests here simply because he has run out of roadway. He is physically, emotionally and ideologically bound to the roadways of Huntercombe.

In fact, Hawkin's identity is readily integrated into the roadway topos. This is most apparent when Will and Paul find him slumped in the snow on Christmas morning. He lies beside the church wall, close by the roadway he first appeared on. His position is significant as it indicates that as a cursed wanderer he can neither enter the sacred space nor leave the road. Although he retains the 'hunched' quality that he had on his first appearance, he is, for the first time, motionless.[186] In earlier descriptions, he 'scuttles like a beetle,'[187] 'scuffles'[188] and 'shuffles.'[189] Here, he just lies still. The layer of snow that covers him robs him of any distinguishing features—it takes Will a moment to identify him—effectively blurring the distinction between Hawkin and his environment. This passage moves him beyond the paradigm of the medieval wanderers; here his identity not only 'concatenate'[190] with territory but is absolutely subsumed by the topos. Here, he ceases to wander and becomes instead part of the road.

If Hawkin is accepted as part of the roadway topos—almost as a kind of *genius locus*—the function of roads in the *Sequence* must be reconsidered. As 'a child of the thirteenth century,' Hawkin is a living remnant of the past. Through him, the present, consensual reality of *The Dark Is Rising* is connected to a distant but still localised past. When Hawkin dies, Will feels certain that

> in his own time, somewhere in the village church-yard, covered either by more recent burials or by a stone crumbling into illegibility now, there would be the grave of a man named Hawkin, who had died some time in the thirteenth century and lain there in peace ever since.[191]

Through Hawkin, Cooper allows different time periods to co-exist and to be layered on top of one another. He represents the intersection of both synchronic and diachronic axes. Some of the roads in the *Sequence* share this function and by connecting different and distant times as well as different and distant places. Thus, the road becomes 'a metaphor for historical and narrative processes [...] and implies a dialogical relationship between the past and the present.'[192]

Old Roads and Magic Roads

In Cooper's *Sequence*, time is embedded in the landscape. The surest way to find the past is to look for it within the landscape as 'it is clear that landscapes exist as historical texts.'[193] However distant or different the past may be from the present, some trace of that time will be held, like an insect in amber, within the palimpsestic layers of the landscape. Being etched into the surface of the landscape, roadways lay bare these palimpsestic layers which lie underfoot, enabling characters and readers to access part of the past. Thus, roads do not simply connect geographical sites, but also connect temporal sites. The characters in the *Sequence* are not breaking new paths but 'retreading ancestral ground' where 'deep-rooted cultural symbols [...] lie, sometimes literally, underfoot.'[194]

The sense of an embedded past is not unique to Cooper's work. Butler identifies the same sense of stratified time in Penelope Lively's novels. Lively, who trained as an historian, shares with Cooper an interest in historical geography and was a particular admirer of W. G. Hoskin's work.[195] In her guide book to the geological and cultural geography of Britain, *The*

Figure 3.4 Ghostly track leading towards the Nine Maidens, Cornwall. ©Jane Carroll.

Presence of the Past, she suggests that 'an awareness of the past has added another colour, or an extra dimension'[196] to her understanding of landscape. Lively invokes these same principles in her fiction, most notably in *The Driftway* (1972). The novel focuses on two children, Paul and Sandra, who decide to run away from home to their grandmother's house. On their way there, the children are met by a tramp, Old Bill. Together, they travel along an old road, the Driftway, and move through various stages of self-discovery. Early on in the novel, Lively has Old Bill explain the significance of the Driftway to Paul. He says:

> 'This road. The Driftway. This is an old road, son. Older than you or me, or the houses in this village, or the fields round about, or anything that we can see now, or even think about [...] This is a road that was made when there was first men in these parts, trodden out by feet that had to get from one place to another, and it's been trodden ever since, year by year, winter and summer. Stands to reason it's got a few tales to tell. There's been men passing by here, and women, and children, over thousands of years, travellers. And every now and then there's someone does an extra hard bit of living, as you might call it. That'll leave a shadow on the road, won't it?'[197]

Being primeval, the way is deeply impressed with a sense of time and with a sense of the passage of time. Even though the road predates any formal civilisation, it is bound up with a sense of human history, the passing travellers making their imprint on the landscape by forming the road, just as the road affects them, prescribing the course of their journeys and, in Paul's case, carrying him from selfishness to sympathy and from innocence to experience. The Driftway is both a geographical road and a temporal scar, operating horizontally through space and vertically through time so that Paul's journey towards maturation is both diachronic and synchronic.

There are three old roads in the *Sequence* which, like the Driftway, operate on both synchronic and diachronic levels; two in *The Dark Is Rising* and one in *The Grey King*. Diverging from the normal paradigms of my discussion, I will treat these roads in order of their importance rather than sequentially. Although Cooper never refers to them as 'leys,' it is useful to understand them in terms of the old straight tracks identified by Alfred Watkins.[198] They connect important, sacred spaces in the landscape and behave more like aspects of the sanctuary topos than other roadways.

The first of the old roads is the Ridgeway. Although Cooper never names it, the presence of Wayland's Smithy[199] and the road's proximity to the Chiltern Hills[200] confirms its identity. Cooper describes it as 'a narrow path leading away' from the Stantons' house and merging

> into the road, paved smooth with snow and edged everywhere by the great black trees [...] that in his own time was called Huntercombe Lane. It was the way that he and James had taken to the Dawsons' Farm, the same road that he had trodden almost every day of his life, but it was very different now. Now, it was no more than a track through a forest, great snow-burdened trees enclosing it on both sides.[201]

By using three words—path, road and track—that are not quite synonymous, Cooper evokes a sense of how the road has changed through time even though it occupies the same geographic and physical space. She suggests the bounded nature of the road by drawing attention to the trees bordering its edges. This road is an enclosed and, therefore, sacred space. Like other sanctuaries, the road protects people from harm. Wayland says to Will that 'Their [the Dark's] power can work no harm on the road through Hunter's Combe.'[202] Indeed, the road is so resistant to the power of the Dark that it bears 'no sign of the Rider; [Will] could not even see any tracks left by the black horse's feet.'[203] It is only when Will wanders off down a side-track (the one that leads to Hawkin's hut) that the Rider is able to catch up with him.

Another of Cooper's sacred roads is Cadfan's Way, which appears in *The Grey King*. Like the Ridgeway, Llwybr Cadfan, Cadfan's Way, has a geographical reality as a 'path or track, along which [St. Cadfan] is popularly said to have habitually travelled between Towyn and Llangadfan during his missionary labours' which 'is still traced by the country people at various points on the route.'[204] In the 1920s Llwybr Cadfan was still 'used by miners and its name well known'[205] but Cooper amends the miners' shortcut to something more mystical, suggesting it has fallen out of use and memory. Cadfan's Way, then, is distinctly part of the mythic heritage underscoring the *Sequence*. Once Will is on the ley-line, on the old straight track, he remembers

> everything that his illness had taken away from him. He remembered the verses that had been put into his head as a guide for the bleak, lone quest he was destined now to follow; remembered who he was and what he was [...] and at the same time another kind of innocence fell away, and he was aware too of immense danger, like a great shadow across the world, waiting for him all through this unfamiliar land of green valleys and dark-misted mountain peaks.[206]

Cadfan's Way is a repository of time and of human understanding. Like all roads, it allows the traveller to gain an understanding of the landscape as a whole and, to develop a corresponding self-awareness. As it is a magical road, a ley, it allows Will to understand the landscape, and himself, suddenly and completely. It forges such a deep connection between Will and the 'unfamiliar' landscape that he could 'now walk blindfold all the way from Tywyn to Machynlleth over the hills on Cadfan's Way, even though [he had] never been to this country before.'[207]

A similarly deep connection between time, place and person is created by Oldway Lane in *The Dark Is Rising*. The scene set around Oldway Lane is instrumental in showing the development of Will's character from a blissfully unselfconscious child to an Old One with a profound awareness of the landscape and of his role within time. Cooper signposts Will's changing personality by showing how his attitude towards the road develops through the scene.

Although the Lane is bordered, like the Ridgeway, by trees and so set apart from the rest of the countryside, Will sees the Lane as a mundane, ugly track, nothing more than a shortcut from the bus-stop. He sees himself as dominating his environment and casts the landscape in a passive role:

> Will plodded along, passing garden walls, trees, and then the top of a small unpaved track, scarcely a road, known as Tramps' Alley, that wandered off from the main road and eventually curled round to join Huntercombe Lane close to the Stantons' house. The children used it as a short cut sometimes. Will glanced down it now, and saw that nobody had been along the path since the snow began; down there it lay untrodden, smooth and white and inviting, marked only by the picture-writing of birds' footprints. Unexplored territory.[208]

The Lane in this manifestation is *terra incognita*, a space to be colonised and impressed by Will's passage. The Lane is newly made strange by the fall of snow, just as Will himself is newly made. The landscape is a blank space which reflects Will's own new impressionable identity. Yet even as he makes his mark on the landscape, it simultaneously leaves its impression on him, and 'fragments of [snow] clung in a fringe to the trousers tucked into his boots [...] the walk down the Alley began quite soon to be less fun than he had expected.'[209] Will is forced to admit that he is not the master of his environment and to accept that the landscape has a certain agency; even as he impacts upon it, it can directly influence and impact upon him.

Will's understanding of the power of the landscape is completed when he is attacked, first by the Walker and then by Maggie Barnes, an agent of the Dark. Merriman appears and drives Maggie from the road. With his power, Merriman reinforces the natural borders of the road, making

> a great barrier of light spring up on either side of the road, edging it in both sides with leaping fire, stretching far into the distance in both directions—a great deal further than the length of the track that Will knew as Tramps' Alley [...] he and Merriman and the Walker stood in a great endless tunnel of cold white flame.[210]

The barrier of light transforms Oldway Lane from an ordinary road into a sacred space. Not content with demonstrating the agent power of the road, Merriman impresses on Will a respect for the landscape, and for the history that is bound up in the landscape. He lectures Will:

> 'Do you know the name of this track?'
> 'Tramps' Alley,' Will said automatically.
> 'That is not a real name,' Merriman said with distaste.

'Well, no. Mum won't ever use it, and we're not supposed to. It's ugly, she says. But nobody else I know ever calls it anything else. I'd feel silly if I called it Oldway–' Will stopped suddenly, hearing and tasting the name properly for the first time in his life. He said slowly, 'If I called it by its real name Oldway Lane.'

'You would feel silly,' said Merriman grimly. 'The name that would make you feel silly has helped to save your life. Oldway Lane. Yes. And it was not named for some distant Mr Oldway. The name simply tells you what the road is, as the names of roads and places in old lands very often do, if only men would pay them more attention. It was lucky for you that you were standing on one of the Old Ways, trodden by the Old Ones for some three thousand years [. . .] Look hard, at this road now, boy, and do not call it by vulgar names again.'[211]

Oldway Lane is a ley, made for a special purpose many years ago. Like all roads it provides a route between one place and another—this is the only level that Will can appreciate at first—but, unlike normal roads, it also provides a route between one time and another and Will only recognises this after Merriman reminds him that landscapes are historic as well as geographic. For Merriman an understanding of the landscape is intimately connected to an understanding of the history of a place, a history that may be traced and appreciated through etymology.[212] Penelope Lively suggests that 'just as the landscape has its visible layers of time, so place-names have left indestructible evidence of who was where—and sometimes of when they were there, and what they did there.'[213] For Lively, as for Cooper, these place-names are primarily indications of the human presence within the landscape and express a correlation between place and identity. By emphasising the importance of place-names, Merriman encourages Will, and Cooper encourages the reader, to develop an awareness of the synchronic as well as diachronic functions of landscape.

Conclusion

These old roads offer the means to understand landscape 'in terms of its time relations as well as of its space relations'.[214] In old places, the past is not gone, merely buried, and by walking on roads such as Oldway Lane, by wearing down the surface of the landscape and revealing the hidden strata of time, place, and memory, one can gain access to, and ultimately an understanding of the past. The names of the ways, properly understood, offer an indication of their previous uses, thus connecting footfall understanding with oral or inscribed historical understanding. In my next chapter, I will discuss how certain spaces expose the buried layers of both time and space making the chronotopic correlation apparent without the need for excavation.

Figure 4.1 Ruined house in Cwm Maethlon, Wales. ©Jane Carroll.

Chapter Four
The Lapsed Topos
Caves, Graves, and Ruins

The past is intrinsic to the *Sequence,* forming a large part of the cultural background from which Cooper's plots, characters, and landscapes emerge. Cooper speaks of the five texts, and the landscapes they are set within, as being made up of 'layers and layers of time'[1] and even the most cursory reading of the *Sequence* reveals that the past—real or imagined, historical or mythological—is central to the texts. Many of the quests and tasks in the *Sequence* are, at their most basic, attempts by living characters to reconnect with the lost and lapsed past; the quests cannot be completed except through gaining awareness of the past and informing the present with a knowledge of the past. Through the medium of the landscape, the children in Cooper's *Sequence* learn to negotiate a relationship between the past and present. It takes a special effort, and a profound understanding of the landscape, to reabsorb and refresh the history and culture that are so 'deeply rooted'[2] in the landscape. Far from being regressive, acknowledgement of and engagement with the past enables progress; as David Staines claims, 'searching into the past offers a perspective on the present and can "take us higher."'[3] Tuan asserts that anyone seeking to understand the present must first 'shore up the crumbling landscapes of the past.'[4] So, if we are to understand a fictional or imaginary present, as in the consensual reality of a novel, we must first shore up its past: 'the past must be rescued and made accessible.'[5] The first step on this rescue mission is the realisation that the past has not really disappeared; it has just slipped out of sight.

The surest way to find the past is to look for it within the landscape. However distant or different the past may be from the present, some trace of that time will be held, like an insect in amber, within the palimpsestic layers of the landscape because 'landscapes exist as historical texts.'[6] Whereas the many memory lapses in the *Sequence*, whether accidental or engineered by the Old Ones, signify a disconnection between the past and the present, there are 'lapsed' aspects of the physical landscape which actually provide a connection between the past and the present. Damaged, submerged and even subterranean spaces allow characters to reach out towards and to engage with the past. Aspects of this topos include ruins, which are in the process of collapse and decay, and chthonic spaces which have physically subsided into the earth. Even though these lapsed spaces may seem disparate, ruins are 'akin to caves'[7] because both spaces, like all aspects of the lapsed topos, 'remain essential bridges between then and now [and] illume the process of history and memory.'[8]

Being embedded within or slowly becoming one with the landscape palimpsest, the lapsed topos opens up passages to the forgotten 'deep past',[9] to repressed memories or simply to those aspects of history that have been forgotten and overlooked. Refuting the linearity of time, these spaces permit a disorderly meshing of past and present and of memory and potentiality. These are geographically and temporally liminal spaces, which 'resonate backwards and forwards, splice the personal and the collective [creating] a landscape of juxtaposed asynchronous moments.'[10] The lapsed topos is richly connotative and as a result of its ability to 'resonate backwards and forwards' it becomes one of the most important topoi in the imaginative landscape.

Critical Attempts to Rescue the Past

Parallel to the textual attempts to rescue the past are the critical attempts to rescue the past of the *Sequence* and, through analysis and explanation, to make it more accessible to readers. So far there have been two main critical approaches to the past and the idea of heritage in Cooper's *Sequence*: archaeology, which views the past as being mediated by objects, and genealogy, which regards the past as being mediated by and through people.

Archaeology

The first approach originates with Butler's *Four British Fantasists* (2006) which views the past as something which is physically embodied and may be handed down in the form of objects. Butler highlights Cooper's own interest in archaeology saying: 'Cooper's enthusiasm, sparked by reading Jacquetta Hawke's book *A Land* (1951) in her teens has led her to introduce archaeology repeatedly into her fiction—most notably through the archaeologist Merriman Lyon, a central figure in *The Dark Is Rising* sequence.'[11] Merriman is the only character to appear in each of the five books, and because he is an archaeologist, there is a certain implication that archaeology is a means of connecting people and events in diverse places and times.

Archaeology also has a more literal function within the *Sequence* and the recovery of lost treasures and artefacts is central to its quest-driven narratives. Butler emphasises the symbolic value of the treasures which are 'possessed of a [...] kind of power conferred by age, rarity and historical significance.'[12] In the *Sequence* many of the treasured objects carry a sense of heritage, that is, of social and symbolic value passed from one time into another through the medium of an object. In literature there are many examples of treasure-giving as a social action. Treasure-giving ceremonies also form an important structural element in the arrival and departure scenes in *Beowulf*. The final departure scenes—if they may be so characterised—are Beowulf's death and burial which place unprecedented emphasis on the social significance of treasure. Treasure commonly reinforces social relationships in children's literature too; in *The Lion, The Witch and The Wardrobe* (1950), the Pevensie siblings receive splendid gifts from Father Christmas which cement their roles as kings and queens of Narnia. In Alan Garner's *The Weirdstone of Brisingamen* (1960), the 'bridestone' is passed from mother to daughter, and in J. K. Rowling's *Harry Potter and the Half-Blood Prince* (2005), Tom Riddle becomes obsessed with finding objects that belonged to the founders of Hogwarts, believing that these objects can bestow some of their owners' power upon him. Here archaeology and genealogy intersect and provide an exceptionally strong link to the past. Similarly, the Signs Will Stanton collects serve to connect him to the past because they have been passed down among the Old Ones for centuries.[13] Similarly, the grail the Drews discover in *Over Sea, Under Stone*, is richly connotative of an inherited cultural symbolism. Because the Drews insist on calling the object they discover a 'grail' rather than a 'cup' Cooper invokes the cultural values of the Holy Grail. The cultural significance attached to the grail is especially evident when Simon admits that he had envisioned the Arthurian cup being a different shape.[14] That is to say, Simon has a deeply embedded preconception of what the grail ought to look like, and thereby the cultural significance of this treasure is affirmed.

However, a certain amount of the power and significance of these objects found within the five texts of the *Sequence* rests upon the characters' and readers' recognition of their value and age. For the readers' benefit, the age, beauty and rarity of the treasures must be explicitly remarked upon. For example, when Jane Drew first sees the grail her brothers have found, she says 'it's terribly ancient'[15] and the Sign of Iron is described as reminding Will Stanton 'of a certain place in the rough stone floor of the kitchen, where all the roughness had been worn away by generations of feet.'[16] Rather than providing proof of the importance of archaeology in the *Sequence*, these examples serve to undermine Butler's argument. Will is only able to intuit a sense of the past because he is an Old One and has a latent knowledge of all things. Jane, on the other hand, is not special or gifted and is certainly not an antiques expert or an historian, so it is unclear how exactly she knows that the grail is old. Furthermore, there is little textual evidence to support Butler's reading; the only real archaeological incident occurs in *Silver on the Tree* when Will and Merriman speak with an American archaeologist in Caerleon. It must be noted that Merriman is not really an archaeologist, but rather an Old One performing a role within human society which allows him to act on behalf of the Light. He poses as an archaeologist only when he has to recover lost objects. In *The Dark Is Rising*, he claims to be Miss Greythorne's butler so that he can be close to Will. The lack of convincing textual evidence weakens the status of treasure as the sole signifier of the past in the *Sequence* and undermines the role of archaeology as the sole means of accessing it.

Genealogy

The second approach to the past of Cooper's *Sequence*, genealogy, originates with Michael Drout's 1997 essay "Reading the Signs of Light."[17] Under Drout's analysis, the past is something that must be repeated, or at least echoed, throughout time and thus genealogy structures the narrative. Indeed, genealogy and inheritance are important motifs in literature and elaborate genealogies occur in many canonical children's texts; the Pevensie children in the Narniad are 'daughters of Eve' and 'Sons of Adam'[18] and in Alan Garner's *The Owl Service* (1967), which is discussed in detail in Chapter Five, three teenagers become the symbolic heirs to Gronw, Blodeuwedd, and Lleu Llaw Gyffes and find themselves re-enacting an ancient cycle of love, jealousy, and violence that has been repeated for generations. For Drout, a sense of the past is mediated most eloquently within the *Sequence* through intertextual references to exceptional figures, especially literary and historical kings. Just as Merriman Lyon is presented as a version of Merlin,[19] and so personifies a direct connection between the action of the narrative and the legendary past, the child-characters of Cooper's *Sequence* are seen as the literal and metaphorical heirs of these long dead kings. Will is an Old One, Bran is the 'Pendragon' and the son of King Arthur, and although the three Drews are not genetic heirs, they are, Drout argues, chosen to participate in the quests because they are 'culturally English'[20] and follow in the heritage that has been established historically by individuals like Alfred the Great and culturally through stories about heroes like Scyld and Beow and Beowulf. The reader, presumably, is invited to participate in this heritage through the act of reading a text which is so richly imbued with cultural and genealogical significance.[21] By shifting the focus from things to people, Will's comment about the Sign of Iron may be read in an entirely new way. As we have already observed, the Sign reminds Will of 'a certain place in the stone floor of the kitchen which had been worn smooth by generations of feet.'[22] Whereas archaeology is interested in the stone floor, and other physical objects which bear witness to the passage of time, genealogy is interested in the 'generations of feet' and their relationship with the living characters in the *Sequence*.

Figure 4.2 Stratified layers of rock, Boscastle, Cornwall. ©Jane Carroll.

However, this genealogical approach to the past is not unproblematic. Lois Kuznets claims that the *Sequence* may be 'fatally weakened by too close a focus on heredity'[23] but the fundamental problem with Drout's argument is an over-dependence on intertextual references. Whereas it is possible that 'readers might intuit the echoes'[24] of these intertexts, Drout admits that many child readers do not have the 'cultural literacy to reconstruct a reference from an allusion'[25] and so the rich intertextual background that a genealogical reading of the *Sequence* depends upon may be lost on the inexperienced reader. Even though young readers may intuit the presence of an intertext, there is no guarantee that the reader will intuit a sense of the correct historical period. The ring-bound ship and the boar-helmet which Drout describes may well conjure a sense of fantastic otherness before they connote a true sense of the Saxon seventh century through intertextual references to Sutton Hoo.[26] At worst, this genealogical approach is elitist as it focuses on a particular kind of reader—a reader with a certain kind of education and knowledge—at best, it is unreliable because it is focused on intertextual rather than textual evidence for the past and therefore cannot provide consistent access to the past for all readers.

The Argument for Topoanalysis

Given Cooper's interest in and focus on landscape within the *Sequence*, it is appropriate that the landscape—or a particular topos within the landscape—provides the means by which the past of *The Dark Is Rising Sequence* is 'rescued and made accessible.' Whereas archaeology and genealogy provide a means of access to the past, these means are not reliably and consistently accessible to readers of all ages or levels of experience. These approaches rely too much on context and intertext rather than the texts of *The Dark Is Rising Sequence* themselves and so in identifying treasure and kingship as two great signs of the past within the *Sequence*, both Butler and Drout have identified the symptoms but not the true cause of Cooper's 'layers and layers of time.' In focusing on genealogical intertexts, Drout has overlooked the text itself and although Butler acknowledges that there is 'a systematic correlation between space and time'[27] in many children's books written during the same period as the *Sequence*, his focus is on the results of archaeology, not on the process of excavation itself. Through close analysis of the lapsed topos, and specifically through the analysis of chthonic spaces, I will redirect critical focus towards this process of excavation because even though kings and grails and ring-prowed ships are undoubtedly signs of the past, they are mere foils for the true vehicle of history and culture. In Cooper's *Sequence* the landscape is the true focaliser of the past.

In keeping with the established motifs of northern European literature,[28] all of the treasures mentioned in *The Dark Is Rising Sequence* are buried at some point. In *Over Sea, Under Stone*, the Arthurian grail is buried beneath Kenmare Head. The manuscript found in *Greenwitch* is beneath the ocean, as is the crystal sword which is found in *Silver on the Tree*. The Silver Harp is found inside the cave at Craig yr Aderyn and the six Signs of the light which Will Stanton collects in *The Dark Is Rising* are buried for safekeeping in the ruins at Caerleon. Further evidence for the importance of landscape as a means of rescuing the past is provided by the fact that all of the kings mentioned in the *Sequence* are buried or are associated with the underground. In *Over Sea, Under Stone*, King Mark of Cornwall is buried in the cave at the headland near Trewissick. In *The Dark Is Rising*, the unnamed King of the Light is found in an egg-shaped barrow near the Thames. In that same text, Herne the Hunter who appears at the head of the Wild Hunt is at once a version of Cernunnos, a Celtic god of the underworld, but his red-eared hounds indicate that he is also a version of Annwyn, Son of Annan the king of the underworld who appears in the *Mabinogion*. There are no kings mentioned in *Greenwitch*, but the next book, *The Grey King*, is almost overpowered by the number of references to kings, kingship, and chthonic spaces; the Brenin Llwyd is strongly associated with the land beneath the mountains near Aberdovey and it is in a nearby cave that King Arthur lies waiting with the Seven Sleepers. Bran, who is the Pendragon, and son of Arthur, enters into this cave to recover a magical harp. In *Silver on the Tree*, Bran again enters a chthonic space to recover a treasure; out in the Dyfi estuary, the king of the Lost Land and his people lie buried beneath the sea in the Drowned Hundred.

There is one more king in *The Dark Is Rising* whose appearance is brief and obscure but affirms the connection between kings and chthonic spaces within Cooper's work. It is the wren that Will Stanton glimpses in a dream. The wren is, of course, according to European myth, the 'king of all birds.' The title 'king' is given to the wren all across Europe. In France, it is called the *Roi de Froidure*, 'king of the cold'; in Spain, *Reyezuelo*, 'little king'; in Italian, *Re di Siepe*, 'king of the hedge.' In Denmark, it is *Elle-Konge*, 'alder king'; in Germany, *Dornkönig*, 'thorn king'; and in the Netherlands, *Konije*, 'little king.' In Welsh, *Bren* means both 'wren' and 'king.'[29] Cooper does not quote the traditional rhyme of the Wren-Boys, but if she had, it would serve as unquestionable proof of the connection between kings and chthonic spaces in the *Sequence*;

> The wren, the wren, the king of all birds
> Was on St. Stephen's day caught in the furze
> Up with the kettle and down with the pan,
> Give us a penny to bury the wren.[30]

This ritual of the Wren-Boys is not just a quaint country custom Cooper refers to for a sense of rustic authenticity; it serves as a sure reminder that wrens, like all kings, are to be buried. Like many of Cooper's other kings, the little wren is also associated with caves; its Latin name is *Troglodytes troglodytes* or 'cave-dweller, cave-dweller.' It is clear that Cooper's emphasis is not just on kings, but on buried kings, which suggests that it is not the king but rather his grave that we should be looking at. It is clear that topoanalysis rather than archaeology or genealogy provides the means to understand and analyse Cooper's 'layers and layers of time.'

140 • Landscape in Children's Literature

Figure 4.3 Cave at Pentewan, Cornwall. ©Jane Carroll.

The Chthonic Space

The 'layers and layers of time' indicate that the books in the *Sequence*, and the landscape the texts are built upon, are constructed as a vast palimpsest, a text in which the correlation of space and time is realised through stratification. The metaphor of stratification is a useful one when it comes to understanding the relationship between time, place, and memory and it is one favoured by Jacquetta Hawkes, whose influence on Cooper's writing, as we have seen, is well documented.[31] Hawkes writes that 'lost memories lie in unconscious strata of [the] mind itself, these dark, rarely disturbed layers that have accumulated, as mould accumulates in a forest, through the shedding of innumerable lives since the beginning of life.'[32] Over time, soil, like memory, is deposited in layers. The deepest of these layers are the oldest; the shallowest ones are the most recently laid.

So, just as time is not a single moment, but a synchronic mesh of instances, the landscape is not a two-dimensional unit, but rather a kind of thick palimpsest where time and space are directly correlated. Caves, graves, and holes in the ground open up and expose the buried layers of both time and space, making the chronotopic correlation between time and space apparent without the need for excavation. The grave, with its etymological root in *grafan*, which also gives us the verb 'to engrave,' is literally and symbolically engraved in the earth, cut into and written upon the palimpsest of soil and time.[33] The chthonic space, therefore, becomes synonymous with the relationship between past and present.[34] By exposing the buried layers of soil and time, caves, graves, and chthonic spaces allow both characters and readers to engage directly with the landscape-text rather than indirectly with an intertext.[35] Whereas houses in literature are very much beginning or opening spaces, the spaces which make up the lapsed topos are often the end point of a quest,[36] and are described by Cooper as being 'very much the end of a place,'[37] and so it is appropriate to conclude an examination of landscape with a discussion of their significance within her work.

The Symbolic Function of the Chthonic Space

The chthonic space is sub-divided into various forms such as caves, mines, and graves, which, although all marked by descriptions of depth and often of darkness, have some distinguishing characteristics. The cave, for example, is organic; it is not created for a particular reason but formed as a consequence of the action of environmental factors such as water or frost. The mine, like the grave is artificial, but whereas the mine is opened for the purposes of extracting something from the earth, the grave is opened for the purposes of interring something in the earth, usually to house a corpse. Furthermore, even though all chthonic spaces are openings in and beneath the surface of the earth, the cave opens horizontally whereas the grave and the mine open vertically. The primary movement associated with these vertical spaces is downwards; however, the primary movement corresponding to caves is an inward u-turn: the hero enters and moves down the tunnel and when s/he finds what s/he was looking for, s/he turns around and re-emerges into the light. The entrance to a mine may resemble a cave, and therefore encourage movement inwards, but it soon deepens and broadens and becomes vertical. Moreover, the mine offers a passage through rather than a u-turn, as in *King Solomon's Mines* (1885) or *The Fellowship of the Ring* (1954). Graves occur far less commonly in children's literature than caves and very often a scene may be set in a graveyard rather than around an individual grave, resulting in a displacement of the chthonic and chronotopic connotations of the space.[38] There are several possible reasons for this: the grave is a restrictive space, allowing for static scenes rather than for movement and narrative development; the grave is a morbid space, with connotations which some authors may prefer to avoid but it is most likely that the grave, as a void which is covered over with earth rather than being left open to the elements, presents characters with the problem of moving the soil away before gaining access to the buried past. On the other hand, caves, as natural, horizontal and open incursions in the earth, allow characters an easy route to the deep past without the effort of having to move earth away.

In spite of their physical differences, all chthonic spaces carry the same connotations and fulfil the same symbolic functions in literature. The chthonic space serves as a bridge between the past and the present. This symbolic function has remained rigidly in place for a long time. As with the green topos, the lapsed topos has antecedents in classical literature as well as in Northern literature, and the chthonic space often provides passage to a secondary world. Sometimes, this other world is figured as a fairy-land and sometimes it is a kind of underworld where protagonists come face-to-face with the dead.[39] The journey to the underworld 'enabl[es] the hero to contemplate the fate of those who have lived before'[40] and thereby to interact with a very human aspect of the past. The past may also function as a kind of secondary world, as a fantastic Other space. Clare Bradford has outlined the theory that the past is itself a cultural space, open to colonisation and orientalising discourse.[41] Indeed, post-colonial theory provides a particularly appropriate means to read and understand the function of the chthonic space. The present, consensual reality of the text and the primary world stands in contradistinction to the distant, subaltern, other past. The Other is a 'site of desire'[42] but also a locus of suspicion and dread; it both fascinates and repels. This explains why chthonic spaces are often marked in literature by the strange and deeply connotative pairing of treasure and monsters.

The process of colonisation is fundamentally a 'rite of power' enacted upon a 'site of desire.'[43] In literature, this 'rite of power' is often highly stylised. The hero enters, perhaps even penetrates, the chthonic space, overcomes the monster and then forces the past to give up its treasures and its secrets.[44] The past is plundered by the hero to satisfy the demands of the present time. Given the darkness and the deathly associations of the chthonic space, it seems reasonable that the space should contain something that the protagonist wants; otherwise he should not bother to enter such a grim and uninviting place. Ideally, the object of this quest into the underworld should be something of both material and spiritual value.[45] However, it would be too easy if the protagonist were simply to enter the cave, snatch up the thing he or she desires and stroll back out. The passage to the underworld is a kind of initiation rite; there must be some condition to fulfil or an obstacle to overcome. In Philip Pullman's *The Amber Spyglass* (2000), Lyra must be separated from her beloved daemon before she can enter the world of the dead to look for her lost friends.[46] J.R.R. Tolkien notes in *The Hobbit* (1937) that Bilbo's real battle was in making himself go down the passage way into Smaug's lair: 'going on from there was the bravest thing he ever did. The tremendous things that happened after it were as nothing compared to it. He fought the real battle in the tunnel alone, before he ever saw the vast danger that lay in wait.'[47] In *Over Sea, Under Stone*, Barney Drew has to overcome similar fears—his fear of the dark and of getting trapped in the cave[48]—and in doing so he proves that he is 'the proper man in the proper place'[49] to retrieve the Arthurian cup. In these instances, the greatest conflicts are internal; the greatest obstacle to overcome is one's own fear of death, or perhaps, more accurately, of being a living being among the dead. The fear of being alive among the dead is, essentially, the fear of being in the wrong place at the wrong time, of not being in harmony with one's environment. For Barney, being the 'proper man in the proper place' means overcoming his fear of intruding in the realm of the dead and assuring himself that he too belongs in this chthonic space. Thus, by the time Lyra, Bilbo, and Barney meet the real monsters they have already, symbolically, overpowered them. This rite of power is a narrative trope (enter chthonic space, overcome monster, retrieve treasure) integral to the lapsed topos. Along with the physical and symbolic characteristics of the topos, these narrative tropes may be seen in the earliest inceptions of the topos in medieval English literature.

The Chthonic Space in Medieval Literature

The lapsed topos is a regular feature in the landscapes of medieval literature and, after sacred and domestic spaces, is perhaps the most common kind of topos and its appearance is a characteristic feature of the elegiac poetry of the period. As I will now demonstrate, the associations of the lapsed space with the past, with monsters and with treasure were firmly in place in medieval literature where, as in modern texts, the lapsed space takes three distinct forms; the grave, the cave and the ruin. I will deal with this last aspect at a later point in this chapter.

The underground is the space of the dead. In the First Branch of the *Mabinogion*, Pwyll encounters Arawn king of Annwfn, the lord of the dead, out hunting with his red-eared hounds. They agree to exchange residences for a year and Pwyll goes to live underground among the dead although Arawn's kingdom has 'halls and rooms and the most beautifully adorned buildings that anyone had seen.'[50] As such, Annwfn is not typical of literary underworlds. A more typical representation of the lapsed topos may be found in the contemporary *Snorra Edda*, when Hermóþ tries to rescue his brother Baldr from death, he rides northwards and downwards into the Niflheim where those who die of sickness or accidents go. He rides 'for nine nights through dark dales and deep so that he saw nothing.'[51] Like many chthonic spaces, Niflheim is populated by monsters, in this case Hel, whose lower half is a decaying corpse, and her corpse-like servants.[52] Hermóþ fails to persuade Hel to relinquish his brother but Baldr and his wife Nanna send gifts back to the world of the living, including a bracelet and a gold ring, thus fulfilling the connection between treasure and the chthonic space.[53] Treasure makes cyclical journeys, repeatedly moving from the earth, its place of origin, up to the light. In death, treasure is consigned to the earth only to be uncovered or returned. However, Hermóþ has not come for treasure, but for his brother; and in trying to rescue Baldr, his journey may be seen as a reprise of the myth of Orpheus, or even that of Heracles who enters the hell-mouth in Euripides' *Heracles*.[54] As in the classical tradition then, the underworld is the space of the past.

Whereas the classical tradition places emphasis on the underworld as a whole, in northern medieval literature stories often focus on the graves of individuals which carry the same connotations of treasure and the past. Just as the underworld seems open to the comings and goings of the living, graves are similarly restless sites. There are four prominent haunted graves in the Northern tradition; three are from Old Norse and one from Old English. E.V. Gordon notes that the 'typical Icelandic 'ghost' [is] more material than the ghosts of English tradition'[55] and these restless, corporeal ghosts, along with their barrows, provide a clear and irrefutable link with the past. They include the murdered Gunnar of Hliðarendi who sits up in his barrow, cheerfully singing by moonlight.[56] In the *Grettir Saga*, Glám refuses to lie in his grave and becomes an *aptr-gongu-maðr*, an 'after [death] walker' that goes 'riding roofs and breaking down doors' at night.[57] In 'The Waking of Angantyr,' a poetic fragment taken from the *Hervorsaga*, Hervor deliberately wakes the dead, demanding her father's sword so she can wreak vengeance on his murderers. The poem is deeply atmospheric and clearly feeds into a tradition where graveyards and barrows were considered frightening and so Hervor demonstrates great courage in walking up to her father's grave alone and at night:

> She saw now fire from the graves and living dead standing outside, but she went to the graves and was not scared; then as if the fire were smoke she went on until she came to the berserkers'' barrows. The she said: 'Wake, Angantyr! Wake! I am Hervor / The only daughter of you and Tofa. / Give up from the grave the keen sword /That dwarves forged for Svafrlami.[58]

Angantyr's grave is the locus of both archaeological and genealogical associations; the sword Hervor demands from her father is not just a tool but an ancestral weapon and proof of her legitimacy.[59] But Hervor is determined and no monsters or ghosts will dissuade her from taking the treasured sword. Throughout the poem her language is violent and aggressive. She associates herself with Vikings, implying that her intention is to plunder the grave if Angantyr refuses to give up the sword. When Angantyr expresses reluctance, she threatens him and his brothers: 'may you all writhe within your ribs/As if you rot in an anthill.'[60] Angantyr's grave represents a site of desire for Hervor and she is willing to enact a none-too-gentle 'rite of power' upon it in order to claim what is rightfully hers. For Hervor, the dead are subaltern and their needs and wishes are inferior to those of the living.

On the other hand, the tone of the Old English elegy, 'The Wife's Lament' is very different, and even though the ghostly speaker is restless and 'possessed with longing'[61] she does not have the corporeal quality or desire for violence exhibited by her Norse counterparts. Unlike Glám, she is tied to her barrow, 'ordered ... to live alone in the bare wood/ under an oak tree in a grave.'[62] As a ghost, she is very literally a remnant of the past, but it is her grave, 'an ancient hole,' that enables her past to have a continuous presence in the world. The verticality of the grave is given further emphasis, even exaggeration, by the oak tree which stretches both above and below the earth. The oak tree is described as growing out of the hole—it has sprung from the rich soil of the grave—and is thus a reflection on the tropes of the green space topos. But whereas the green topos is a space for restful death and for the acceptance of the natural cycles of decay and rebirth, the speaker in this poem is uneasy and weeps 'for my exile/ and my misery, because I may never/find rest from my grief /nor from all this longing that beset me in this life.'[63] Despair overwhelms her; 'here I often surrender myself to grief/ at my lord's parting.'[64] At a remove from the peace and order that defines the green topos, the speaker of 'The Wife's Lament' is denied the possibility of rebirth or resurrection. Confined to her grave, to the lapsed topos, she is unable to do anything except dwell on the past.

The same sense of grief motivates the 'last survivor' in *Beowulf*, although he does not haunt a grave like the other ghosts I have discussed here. Nevertheless, he is restless in his grief. 'So, sad of mind, sorrow spoke / one left behind, joyless, restless/ days and nights until death welled/ in body and heart.'[65] He is the last of his people and, despairing, consigns all of their riches to the earth saying 'hold you, now, earth, since heroes could not, the property of earls.'[66] His words have the same elegiac quality as those expressed in 'The Wife's Lament': 'I have no one to wield the sword or polish the fretted cup, the precious drinking-cup, the host have hastened elsewhere.'[67] Here, the treasure and the people are treated as equivalents. The poet does not show the last survivor digging graves and laying his people to rest, but burying their possessions. By bringing the features of the hall—cups, retainers, and music—into conjunction with the bare cave, the poet establishes a complex juxtaposition between halls and caves which, as I will now show, is a recurring feature of *Beowulf*.

In *Beowulf*, the cave sub-topos is particularly sophisticated, and the poet draws together the associations of monsters, treasure, and the past elegantly in the two representations of caves in the poem. Grendel 'holds the moors, the fens and the fastness,'[68] but his stronghold is 'a hostile hall'[69] beneath a lake. Deprived of the qualities of a domestic space, Grendel's hostile hall is endowed with the characteristics of a chthonic space. It is fitting that when Beowulf dives down into the mere, he discovers that the cave is full of old treasures and weapons, including 'a mighty ancestral sword.'[70] The sword is 'wrought by giants,'[71] a sure sign of its great antiquity. When he brings the sword up to the surface, he sees that its hilt 'bright in gold/ with runic letters, rightly engraved/ that set out and said for whom the sword was made/ the iron first cast/ the wrapped hilt and ornamented blade.'[72] The sword is instantly recognisable as both an archaeological and a genealogical token; the inscribed name connects an ephemeral human past with the artefact's enduring presence.

The certainty that human life will pass but treasure will endure is the prime motivation behind Beowulf's decision to fight the dragon later in the poem. As a king, his reign is characterised by peace, but when he realises that 'the precious hoard [may be] bought with my old life,'[73] he decides to seek out the dragon, believing that the treasure will benefit his people long after he is dead.[74] It is especially appropriate that the treasure Beowulf will fight for is the same hoard abandoned by the last survivor. Beowulf's actions invert those of his predecessor; where one consigns the gold to the ground in despair, he, in hope, will raise it up again and so the treasure which outlasted one nation will come to sustain another. Beowulf's final 'rite of power' is to kill the dragon, enabling his young retainer, Wiglaf, to enter the cave and bring the treasures out into the light and into the present time.[75] Here human life and ancient ornaments are intricately connected. Beowulf clearly sees the treasure and his life as direct equivalents. This treasure is a *memento mori*; it serves as a reminder of the dead generations who made it and, he believes, will come to serve as a reminder of his own life. It is a deep and poignant irony, then, that after Beowulf's death the Geats turn to despair and bury the treasures he has won for them in his grave mound, thus undoing all his efforts. Here, as in *Snorra Edda*, treasure perpetuates a cyclical, and ultimately futile, movement of burial and recovery.

As I have shown, the chthonic space is a common feature of medieval literature where it functions as a link to the past. Often, this topological connection with the past reinforces the impact of a genealogical or archaeological connection and the chthonic space acts as a burial site for both people and their treasures. In many cases, the past is treated, however subconsciously, as a subaltern space which must yield to the demands of the present age and give up its treasures. However, the chthonic space is often the realm of monsters or the restless dead which, being a part of and belonging to the past, naturally resists the will of the living. So the lapsed topos is at once a site of a desire and a site of dread, a place of hope and of despair. These complex and interlinking associations become the foundational features of the lapsed topos in modern children's literature.

The Chthonic Space in Children's Literature

The primary function of the chthonic space, as with all aspects of the lapsed topos, is to provide a connection with the past. Nolan Dalrymple has noted that in David Almond's fiction, children move underground 'in order to connect with a more primal way of life'[76] and that 'entering into the earth leads children to reassess the landscape [...] in light of those newly uncovered depths it reveals'[77] In *Kit's Wilderness* (1999), *Clay* (2005), and *The Savage* (2008), underground spaces become sites where the boundaries between the past and present are dissolved, full of raw emotion and rage.

In children's literature, chthonic spaces are deeply associated with the past and are also marked by the twin symbols of treasure and monsters and invite a character to enact the 'rite of power' upon the 'site of desire'. Even a relatively simple text such as Michael Rosen's *We're Going on a Bear Hunt* (1989) playfully extrapolates this association; the bear is at once the ultimate object of the quest, an object of desire and therefore a kind of treasure, and also a frightening monster who resides in 'a narrow, dark, gloomy cave.'[78] In Alan Garner's *The Weirdstone of Brisingamen* (1960), Colin and Susan stumble upon a cave filled with savage goblin-like creatures that 'emerge like ants from a nest'[79] and pursue the children. The ugliness of the creatures, their distorted and misshapen bodies, and the animalistic imagery Garner uses deepen the dialectical rift between Self and Other, Normal and Abnormal which govern all relationships between the past and the present. The children are rescued by a wizard, Cadellin, who then takes them to the Fundindelve, 'a long low cavern' filled with 'jewels, and gold and silver, which stretched away into the distance like sand-dunes in a desert.'[80] The Fundindelve is also the cave in which the legendary Sleepers lie[81] and so, despite the monsters and the treasures Garner mentions, the primary function of the chthonic space is to connect the present time (Susan and Colin) to the past (Cadellin and the Sleepers).

Monsters, particularly dragons, feature strongly in the chthonic spaces in children's literature where they are very frequently associated with treasure.[82] In C.S. Lewis's *The Voyage of the Dawn Treader* (1950), Eustace finds an ancient treasure hoard in a cave and falls asleep dreaming greedily about his riches. When he wakes, he finds that he has been transformed into a dragon.[83] In J.K. Rowling's *Harry Potter and The Deathly Hallows* (2007), the underground vaults at Gringotts bank are guarded by a 'gigantic dragon' that roars 'with a noise that made the rock tremble, opened its mouth and spat a jet of fire that sent them running back up the passageway.'[84] In Neil Gaiman's *The Graveyard Book* (2008), a magical serpent, the Sleer, guards the few remaining treasures in an ancient underground tomb[85] and in Philip Reeve's *There's No Such Thing as Dragons* (2009), dragons, like magpies, assiduously hoard shiny and reflective objects.

In terms of canonical examples of the chthonic space, one need look no further than J. R. R. Tolkien's *The Hobbit* (1937). Tolkien's expert immersion in medieval literature means that *The Hobbit* provides an obvious link between the representations of caves in medieval literature and those in children's literature. Echoing and even parodying *Beowulf*, Tolkien's unlikely hero Bilbo enters two caves and encounters two monsters; Gollum and the dragon Smaug. Each of the monsters guards a treasure. Tolkien's descriptions of the caves adhere to the conventions of medieval literary depictions of the space. The caves are old; they 'go back in their beginnings ages before the goblins'[86] and, as might be expected, their chief characteristics are darkness and narrowness. The network of tunnels which Bilbo first enters is full of 'nasty slimy things, with big bulging blind eyes, wriggling in the water'[87] the worst and most monstrous of which is Gollum who is 'as dark as darkness.'[88] Like Grendel, Gollum has been cast out of society and lives in an underground lake, only venturing forth to hunt, but unlike the Grendel-kin who have amassed a great amount of treasure, Gollum's treasure is a single ring of power, his 'precious.'[89] Bilbo enacts the standard rite of power within the cave and overcomes the monster—quite literally, as he jumps over Gollum—and takes the treasure for himself.[90]

Being a dragon, Smaug is a more conventional chthonic monster and he is surrounded by a more conventionally-sized treasure: 'on all sides stretching away across the unseen floors, lay countless piles of precious things, gold wrought and unwrought, gems and jewels, and silver red-stained in the ruddy light.'[91] Apart from this, Smaug's cave is very much like Gollum's and it is introduced with the standard description of darkness and depth. Tolkien writes: 'it seemed as if darkness flowed out like a vapour from the hole in the mountain-side, and deep darkness in which nothing could be seen lay before their eyes, a yawning mouth leading in and down.'[92] As might be expected, Smaug's hoard is an ancient one and the cave functions as a means to connect the characters—particularly the dwarves—to a sense of the distant past and of an ancient heritage. Through the dwarves' romanticisation of the past, their idealisation of the hoard, and their valorisation of the deeds of their ancestors, this passage hints at the orientalisation of the past. Here, archaeology (the mention of artefacts) and genealogy (the mention of long-dead nobles) both occur as signifiers of the past, but Tolkien maintains the integrity of the chthonic space as the true vehicle of the past by setting both the hoard and the conversations about it, within a cave.

Chthonic Spaces in The Dark Is Rising Sequence

In Cooper's work, as in Tolkien's, Garner's, and Almond's, culture arises from the earth, is deeply tied to the earth and whenever characters have to connect to a sense of the deep cultural past, they must first come into contact with a chthonic space. Caves, graves and mines do not simply conjure a sense of the past, like archaeological artefacts or genealogical inheritance; they allow characters to enter into and participate in the spaces of the past and, moreover, to engage in footfall continuity with the past. Even though intertextual references may be misconstrued or overlooked and objects cannot in and of themselves inculcate a sense of the past for the reader or for a character, these scenes show characters going down into the earth and connecting with a lost and buried past. In the *Sequence*, chthonic spaces are never merely the background to encounters with the past, but rather the fundamental spaces necessary to their manifestation. If the past of the *Sequence* is to be rescued and made accessible, it must be rescued through the exploration and understanding of the landscape.

As in her use of other topoi, Cooper is clearly aware of the symbolic and narrative functions of chthonic spaces and within the *Sequence* the chthonic space is used regularly and with great dexterity. At this point it is essential to note that in spite of their physical differences, Cooper uses caves and graves as interchangeable elements in the lapsed topos, thereby missing out on an important and potentially rich distinction in the landscape. Cooper conflates caves and graves by having bodies buried inside caves (as in the Gravestones at Trewissick, and the cave at Bird Rock, Craig yr Aderyn)[93] and by all but destroying the verticality which marks the grave as distinct. In fact, there is only one true grave in the *Sequence*—the grave of the unnamed king in *The Dark Is Rising*—and even that designation is precarious as it soon collapses into another aspect of the lapsed topos, the ruin. However, given Cooper's awareness of and interest in landscape, it may be that the merging of the various kinds of chthonic space is the result of an astute choice rather than an accident or oversight. In all, there are six chthonic spaces in the *Sequence*; the two caves, one at Trewissick and one at Cader Idris; the archaeological excavation at Caerleon; the ship burial of the King of the Light; and two submerged spaces, the Lost Land and the realm of Tethys. These submerged spaces are included as they adhere perfectly to the symbolic function of the chthonic space even though they do not share all of the physical characteristics of the other spaces. The archaeological site contains treasure, but no explicit reference to a king. Four of the other spaces contain treasures and a king, and the fifth, the realm of Tethys, contains treasure and a queen.[94] I will now treat of the function and significance of each of these spaces in turn.

Over Sea, Under Stone

The most intricately constructed chthonic space within the *Sequence* is, perhaps surprisingly, the very first one we encounter, the cave at Kenmare head in Cornwall. The headland is strongly associated with King Mark, as is, of course, the whole region. This particular area, just north of Trewissick, is referred to as the 'gravestones' by locals who believe the headland to be haunted,[95] and thus Cooper conflates caves and graves, creating a homogenous chthonic space. This space is already strongly associated with a king so when the children find a map of the headland, the reader does not doubt that there will be some treasure buried there too. When Barney first sees the old map he says, 'I bet old King Mark left some treasure behind somewhere and that's why there's a map.'[96] Here, Barney connects three elements—the treasure, the king, and the landscape—but of the three, it is the landscape that is most important as it will lead on to the other two.[97] Before the children can find the treasure they must first explore the whole headland and 'learn what it looks like.'[98] They must acquire footfall knowledge of the territory. Once they understand the landscape culturally, geographically, and, above all, topologically, they will find the treasure.

On one of their exploration-games, they find a 'dark shapeless hole'[99] beneath a rock. Simon leans over and puts his hand in:

> His arm disappeared up to the shoulder, until he was lying flat, and he could feel nothing but rough rock at the sides. He blinked up at Barney and Jane. 'I can't feel any bottom to it,' he said, hushed. [. . .] 'This must be it, mustn't it? It must be where [they] hid the grail!'[100]

Here, ancientness is directly equated with depth; the deeper the layers go, the further the space reaches back in time. Simon knows there is little point searching for treasure that has been buried for a thousand years anywhere except very deep in the earth. Cooper is careful to impress a sense of the depth, and thereby the ancientness, of the cave upon the reader by having the Drews drop little stones into the hole and listen for echoes and then unwinding a reel of thread to measure the depth. The cotton breaks but they deduce that the hole is at least a hundred and fifty feet deep.[101] The reader, like the Drews, may deduce that the deeper the hole, the older it is or—more correctly—the older the soil at the bottom is according to the law of stratification.[102] Returning to the idea of stratification, it becomes clear that a hole, a cave, a grave, a void in the earth allows people standing on the surface or in the present time to look down through its layers into the past and—as Simon does—to reach back down into and even enter into the past.

Eager to reach into and to rescue the past by taking the grail from its hiding place, the three Drews run around onto the beach when they can get in at the cave and at the treasure they are certain lies within. One might expect that the grail is the most important aspect of this whole scene but close examination of the four hundred lines between pages 184 and 203 reveals that two hundred and forty one of the sentences—just over sixty percent of the writing—are devoted to descriptions of the cave. By comparison, twelve percent of the lines are given over to the grail itself and a scant one percent to King Mark. Cooper presents this cave as a space which both adheres to the topological conventions and disappoints them. For the Drews, the cave is 'not the kind of cave they had pictured in their minds,'[103] yet Cooper maintains the characteristics of the topos by referring to the low ceiling and the darkness within. She writes:

> narrow and triangular, it rose barely high enough for Barney to stand upright inside, and they would certainly have to crouch to go in. Rough boulders lay heaped round the entrance, and water dripped from the wet green weed coating the roof. They could not see very far inside.[104]

With the physical signs of the topos in place, it may be expected that the symbolic attributes will also be present. Sure enough, Barney's assertion that it is 'just a hole'[105] soon proves to be misguided for when he and Simon enter the cave they discover a long narrow tunnel which broadens into the expected bowl-shaped ending. The further the boys go into the space, the more signifiers of 'cave' they encounter. Cooper mentions that 'the silence, like the darkness, seemed almost solid'[106] and that 'the ground, when Barney stooped to touch it, was covered with a kind of dusty sand'[107] and soon the 'caveness' of the cave is fulfilled by a description of 'narrow shadow-swung walls tunnelling into the dark, holding them in a cramped, unfriendly grip. [Barney] moved hesitantly forward, and then some instinct told him to stop. He put out his hand in the silent darkness. It met solid rock a few inches from his face.'[108] Indeed, Cooper's description of the cave at Kenmare Head covers all the expected elements of the space; silence, darkness, narrowness, rock, and dust.

By the time Barney's hand meets 'solid rock' and the end of the tunnel, the informed reader expects that, somewhere in the vicinity, the boys will find the treasure they have been seeking. Before Barney can find the treasure, however, he must overcome the monster and prove that he is 'the proper man in the proper place.'[109] This time the monster in the cave is figurative, composed of Barney's own fears, his panic and his uncertainty. Nevertheless, Barney's fear almost overwhelms him:

> It was as if they were all around him in the silent darkness, evil and unseen, willing him to go back. [...] he felt that something was pressing him down, calling him incessantly to turn away, Who are you to intrude here, the voice seemed to whisper [...] Go away, go back to where you are safe, leave such ancient things alone ... .[110]

It is only through great strength and great selflessness that Barney is able to overcome these terrible fears. He draws courage from thinking about Arthur and his knights, drawing on memories of ancient good in order to combat an ancient evil. It is only when he demonstrates this courage that he is permitted to see 'the glint of candlelight reflected back from a shape that was not part of the rock.'[111] It is, in fact, the grail, 'dusty and dirty,'[112] but recognisable by its shape. Barney and Simon then execute the u-turn which is so typical of the space and emerge once again into the sunshine and the present time.

Because the grail is an object from the past, it cannot be found or preserved without the medium of the chthonic space. So when Jane first sees the grail and exclaims 'it's terribly ancient!' she is not revealing a hitherto unknown interest in medieval antiquities but rather the end of a logical thought process; Jane knows that the grail is ancient because it has just come out of the ground and because it was buried very deeply in the earth it had, therefore, been buried a long time ago. Although Cooper's use of the chthonic topos is intricately planned, the revelation of the complex 'layers and layers of time' is actually very clear and straightforward. As with the other chthonic spaces in the *Sequence*, this cave is a locus for the past and it fulfils its symbolic function by allowing both characters and readers direct access to the past, thereby establishing and mediating a relationship between the present and the past.

The Dark Is Rising

The second chthonic space is in *The Dark Is Rising*, the second book in the *Sequence*. Towards the end of the book Will finds a king's grave when the mound he is standing on breaks apart after a flood. The land 'fell away'[113] and a ship appears, laden with the body of the king who holds the last of the six Signs in his hands. The ship contains masses of treasure 'piled around him [the king] in glittering mounds.'[114] For the informed reader, the scene has connotations of the burial of Scyld Shefing in *Beowulf*,[115] or the death of Baldr in the Eddas[116] and Cooper's description of the ship with its 'high curving prow' and central raised canopy is reminiscent of the Sutton Hoo ship burial or the ship-burial at Taplow.[117] But not every reader can know this and the descriptions of the king and the treasure bestow a sense of magic and fantasy before they convey a sense of a particular time-period. The past is, however, definitively evoked when Merriman says that the king 'has lain here in his burial-ground for fifteen hundred years, waiting' and remarks that the sign he holds 'is one of the oldest.' We can be certain that the Sign is old, not because the ship-burial reminds us of Sutton Hoo or because the king with his boar-crested helmet recalls images of Scyld Shefing, but because it has been buried for fifteen hundred years. Furthermore, Cooper places specific emphasis on the landscape in this scene, drawing the reader's attention to the fact that the island the ship lies on is 'sinking towards the river' and the earth around the ship 'slid and crumpled' and when Will approached, it 'lurched to one side [. . .] creaking and rattling.'[118] Thus, the king's barrow, through its physical instability and imminent collapse, is marked as part of the lapsed topos. Like Barney, Will must also overcome a series of obstacles—Hawkin, Mitothin, and finally his own fear of death—before he can take the Sign of Water from the king's hands. Here, through the medium of the chthonic space, Will is enabled to connect with the distant past and thereby to enact a familiar 'rite of power' over the 'site of desire' and claim the treasure as his own.

The Grey King

Given the role of the chthonic space as a medium between past and present in the *Sequence*, it is especially appropriate that in the *The Grey King*, the riddle-scene in which Bran and Will are tested on their knowledge of Britain's mythological past takes place within a cave at Craig yr Aderyn. This cave is deeply impressed with a sense of time; the boys walk along a stairway which been 'worn by centuries of passing feet'[119] and into a hall where three lords sit, one of whom is King Arthur. The lords ask the boys three questions which test their knowledge of British and Welsh mythology. Bran must name the Three Elders of the World and Will names the Three Generous Men of the Island of Britain and then answer a riddle.[120] These questions, and their enigmatic, formulaic answers, reiterate the central importance of myth and folklore within the *Sequence* and serve as a reminder that, for Cooper, a proper understanding of landscape and of one's role within the landscape must entail an understanding of history and culture. Both questions combine human life with geographical setting; they are not simply three generous men, but the three generous men of Britain. By answering these questions correctly, Bran and Will prove that, like Barney, each is 'the proper man in the proper place.'[121]

By establishing the boys as cultural heirs, Cooper draws on genealogical connections with the past, which deepens when Arthur is revealed as Bran's birth-father. And once these genealogical ties are established, the boys can claim the harp, thus establishing an archaeological link with the past. Cooper makes it clear that these connections would be meaningless without the surrounding and supporting topological connection provided by the cave. The cave allows Cooper to demonstrate that within the *Sequence* culture is autochthonic; it is embedded within and emerges from the landscape.

Anomalous Chthonic Spaces: The Realm of Tethys and The Lost Land

There are three anomalous lapsed spaces in *The Dark Is Rising Sequence*; the realm of Tethys, the Lost Land, and Caerleon. The realm of Tethys and the Lost Land both fulfil all of the expected symbolic criteria of the topos by providing connections to the deep past. These two spaces contain treasures and monsters as well as noble figures; in one there is a king, in the other, a queen. However, instead of being below the surface of the earth as with the other chthonic spaces in the *Sequence*, they are below the surface of the sea. In this way, both the realm of Tethys and the Lost Land are anomalous.

The realm of Tethys appears in *Greenwitch* when Will and Merriman dive into the sea, hoping to regain the manuscript that was lost at the end of *Over Sea, Under Stone*. Even though the dark space beneath the surface of the sea is fluid rather than solid, it shares many characteristics with more typical chthonic spaces. Cooper emphasises the sense of deepness and darkness, referring to the sea euphemistically as 'the deeps.'[122] Furthermore, Tethys, the sea goddess, does not merely live at the bottom of the ocean but in 'a great crack in the bed of the sea, an abyss deeper than all the ocean deeps.'[123] Here, as in the other submerged spaces, 'only a little of the day' can penetrate.[124] As with all aspects of the lapsed topos, the realm of Tethys is replete with the past. Tethys is 'older than the land, older than the Old Ones, older than all men.'[125] Tethys is keen that the past should influence the present time and she praises the fishermen who, in naming a boat *The White Lady*, perpetuate ancient customs.[126] As with the other chthonic spaces in the *Sequence*, the realm of Tethys is guarded by monsters; Merriman and Will must pass through shoals of ugly, malformed fish in order to reach this depth:

> Will saw huge toad-like fish with bright tipped fishing-lines curving up from their backs, to hang cruelly alluring over wide mouths bristling with

teeth. He saw a dreadful creature that seemed all mouth, a vast mouth like a funnel with a lid, and a puny body dwindling into a long whiplash tail. Beside it, the body of another began to swell horribly, as a big fish, struggling, disappeared inside the trap-like mouth. Will shuddered.[127]

Will's shudder echoes Barney's fear in the cave below King Mark's Head and pre-empts the shudder Bran gives upon entering the cave at Craig yr Aderyn. His discomfort stems from the monsters, but also from the realisation that the realm of Tethys is 'an alien world', an Other space in which someone from the present time must always feel uneasy.[128] The Otherness of the space cuts both ways; even as it is a frightening space, it is also a vulnerable, and therefore subaltern, space, open to the rite of power which Will and Merriman must enact upon it in order to retrieve the manuscript. Remarkably, their rite of power is unsuccessful and they leave Tethys empty-handed. Tethys is the only chthonic space which does not surrender the secrets and treasures of the past.

The Lost Land
Although it is submerged rather than strictly chthonic, the Lost Land may also be considered in terms of layers of time, which, although not rendered as visually as in the stratification of rock and soil, are just as applicable here as to the other chthonic spaces I have discussed. Even though Will and Bran cross a rainbow bridge to get to the Lost Land, it brings them 'down through the bright haze.'[129] This downward movement reinforces the sense that the Lost Land is beneath the surface of the present time. Will and Bran's journey into the Lost Land is unquestionably a rite of power; they are there to find the crystal sword Eirias and to take it back with them to the present time. The Welsh word *eirias* means a fire or a blaze and is, therefore, a true weapon of the Light. For Bran, the quest is one of self-discovery but for Will, Eirias, the Light, is 'the meaning'[130] of their quest. As with the other chthonic spaces in the *Sequence*, the events in the Lost Land are very much an initiation rite and the boys have to overcome various trials and challenges before they win the right to claim the sword. Some of these challenges take the form of puzzles, whereas others are direct, physical encounters with monsters such as Mitothin and the Mari Llwyd. These trials and challenges form the basis of the narrative tropes which are so inherently characteristic of the chthonic space in literature.

The Lost Land as Ruin
Although the Lost Land contains many sub-spaces and sub-topoi, including a garden, which is discussed in Chapter Two and a small ruined cottage, which will be discussed later in this chapter, if the space is regarded as a whole then its position within the lapsed topos becomes clear. As well as bearing the hallmarks of the chthonic space, the Lost Land may also be described as a ruined

space. In having the characteristics of both a chthonic space and a ruined space, the Lost Land, like Caerleon, which I will discuss presently, bridges the ontological gap between the two aspects of the lapsed topos. From the outset, Cooper makes it clear that this land is not 'lost' in the sense that it is gone astray or that its location is uncertain or unknown; it is a folkloric commonplace that the Drowned Hundred lies in the Dyfi estuary and Bran claims that he has 'known that old story always, as well as [he knows his] own name.'[131] Rather, the Lost Land is 'lost' because it has been destroyed; it is ruined physically, morally, and spiritually. Even though Cooper provides a rather straightforward explanation for the Drowned Hundred, having Bran explain to the other children that *'Cantr'er Gwaelod*, the Lowland Hundred, the lovely fertile land of the King Gwyddno Garanhir, centuries ago [...] was so flat that the seawater had to be kept out by dykes, and one night there was a terrible storm and the sea-wall broke, and all the water came in. And the land was drowned,'[132] other versions of the story have close parallels with the Hebrew deluge myth. W. Jenkyn Thomas relates a version of the story in which the citizens of the Lost Land are too careless to keep watch on the tides and to maintain the sea-walls. The piles are 'rotten, broken and out of their places'[133] and when the storm comes the city is easily overpowered. In other versions of the tale, the fault lies solely with the king, and Robin Gwyndaf writes that the land is 'drowned because of the wickedness of its ruler.'[134] So, the Lost Land is lapsed in several ways: it has fallen into error and sin and, as a direct result, into decay, and it has also sunk into obscurity. In bridging the division between the chthonic space and the ruin, the Lost Land comes to epitomise the lapsed topos.

Caerleon as Lapsed Space

As Caerleon is both a chthonic space and a ruined space it presents a perfect and unique connection with the past in the *Sequence*. In addition, Cooper evokes both archaeology and genealogy as signs of the past within this space. Merriman notes both the archaeological and genealogical effects of the Roman settlers which mark passage of time through the 'transform[ation of] our cities [...] and the pattern of our lives.'[135] The Romans make sure to leave physical traces of their presence and Marcus, the centurion, shows Will and Merriman a carved block of stone: 'It was much larger than the rest [of the stones] [...] with one broad, unusually flat surface for the front side. Will saw the incised letters: COH. X. C. FLAV. JULIAN.'[136] In the twentieth century, the archaeological connection to the past is completed and its value confirmed when an American archaeologist proudly shows his discovery to Will and Merriman. Will recognises the stone with its 'inscribed letters battered now by age'[137] as the same one shown to him by the centurion.

The centurion and the archaeologist are connected by the inscribed block, but they are also connected emotionally through a shared sense of homesickness. The sympathetic relationship between the Roman centurion and the American archaeologist forges a kind of genealogical and emotional connection between the two time periods. By having the twentieth-century archaeologist finish the first-century centurion's sentence Cooper gives the impression that a great quantity of time has been compressed.[138] Even though Caerleon does not mean the same thing to both men, the place inspires identical emotions for them and both express exactly the same sentiments: 'in the new voice, the ache of longing was exactly the same.'[139] Thus Cooper suggests that even though the people of the past and the people alive in the present day may not belong to the same geographical or temporal space, or even share a language, they share social and emotional connections.

Merriman reminds Will, perhaps unnecessarily because Will too has witnessed both the construction of Caerleon and the excavation of its ruins, that 'the times are linked, by our [the Old Ones'] presence and by the place.'[140] There can be no doubt that it is the lapsed topos itself that provides the strongest connection between past and present. In and of themselves, neither the stone block nor the expressions of homesickness convey any sense of the passage of time; it is the physical context for these signs that imbues them with meaning. Whereas the inscribed stone was once part of a 'vaulted arch,'[141] it is now only 'shoulder high.'[142] The great amphitheatre has lapsed into the earth and even the newly excavated sections still bear 'an inch of earth.'[143] The stones are literally and symbolically covered by the layers of time.

Caerleon is unlike the other lapsed spaces which I have discussed so far in that it is not entirely submerged within the earth and that it does not adhere to the narrative patterning associated with the chthonic space. Although this space contains treasure, Will and Merriman enter it without completing any initiation rite or overcoming any monster. Caerleon is not simply a chthonic space, it is also a ruin. In Cooper's description of the excavation it is not just the layer of earth that indicates the passage of time but also the physical deterioration of the stones themselves. Thus, 'the ruin itself embodies the events which led to its present state.'[144] The ruin also entails an emotional quality which is absent from the other aspects of the lapsed topos. Here, the image of the great amphitheatre worn down into the earth by age and neglect serves as a poignant reminder of the frailty of human life and human endeavour. Ruins 'embody the historical process and the temporality of existence.'[145] Cooper intensifies this sense of the passing of time by ensuring that the reader never sees the completed amphitheatre; it is half-built and then half-destroyed. The partial presence of a building within a series of texts that are so fundamentally rooted in a sense of place creates a sense of unease, which in turn invests the space with a sense of the uncanny, here imparted by the echoing voices and emotions of the centurion and the archaeologist.[146] They form a double, an almost ghostly reflection of the past within the present. These uncanny qualities are not part of the chthonic space, but are the hallmarks of the ruin.[147]

Figure 4.4 Ruined house at Pentewan, Cornwall. ©Jane Carroll.

The Ruin

All ruins are 'haunted by the presences of another age.'[148] By showing outward and visible signs of ageing, the ruin epitomises the passage of time, thus connecting us to the time in which it was built, and through its various processes of decay and collapse, illustrates the time that has lapsed between then and now. Being artificial, the ruin entails a human past and by physicalizing the human past the ruin, like the grave, becomes a *memento mori*; a stark reminder of the inevitability of death and the inexorability of time. The human connection with the ruin produces emotional effects ranging from the morbid 'contemplation on collective self-annihilation'[149] to a poignant 'nostalgia for a place [one has] never visited.'[150] So, like all aspects of the lapsed topos, ruins are the subject of both fascination and revulsion. They are simultaneously sites of desire and part of the 'geography of despair.'[151] Like other lapsed spaces, ruins are potential spaces of colonisation; their disordered boundaries make them physically and ideologically vulnerable, open to the rites of power which intruders or visitors from the present time may wish to enact upon the past which is housed within them.

Ruins are in the process of collapse and it is this process that distinguishes them from any other kind of space.[152] The other spaces and topoi I have discussed are complete spaces in the sense that their boundaries and their functions are relatively stable. Formed through the disordering of material and metaphysical boundaries, ruined spaces are always ontologically and physically unstable and, in literature, these instabilities always foreshadow the collapse of other boundaries such as that between the normal and the fantastic, between the present and the past, between safety and danger. For instance, a house is built to provide safety and shelter, but a ruined house fails to provide either adequately. As the physical boundaries of a space are destabilised, the space itself is laid open to multiple and conflicting functions. The ruin functions as a kind of hybrid space, a 'partial presence,'[153] which, as with the cave and the grave, becomes a site of desire upon which colonial rites of power may be enacted. One of the most obvious rites of power enacted upon the ruined space is 'the botanical colonisation of derelict land and buildings.'[154] As a result of these spontaneous and uncontrolled invasions, the ruin comes to occupy the boundary between organic and inorganic space, bringing elements of the lapsed topos together with elements of the green space and becoming something more than the sum of its parts. Whereas the chthonic space only looks to the past, the ruin, in supporting botanical growth, also 'hint[s] at potential futures.'[155] The ruin, unlike the other lapsed spaces, not only connects the past to the present, but also the present to the future.

The Ruin in Medieval Literature

Ruins are 'spaces of disorder,'[156] formed through the disruption of previously rigid boundaries. The spatial limits that keep other topological elements in check are, in the case of ruins, disturbed and even dismissed. Thus, the ruined space is 'the antithesis of purified space,'[157] because it does not have distinct boundaries it cannot be completely separated from other spaces. So, when the functional aspects of a space break down we can expect to see a corresponding collapse in its physical and ontological aspects. In literature, every element of the ruined space is shown to be in disarray. Unlike the smooth u-turn which is characteristic of movement within the cave, or the strict verticality of the grave, the ruin presents a more difficult passage to the past and is typically littered with broken and discarded objects which become obstacles. Characters duck or squeeze through small gaps, and clamber over fallen objects, avoiding dirt and hazards. These awkward movements are often echoed by fragmented or damaged language, as the hybrid space opens up a 'cleavage'[158] in linguistic order. Janowitz notes that the ruin enforces 'regression to pre-consciousness and a world without speech'[159] wherein language is threatened and may break down altogether, resulting in silence or awkward conversations full of half-sentences in which voices may overlap, trail off, and fall into silence. This linguistic collapse is central to a sense of the uncanny which, as Punter argues, is brought about by the 'deconstruction and dismemberment of the real.'[160] This deconstruction may take place on a large scale through the appearance of ghosts or supernatural elements, but it also occurs in miniature through the minute cleavages and divisions that open up in language. These cleavages serve to 'deconstruct' the real, creating a sense of the uncanny that goes down to even the smallest elements of a text. Thus, in effecting a breakdown in ontological and linguistic order, ruins come to embody an uncanny force.

This sense of the uncanny is readily extrapolated in fiction, particularly in representations of ruined houses where the structure is *unheimlich*: both unhomely and uncanny.[161] The uncanny space is often the site of revelation for some buried, repressed, or hidden aspect of the past and the ruin's crumbling exterior connotes the deterioration of the powers that kept that thing secret or repressed. As an awesome and even fearsome aspect of the landscape, the ruin is a *locus horribilus*,[162] the opposite of the peaceful, drowsy *locus amoenus* which I discussed in Chapter Two. In the late eighteenth and early nineteenth century it became the fashion to include something of the *locus horribilus* in the landscape gardens of large estates and wealthy landowners often moved ruined buildings stone by stone into their gardens in order enhance the picturesque quality of the view.[163] In the absence of any genuine local ruins, it became the practice to build 'follies', large, fake ruins that were often little more than plastered wood structures.[164] Ruins were also popular in the literature of the same period where architectural collapse came to serve as a metonym for social, moral, psychic and linguistic breakdown.[165] Gothic literature 'revels in ruins.'[166] However, the ruin is an old topos with a long literary provenance and the topological and narrative tropes which are drawn out in gothic literature were in place long before the genre came into existence. Janowitz notes that 'the ruin subject [is] integral to the thetic life of English poetry'[167] and traces the origin of this subject back to the middle ages. It is in the middle ages, specifically in Old English *dūstscēawung* poetry, that the hybrid and dialectical associations of the ruin find their purest expression. *Dūstscēawung* poetry—poetry that 'contemplates the dust' and reflects on the decline of civilisation and power—does not restrict itself to things that have been ruined, but also looks to a bleak future in which objects, buildings and people will be ruined.

Stuart Lee and Elizabeth Solopova note in *The Keys of Middle Earth* that the bleak and pessimistic tone of *dūstscēawung* poetry was quite natural to the Anglo Saxons; 'the passing of worldly glory [...] deeply moved them. This is not surprising, perhaps, when one considers the harshness of life in the period. The evidence of worldly transience was all around them.'[168] Of the surviving literature of the period, a great deal of the poetry falls into, or contains elements of, the *dūstscēawung* genre attesting to the Anglo-Saxon obsession with the past and with the ephemerality of life. Poems such as *The Ruin*, *The Wanderer*, *The Seafarer*, *The Wife's Lament*, *Deor*, *Wulf and Eawacer*, and *Resignation*—all in *The Exeter Book*—may all be described as belonging to the *dūstscēawung* genre and all contain descriptions of ruined and lapsed spaces.[169] These poems form the basis of the ruin as a literary commonplace in English literature and have exerted enormous influence upon the development of the lapsed topos. Other texts, such as *Beowulf*, draw upon the features of *dūstscēawung* poetry to provide a counterpoint within a greater narrative; the lament of the last survivor has much in common with the elegiac narrative of *The Wanderer* and *The Wife's Lament*. The last survivor declares, 'death in battle, ghastly carnage, has claimed all my people [...] Gone is the pleasure of the plucking harp, no fierce hawk swoops about the hall, nor does the swift stallion strike sparks in the courtyard. Cruel death has claimed hundreds of this human race.'[170] There are actual ruins in *Beowulf* too; from the house of the old man whose sons have died described as *eal to rum*, 'suddenly too big'[171] to Heorot, which is built as a feast hall, a place of joy, a *wine-sele*, which is ruined by Grendel's attacks. Moreover, the poet describes Heorot in such as way as to mirror the typical descriptions of ruins in contemporary poetry. Even when the feast-hall is newly completed, the poet predicts its doom: 'The hall towered aloft, high and wide-gabled: it awaited the upheavals of war and malicious fire.'[172] War and fire do not come to Heorot, instead Grendel who is 'at war with God'[173] and with 'a light most like fire'[174] in his eyes (thus combining both threats) attacks the wine-hall. Grendel 'prevailed and, in defiance of right, he contended with them, one against all, until that finest of halls stood useless.'[175] Heorot becomes useless both because it falls into disuse and because it cannot be used for its intended purpose. Heorot is a ruin.

It is, perhaps, appropriate that the best example of *dūstscēawung* poetry is a short poem now known as 'The Ruin'. Existing only in a number of damaged fragments, it laments the destruction of a Roman city which has been identified as Bath.[176] The poem displays all of the physical and symbolic attributes that distinguish the topos. There is a great sense of time and of the passage of time in the poem. The poet notes that 'a hundred human generations lie dead,'[177] imbuing the landscape with a sense of the human past, and with the sense that a great, almost incalculable, amount of time has passed. The effects of time are two-fold; firstly, the people who made these buildings are all gone and their knowledge and skills have been lost, and secondly, the evidence of those people is at risk as the buildings themselves give way under the weight of time and the elements. The city walls are *'wydre gebraecon'*, 'shattered by fate'[178] and the buildings themselves are 'shorn, fallen, under-eaten by age.'[179]

'The Ruin' establishes many of the symbolic and physical elements associated with the ruin in modern literature. The hybrid nature of the ruin is also evident as the poet is careful to mention the botanical colonisation of the space, noting the slow growth of grey lichen on the walls.[180] Perhaps most significantly to the foundation of the literary topos, the poet places emphasis on the dilapidated boundaries of the city, on the roofs, towers, walls, and gates and uses these elements almost synecdochically to denote the collapse of the entire city. The poet writes 'the roofs are fallen, the towers ruinous, the frost-gate bereft; rime on lime'[181] and later that 'the dwellings grow desolate/ and this red-arch falls away from the tiles/ the wooden-vault's roof. The ruin cringes to the ground'.[182] The downward movement of the ruin echoes the vertical movement associated with the grave. Like the grave, it acts as a *memento mori*. Everything the poet looks at is a stark reminder of the past and of 'the inevitability of life passing, [and of . . .] the inexorable processes of nature.'[183] Falling to the ground and even subsiding into the ground, the ruin is not only merging with the landscape but also taking on the characteristics of the chthonic space; it is sinking out of the present time and becoming part of the past. It has simply become the uppermost layer of the 'layers and layers of time'[184] from which history is constructed.

The Ruin in Children's Literature

Modern children's literature has built on the characteristics of the ruin as established in medieval literature and as developed through gothic literature. The ruin is always a vulnerable and fragile space, and much emphasis is placed on its deteriorating boundaries and on the signs of neglect and disuse which characterise the space. The uncanny aspects of the space are evoked through linguistic collapse and through the revelation of repressed or hidden aspects of the past. Through the revelation of these details, the ruin may also prescribe a course of action for the future. In some cases, as in Susan Price's *The Sterkarm Handshake* (1998), this sense of revelation is thwarted. When Andrea visits the ruins of the Sterkarm castle she once lived in, she is made acutely aware of the huge amount of time that has lapsed between herself and her Sterkarm lover, Per. In C.S. Lewis's *Prince Caspian*, (1951) the Pevensie children come to realise how much time has elapsed in Narnia since their last visit only when they are confronted with the ruins of Cair Paravel.[185] This awareness allows them to locate the entrance to the underground chamber where they had stored their treasures, including the magical weapons given to them by Aslan. Here, the ruin, like the chthonic space housed within it, provides a genuine and beneficial connection to the past. A similarly beneficial connection to the past is provided by a lapsed space in Robert Westall's *Ghost Abbey* (1988). Maggi finds two dilapidated teddy bears which turn out to be 'genuine Stieff bears [. . .] [worth] in the region of twelve or thirteen thousand dollars.'[186]

Maggi believes that the bears 'were a kind of gift the Abbey had given her'[187] in return for her attention and care. Here, respect for the past leads to ample and obvious rewards.

Maggi's relationship with the Abbey, and with the past, is far from straightforward. The majority of the lapsed spaces I have examined so far preserve a connection with a single, fossilised moment from history; however, Westall's Abbey connects Maggi and her family to many different time periods. Westall remarks that the old house 'could whirl you back to 1953 with a bunch of dusty menus; or back to 1850, with a bleating goat; or back to a sniper who died in 1644 with nothing at all. And now back to the Middle Ages and the monks, with a voice in a sunny garden.'[188] Here, time is not envisaged as a single, linear strand, but as an intersecting mesh of 'asynchronous moments.'[189] In other texts, this intersecting mesh of time appears as a network of memories 'crossing, folding, piercing'[190] each other and the ruins provide a space in which these memories may be untangled. For example, even though J. K. Rowling provides only the barest description of the Shrieking Shack in *Harry Potter and the Prisoner of Azkaban* (1999), it clearly functions as part of the lapsed topos, and it is within this space that Harry is able to unravel the knots of the past and understand what happened on the night his parents died.[191] Rowling reveals her awareness of the canonical function of ruins by having the Shrieking Shack operate as a liminal space. Here, the proper division between human and animal falls apart as Lupin admits he is a werewolf and both Sirius Black and Peter Pettigrew are revealed as *animagi*, as people who can turn into animals at will. The collapse of boundaries is extended to the collapse of linguistic order as in the confusion characters shout over one another and interrupt each other constantly. In the thirty-two pages set around or within the Shrieking Shack there are almost one hundred and fifty partial or unfinished sentences. As expected, this ruin also prescribes course of action for the future as Sirius offers Harry a new life with him.[192] So, the Shrieking Shack does not simply offer a connection to the past, it demands that the characters respond to the past and engage with it in order to create a future that is informed by, but not restricted by, what has gone before.

The tension between the past and the future is a central theme in Terry Pratchett's *Nation* (2008). When the village on Nation Island is hit by a tsunami, Mau, who had been looking forward to the safety and hospitality of the village, returns to 'a ruined world.'[193] The village and all of its inhabitants are gone. Here, the dead villagers, like the dead in the underworld in Pullman's *The Amber Spyglass*[194] or in Gaiman's *The Graveyard Book*,[195] are an indisputable link to the past. The village exemplifies the way in which ruins may be 'haunted by a horde of absent presences.'[196] This sense of haunting becomes all the more apparent when Mau starts to hear the long-dead elders of Nation, the Grandfathers, talking to him. The Grandfathers—whose skeletons, perhaps unsurprisingly, are housed in a cave—insist that Mau does 'the things that have always been done'[197] thus turning the present into nothing more than a version of the past. For the Grandfathers the past is sacred and, initially, the grieving Mau agrees with them and tries to make life on Nation resemble the old ways as much as possible. However, Mau comes to recognise that the ruined island has the potential to support a new and better kind of life and by repairing and removing the ruined aspects of the landscape he erases the unwanted traces of the past and establishes new, safe domestic spaces on the island which signal towards a positive future.

The Ruin in **The Dark Is Rising Sequence**

In the *Sequence*, Cooper demonstrates astute awareness of the ruin's position and function in children's literature and provides detailed descriptions of ruined spaces while ensuring that in each instance the connection with the past and the prospect towards the future are always evident. In *Greenwitch*, the children come across a broken down caravan inside a ruined barn; in *The Grey King*, Bran learns about his past in a ruined cottage; and *Silver on the Tree* contains another ruined cottage as well as the ruins at Caerleon which I have already discussed. It is especially fitting that the ruined cottages and the caravan were originally domestic spaces. Cooper's attention to the boundaries and limits of the sanctuary topos ensures that the reader is already aware of the vulnerabilities of these spaces, and understands how they can be disrupted. Moreover, the original homely (*heimlich*) aspects of these spaces allow for a greater narrative impact when these familiar and supposedly safe spaces are suddenly disrupted and rendered uncanny (*unheimlich*).

Greenwitch

The ruined barn and caravan in *Greenwitch* are given particularly detailed and intricate descriptions. The borders of the barn, as with all ruins, are disordered and confused. The stone walls of the barn are 'crumbling,' the windows are broken and it has 'a perilous half-fallen roof' and 'a rotting wooden door, hanging sideways from one hinge.'[198] The limits and borders of this space are extremely fragile but they are made seem even weaker because they stand in contradistinction to the solid and secure limits of the domestic spaces that appear throughout the *Sequence*. By allowing the 'weak framing'[199] of this ruin to echo the solid framing of other buildings, Cooper reinforces the sense of the ruin's fragility while simultaneously strengthening the intertextual connections between the five texts of the *Sequence*. The recovery of the grail for a second time links two major aspects of the lapsed topos; the cave and the ruin, creating a sense of symmetry and continuity between *Over Sea, Under Stone* and *Greenwitch* and reassures the reader that, for Cooper, landscapes are not merely one-dimensional backdrops, but are integral to the texts and to the narrative action that unfolds within them.

The fragility of the ruin is also reinforced by repetition; by placing the caravan inside the barn, Cooper effects a physical and symbolic doubling, creating an uncanny effect and intensifying the connotations of death, decay, and dread.[200] The suggestion of death is made explicit through Cooper's anthropomorphic descriptions; this scene is continually described in terms of the body, the broken windows are like teeth and an old plough is likened to a skeleton. Cooper writes:

> The low grey building seemed even more decrepit than Simon remembered. He looked with more attention now at the beams of wood nailed cross-shaped over the front door; at the new growth of creeper reaching over windows unhindered; at other windows, here and there, black and broken like missing teeth. Long grass rose lush and new round rusting pieces of farm equipment left in the yard: a skeletal old plough, a harrow, the remnants of a tractor with its great tyres gone. In the pen of a deserted pig-sty, nettles grew, tall and rank. [...] There was a wet smell of growing things.[201]

The image of the 'skeletal' plough surrounded by 'lush grass' is especially apt because it suggests anthropomorphic connections and transforms the wrecked objects into poignant *memento mori*. The *memento mori* is extended by the beams of wood 'nailed cross-shaped' which are a subtle invocation of the traditional Christian iconography of death and renewal. A secular reinforcement of this theme is provided by the plants which flourish on top of and beside and around broken and damaged elements of the building, indicating the interconnectedness of decay and regeneration in the ruin.

Cooper deftly works exterior elements into the description of the interior by reiterating the images of dirt, disuse and neglect. When Simon, Barney, and Will enter, they find that the barn is littered with 'the clutter of years' and 'dust and debris' hinder their passage within.[202] The children have to move awkwardly and cautiously within the barn, a prerequisite of the ruin as a literary topos. Once again Cooper emphasises the liminal areas of the space: the overgrown windows, the broken door and the 'splintered edge' that scrapes Simon's arm as he 'wriggled in after Barney.'[203] In a passage that is replete with references to the passage of time, Cooper builds on the anthropomorphic and uncanny imagery established in her description of the barn, writing that

> ghostly in the shadows of corner and roof, stood a gipsy caravan, of exactly the same shape and pattern as the one in which they has met the painter of the Dark. [...] But of course it could not be the same. This caravan was not shiny-new, or newly painted. [...] It was a relic, an antique. Simon stared. It was as if he were meeting the great-great-grandfather of a boy he knew well, and finding that the old man had exactly the same face as the boy but immensely, impossibly aged.[204]

The caravan is an uncanny double; not only is it the double of the caravan Simon encountered earlier, but it also it echoes the barn it stands within in terms of its physical dilapidation. This sense of repetition and replication is deepened by Cooper's use of the adjective 'ghostly' which implies both that the caravan is haunted and that it has outlasted its normal span on earth through its continued and repetitious existence. Thus, Cooper deliberately evokes a sense of the uncanny and also reiterates the anthropomorphic imagery she used earlier. This anthropomorphism culminates the comparison of the caravan with an old man who has the same face as his great-great-grandson. In this image, Cooper recalls genealogy as a connection to the past while making it clear that genealogy is only a metaphor to help Simon—and implicitly the reader—to comprehend the true vehicle of the past; the lapsed space.

The Grey King and Silver on the Tree

There are two ruined cottages in the *Sequence*, although only the first, described in *The Grey King*, was ever a proper domestic space. The latter, in *Silver on the Tree*, is only afforded the briefest description. Will and Bran, running from the nightmarish Mari Llwyd, stumble across a deserted cottage:

> It was a building, [Will] saw. The strangest of buildings: a small low house made of blocks of grey stone, with a once-thatched roof covered in turf and straggling grass and a great swathe of branches blossoming white. A hawthorn tree was growing there in the ancient roof [. . .] a broken shutter hung from the window-frame; there was no glass.[205]

The broken shutter and empty window indicate that the limits of this space have been disrupted, opening it up to potential colonisation. The cottage, like so many ruins, has been colonised by plant life and the hawthorn tree on the roof further disrupts the parameters of the building.[206] In this cottage, Will and Bran confront a repressed aspect of the past; Bran has to admit that he has been afraid of the Mari Llwyd since he was a child. The botanical growth is indicative of the future and, once the Mari Llwyd is gone, the boys have to move on with their quest through the Lost Land.

The cottage in *The Grey King* is more significant in that it plays a more elaborate role in the narrative and is accordingly provided with a more detailed description. This cottage was Owen Davies' home and the place 'where Owen Davies had fought Caradog Prichard for the woman who had borne and deserted Bran.'[207] However, the cottage has been deserted since that time and because it is no longer used as a domestic space and its boundaries are disordered, it has, like Bran's family life, become a ruin. Cooper describes the moment when Will and John Rowlands come across 'a deserted cottage set back from the road: stone-walled, slate-roofed, sturdy-looking, but with the glass broken in its two small windows.'[208] When Will comes to the cottage later with Bran he notices that it has a 'low ruined wall' and that both its front door and back door are broken.[209] Will realises that the cottage is a ruin and that it is haunted, not only 'by the malice of the rising Dark'[210] but also, and more importantly, by the past.

The past is manifested in a number of ways inside the cottage; by memory, by genealogy, and by archaeology. For Bran, who has now lost Cafall as well as his mother, memories of Cafall come

> in a great rush [...] pictures of Cafall as a wobble-legged puppy, Cafall following him to school, Cafall learning the signals and commands of the working sheepdog, Cafall wet with rain, the long hair pressed flat in a straight parting along his spine, Cafall running, Cafall drinking from a stream, Cafall asleep with his chin warm on Bran's foot.[211]

These memories serve to illustrate how the past may be internalised. By using present participles, Cooper suggests that the past can be continuous, ever present, and vibrant once it is successfully internalised. However, readers of the *Sequence* will know that memory is always fragile and is subject to lapses and changes as time passes, especially as the Old Ones have the power to alter or destroy memories. As a result, no matter how vibrant Bran's memories may seem, they will inevitably decline and fail. Memory provides an unstable and unreliable means of access to the past.

More reliable access to the past may be provided—within the encompassing shell of the lapsed space, of course—by genealogy and archaeology. Genealogy focuses the internalisation of the past, focused, not in the mind, but in the body. Drout's arguments in favour of genealogy find new application here as Bran's body, or most specifically his blood, becomes a vehicle for the past. Owen Davies sees in Bran's actions a subconscious but undeniable echo of his mother, Gwen, and says: 'Blood will tell, they say. Blood will tell. She came here out of the mountains, out of darkness to this place, and so this is where you came too. Even without knowing, you came here.'[212] Here, the past is something that is assimilated and internalised unwittingly and, therefore, is unavoidable. In spite of his harsh-sounding words, Owen Davies cannot blame Bran for his genealogical link with the past. Indeed, Owen has made every effort to preserve other connections to the past and the newly apparent correlation between Bran and Gwen prompts him to produce another connection to the past: a letter. As an artefact, the letter provides an archaeological link to Owen's personal history and adds veracity to his story:

> He took a battered leather wallet out of his pocket and drew from an inner flap a small piece of paper. Unfolding it with great gentleness, he handed it to Bran. The paper was creased and fragile, almost parting at the folds; it bore only a few pencilled words, in a strangely rounded hand. His name is Bran. Thank you, Owen Davies. [...] 'It was all she left me of herself, Bran,' said his father. 'That note—and you.'[213]

Owen directly states that he sees both Bran and the note, both genealogy and archaeology, as signifiers of the past which help to reinforce and support memory. He has always been aware of these signs of the past—both Bran and the note are part of his everyday life—but within the lapsed topos these signs become especially relevant and Owen is finally forced come to terms with the past and to talk candidly and openly about the past to his son.

The ruin is the proper space for the past to be brought to light. Cooper makes it absolutely clear that it is the cottage itself that allows Bran to broach the subject of his mother's absence and enables Owen to reveal the details about Gwen that he had so jealously repressed for years. The house is the starting point of their conversation:

> 'This was my house,' Owen Davies said.
> 'No,' Bran said. 'Oh no.'
> 'Eleven years ago,' Davies said, 'I lived here.'
> 'I didn't know. I never thought. It's been empty since I can remember; I never thought of it being a proper house. I come here quite often if I'm out on my own. If it rains. Or just to sit. Sometimes'—he swallowed—'sometimes I pretend it's my house.'[214]

Bran and Owen view the cottage from very different perspectives. Owen speaks of it only in the past tense, whereas for Bran it is much more a part of his present. Their conflicting viewpoints are echoed by their disjointed conversation in which many of the sentences are fragmented, linguistically by hesitations and typographically by the narrator's commentary. Cooper's words visually break up the conversation, reflecting the 'cleavage'[215] in language opened by the lapsed space. For Owen, the cottage represents that which must be forgotten and kept hidden. He wants to enforce a separation between the past and present, and he admits as much to Bran: 'It was over, it was gone, I wanted to keep you away from the past.'[216] For Bran, the past is an enigma, a puzzle that he must figure out. Once Owen tells him the truth about his mother, Bran feels 'as if a door were opening somewhere within him [revealing a] new part of his mind that he had not been conscious of before.'[217] The lapsed space not only provides Bran with a genuine connection to the past, but also unlocks new possibilities for the future. In this space, the proper place for the revelation of buried, submerged, and repressed knowledge, Bran's 'buried and infinitely powerful nature'[218] is released, allowing him to realise his true nature as a 'child brought out of the past to grow up in the future [...] born to a fearsome destiny.'[219] For Bran, the events in the cottage have a large bearing on his future but it is only because his personal past is mediated through the lapsed topos that he is able to come to terms with his identity—and his potential—as the Pendragon.

Conclusion

As these examples show, Cooper reveals the 'layers and layers of time'[220] inherent in the landscape through the medium of the lapsed topos. In the *Sequence*, chthonic spaces and ruins provide the means by which the past may be 'rescued and made accessible.'[221] By including such spaces in her five texts, Cooper demonstrates that landscape is not a superficial covering, but a deeply embedded palimpsest in which the past and the present time are interconnected.

Having covered four fundamental topoi of literary landscapes: the sanctuary topos, the green topos, the roadway topos, and the lapsed topos, in my next and final chapter I will demonstrate the possibility of using these topoi to unlock the significance of landscapes in other children's texts. Topoanalysis allows for a textually supported reading of landscape elements organised in terms of their in-dwelling physical and symbolic features, enabling a reassessment of spaces and places which are so familiar as to be often overlooked. To see the innate significance in the literary landscape is to open new avenues of thought, allowing for the interrogation, investigation and, ultimately, the understanding of place. Whereas landscape had often been considered as of only peripheral importance to narrative action, this new approach allows us to see how landscape not only contains narrative, but supports and shapes it too.

Chapter Five
Applications

The purpose of this book is to provide a robust topoanalytical methodology for reading children's literature, using Cooper's work as a test case and providing a detailed comparative topoanalytical reading of Cooper's work in the process. Having shown how topoanalysis can provide a useful methodology for reading the landscapes of Cooper's fiction, I will now examine how the methodology informs the reading of other children's texts and suggest how the same methodological approach can be usefully applied to other texts. The scope of topoanalysis may be extended through the inclusion of new topoi which are not present in the landscapes of northern literature or through the application of topoi to abstract spaces and imaginary landscapes, and to human spaces such as the body or the mind.[1] However, it is impossible to explore all of these possibilities in such a limited space. Therefore, I will conclude by demonstrating how the structures in this book may be mapped on to other texts by providing three short topoanalytical readings.

John Masefield's *The Box of Delights* (1935), Alan Garner's *The Owl Service* (1967), and Meg Rosoff's *How I Live Now* (2004) are all set within the British landscape. The first two are fantasies, but the third is a fiction without recourse to the fantastic. The first two texts show several points of comparison with Cooper's *Sequence*. Bramwell notes the central importance of the green topos, as evidenced through the presence of Herne the Hunter in both Cooper and Masefield's texts[2] and Butler observes the tension between fantastic and historical spaces embedded within the palimpsestic landscapes of both Garner and Cooper's work.[3] Butler makes the connections between the landscape in Alan Garner's work and Cooper's (alongside Penelope Lively's and Diana Wynne Jones's) the subject of his study *Four British Fantasists* (2006). Like Cooper's *Sequence*, *The Box of Delights* and *The Owl Service* are both informed by a strong sense of landscape and by the intertextual history underlying the landscapes within the text. Rosoff's *How I Live Now* is at a remove from this mythic and ideological background, but nevertheless draws upon and functions through the same set of topoi as the other texts I have discussed.

John Masefield, *The Box of Delights* (1935)

Cooper was familiar with Masefield's work from an early age. In an interview with Leonard S. Marcus, she describes the radio adaptations of *The Box of Delights* and its prequel *The Midnight Folk* (1927) as opening 'all sorts of imaginative doors.'[4] Many of the fantastic elements present in *The Box of Delights* are echoed in Cooper's work, particularly *The Dark Is Rising*. Both texts feature magical artefacts which can transport characters to a world beyond their own. Mikkelsen notes that 'Kay Harker, who slips between past and present as easily as he turns the knob on the Box of Delights, is the forerunner of Will, who slips easily into the past by pressing against a handleless door.'[5] Similarly, the tramp Cole Hawling may act as a predecessor to Cooper's Hawkin; both are connected with the roadway topos and both are invited inside the protagonist's home on a snowy day. Most importantly, Masefield and Cooper share a concern for the relationship between character and environment which is evidenced through their use of tramp figures—Cole and Hawkin—who are deeply connected with the roadway topos, and through their use of Herne the Hunter. As I have demonstrated in Chapter Three, the tramp figure, as *mearcstapa*, is crucial to understanding the function of the figure in the landscape. Both authors make strong use of the figure of Herne the Hunter and emphasise his relationship with the wild green spaces beyond the civilised world. Thus, the clearest connection between Masefield's work and Cooper's is their use of landscape and their shared awareness of topological features. Accordingly, *The Box of Delights* readily responds to a topoanalytical reading, and the four topoi that have emerged in this study are here also fundamental to the text's function.

The Sanctuary Topos

As with many canonical children's books (Grahame, *The Wind in the Willows* 1908; Boston, *The Children of Green Knowe* 1954; Lively, *The Ghost of Thomas Kempe* 1973) the focus of the action in *The Box of Delights* is the house, Seekings, where Kay, the protagonist, lives with his guardians. Rather than providing a single description of the house, Masefield provides small glimpses throughout the novel with particular emphasis on the liminal spaces—the doors, windows, hallways, and thresholds—in the house. This emphasis on liminal sites places Seekings firmly within the tradition of the sanctuary topos. The position of the house within the sanctuary topos is so strong that Masefield toys with it, endowing Cole Hawling's magical play with the effect of dissolving, or appearing to dissolve, the solid boundaries of the house which delights and thrills the children. Masefield writes: '[Cole] walked across to the western wall and tapped the wainscot. It was all dark old wood there, with no hole or cranny in it, yet now, after he had touched it, there was a tiny double gate of bronze, with gilded pinnacles, in the wood'[6] and 'it seemed to the children that the ceiling above them opened into a forest in a tropical night.'[7] Cole's play is delightful and enthralling rather than disturbing and frightening because the children, and the child reader, are already certain that the limits of the house are robust and that the sanctity of the space is in no real danger. Even the mysterious and sinister clergymen who approach the house in search of the Box of Delights cannot pass the threshold, but are reduced to skulking at the windows.[8] Thus the space is kept safe.

A similar focus on limits and boundaries characterises the description of St. Michael's Cathedral where the Christmas Eve mass is celebrated in defiance of the dark and the evil abroad. As a cathedral, St. Michael's is obviously a religious sanctuary, but Masefield strengthens the cathedral's position within the established topos by emphasising the margins of the space and the sacred centre of the building. Thus, Masefield constructs it as a sanctuary on a symbolic as well as physical level. Manlove notes that the service and the church become 'a charmed circle in the midst of a larger and more implacable dark.'[9] Even though his primary interest is not in Masefield's landscapes, Manlove cannot but notice the sense that the cathedral is a 'circle,' a self-contained and complete space. Thus the building functions as separate, closed, and bounded space set apart from the rest of the landscape as discussed in Chapter One. In his description of Kay's arrival, Masefield writes 'the cathedral suddenly rose up in front of them with its enormous black bulk, its windows unlit, its tower transfigured with floodlight, its ledges, mouldings and carvings all topped with snow.'[10] These descriptions focus on the limits of the cathedral, emphasising the building's status as a sanctuary, set apart from the outside world. The distinction between this enclosed space and the rest of the landscape is made abundantly clear when Kay lights all the candles and lamps, creating a visual dichotomy between outside and inside, dark and light, profane and sacred.

The Green Topos
For much of the novel, the landscape is covered and concealed by snow, but despite the winter setting of the novel, the green space topos is a major feature of *The Box of Delights*. Through the magic of the Box, Kay enters an enchanted forest ruled by Herne the Hunter. The forest

> was dark from the great trees yet dappled with light [...] All the forest was full of life: all the birds were singing, insects were humming, dragonflies darting, butterflies wavering and settling. [...] while [Kay] gazed into the heart of summer and listened to the murmur and the singing, he heard another noise like the tinkling of little bells.[11]

The bells signal the arrival of Herne who then leads Kay through a strange, inverted Wild Hunt where they both take the forms of various animals; stags, ducks, and fish. Throughout the hunt, Kay and Herne are pursued by wolves, hawks, and pike, and thus Masefield evokes the patterns of life, death, and renewal. Kay feels great joy although the threat of death is imminent.[12] Herne's ability to shift at the very last moment into a different animal is a kind of symbolic renewal where life takes on different but related forms each time it is re-established after death. This episode bears some similarities to the Forth Branch of the *Mabinogion* where Gilfaethwy and Gwydion are turned into deer, swine, and wolves by Math ap Mathonwy. In the same Branch, Lleu Llaw Gyffes is forced to take the form of an eagle and Blodeuwedd to take the form of an owl.[13] According to Bramwell, Herne is a variation, albeit a restricted one, of the Green Man and so becomes an embodiment of the green space and, like Cooper's Herne, typifies the innate, amoral, primitive, and animal urges which are associated with the green space.[14]

The Roadway Topos

Many of the journeys in the book render landscape insignificant because of the 'go swift' power of the Box of Delights.[15] When Kay presses the little button, he can travel great distances at immense speed and so the landscape which Masefield takes such care to establish in the opening scenes is made almost redundant. However, when Kay travels by conventional means, Masefield reflects this by conforming to the traditional, typological descriptions of landscape. For example, like many personal journeys on the roadway topos, the railway journey, with which *The Box of Delights* opens, serves to establish Kay's character and a perspective on the landscape. Through the conceit of the train-journey, Masefield introduces the reader to many of the important sites in the novel and, cleverly, gives the reader a sense of the distances between places. Through the repeated references to King Arthur, he instils a mythic dimension to his text and a sense of the struggle between good and evil that will soon take place. Kay's introduction to the landscape is very literal; as he travels he studies a map of the area, noting the stations and landmarks that pass by. This scene establishes a connection between landscape elements and between the landscape and Kay. Kay is shown to be aware of and to reflect upon the various aspects of the landscape the train passes through. By using the map to identify the things he sees, he gains an awareness of the textual and metatextual significance of the landscape. The journey inculcates a knowledge and an awareness of the landscape in Kay and in the reader, an awareness which Kay demonstrates through his conversation with the strange clergymen. Kay says: "If you will look there, you will see Condicote Church ... Then, that wooded hill is King Arthur's Court: it's a Roman Camp ... Up there, is Broadbarrow, where there used to be a gibbet."[16] Thus, the railway journey, as with other personal journeys on the roadway topos, instils a sense of the geographical, mythic and historical elements of the landscape and shows how they are intricately and indelibly connected. Physical movement is accompanied by a symbolic trajectory; the train makes linear progress, but there is also a circular and retrogressive movement implied by the landmarks Kay identifies. This circular movement takes the reader from the centre of the modern civilisation out into the landscape and the past, travelling from contemporary religion, through Arthurian mythology, to Roman history, and finally to the pagan gibbet and its implication of the timeless, archetypal hanged man.[17] In articulating the embedded meaning of each element of the landscape, Kay demonstrates a deep cultural, geographical, and historical awareness of the landscape. By taking the reader on this journey, Masefield, through Kay, inculcates this same cultural awareness in the reader.

The Lapsed Topos

There are several lapsed spaces in *The Box of Delights*, from the subterranean cells in which Abner Brown's gang keep their prisoners and talk about the triumphs and disasters of the past, to the abandoned houses lining the Haunted Lane near Seekings which serve to confirm the presence of the past within the landscape. Haunted Lane 'was a way [Kay] did not like, for it was a very dark lane of old houses some of which were still marked with red crosses on the doors to show that within them, two centuries before, someone had lain sick of the plague.'[18] Although the plague-victims are long gone, Kay and the other children still hurry past the houses. The connection between the lapsed topos and the past is affirmed again when Abner Brown recalls that the Box of Delights was buried for a long time within the walls of a ruined castle:

> Before three I was on the site of Stiborough Castle; pitch dark night, gale blowing, rain coming down in torrents, the ivy blowing loose from the wall, bits of boughs flying everywhere, the Castle in such a mess of old broken stones and earth and bramble that I almost broke my neck half a dozen times.[19]

Here, Masefield draws on the hallmarks of the ruined space: the castle is abandoned, it no longer fulfils its original purpose, and there is a confusion of vegetative growth and collapsed masonry which, in turn, enforces a set of awkward movements upon anyone who tries to gain access. A further twist on this inception of the lapsed topos is the Box of Delights itself. The Box is ancient and through its magic, people can 'enter the Past at will'[20] and it is repeatedly buried in the ground or deep inside Kay's pocket and so is in constant association with the lapsed topos. Indeed, as an artefact passed from generation to generation it recalls both archaeology and genealogy, but it is through its association with lapsed and chthonic spaces throughout the novel that the Box is endowed with an indisputable topological connection with the past.

Alan Garner, *The Owl Service* (1967)

Neil Philip remarks that Garner's work is 'not conjured from some airy inspiration, but drawn from the rock, soil and sky of Cheshire.'[21] Hunt has observed, indeed, that 'Garner's countryside is precisely and deeply realized'[22] and that even Cooper 'does not use her backgrounds so faithfully.'[23] *The Owl Service* is set in Wales and is absolutely rooted in the solid forms of the landscape. The valley setting is richly evoked with precise descriptions and deft use of topoi. In this text in particular, Garner demonstrates exceptional skill in merging topoi, leaving the reader with a strong impression of a tightly wrought and claustrophobic landscape.

The Sanctuary Topos

The house at the centre of the narrative action conforms to the tropes of the sanctuary topos yet none of the characters really see the building as home. For Alison and Roger, it is a holiday home, for Gwyn, it is a place he desperately wants to escape. Nevertheless, Garner's descriptions evoke the topos and emphasise the physical limits of the house, windows, doors, stairways. The most significant encounters between characters occur in these liminal areas. Garner establishes the importance of the marginal spaces in the house early on when Gwyn and Alison investigate a scratching noise in the attic above her bedroom. Garner writes:

> Gwyn opened a door by the bedroom chimney. It was a narrow space like a cupboard, and there was a hatch in the ceiling [. . .] He brought a dry mop from the landing and placed the head against the door in the ceiling. The scratching had stopped. He pushed hard and the door banged open. Dust sank in a cloud. 'It's light,' said Gwyn. 'There's a pane of glass let in the roof.'[24]

By focusing on liminal areas such as the doors, the landing, the chimney, and the window in the roof and by drawing attention to these boundary areas, Garner establishes the house firmly within the conventions of the sanctuary topos. However, as I discussed in Chapter One, the attic may stand synecdochally for the house as a whole and the strange scratching implies that the physical sanctity of the house, and thus its rationality, has somehow been compromised. But, as Gwyn discovers, the attic space appears to be intact and undamaged. As the narrative unfolds, it becomes clear that what threatens the house and its inhabitants most is not an external force, but an internal power which needs to be released. Since the owl-patterned dinner-service from which the text takes its name, the sixteenth-century fresco on the billiard-room wall, and the stuffed owl all represent Blodeuwedd, and since Blodeuwedd is made of flowers we see that, like Cooper's Greenwitch or Masefield's Herne, she is essentially part of the green space. Through the dinner-service, the painting, and the stuffed owl, she has been unnaturally imprisoned within the sanctuary topos, and, working through Alison, she now tries to escape.[25] Thus, the forces that threaten the stability and security of the house are paradoxically enclosed within it. Whereas the normal narrative pattern involves reinforcing the boundaries of the sanctuary to keep danger out, Garner subverts this, showing a threatening force pent up within the house that needs to be channelled out. As a result the house, unlike the other sanctuaries I have discussed, becomes a place of extreme tension, danger, and violence.

The Roadway Topos

In this isolated valley, the urban landscape is condensed into a single shop 'in the front room of a cottage [...] [that] was furnished to be lived in',[26] but even in this greatly reduced space, Garner adheres to the conventions of the topos. In their conversation, Mrs Richards and Mrs Lewis-Jones conflate Roger, Gwyn, and Alison's identities with those of Gronw, Lleu, and Blodeuwedd.[27] It must be noted here that both Roger and Gwyn can take the parts of either Gronw or Lleu. Both are seen separately beside the Stone of Gronw and even at the end of the novel it remains unclear which of them is really Gronw. As if sensing this, the women dismiss the teenagers' status as individuals. Roger, as a stranger to the valley, also feels that his identity and status is impinged upon by the fact that the women speak Welsh instead of English.[28] From the snatches of conversation he overhears in English, Roger gleans the assumption that the women were talking 'about some Bigwig coming. I didn't catch it. They clicked into Welsh when they saw me. Some kind of centenary, is it? A festival? A May Queen, or something? I don't know.'[29] Through these seemingly off-hand comments, the carnivalesque associations of the roadway are apparent.

The roadway topos also presents itself in the form of the peat road that Alison and Gwyn walk. During this walk, Gwyn tells Alison what he knows about the valley, touching on elements of landscape, history and culture. Questions of personal identity also arise as the roadway encourages self-reflection through the presentation of a perspective on the landscape. Garner writes:

> The track was a peat road, now a sunken line on the mountain, and [Alison] climbed the bend that she had seen from the river [...] and soon she was round the shoulder and the house was hidden. Alison rested on a slate outcrop. The peat road went up a fold in the mountain made by the stream, but led away from the water.[30]

In this text, the house and its garden are secluded and so are isolated from the rest of the landscape. Here, for the first time, Garner allows his reader a panoramic view of the whole valley. The roadway topos enables the reader to see how the fictional landscape is constructed; it provides a sense of the distance between the other spaces. The roadway topos, being part of the built environment, also allows Garner to articulate the geographic, social, and economic culture of the landscape without recourse to lengthy descriptions. The fact that the peat road is 'sunken' in a 'fold in the mountain' draws on the historical connotations of the lapsed topos. Indeed, Alison feels 'it could be a thousand years ago'.[31]

But the roadway topos, as I have discussed, does not just provide a perspective of the landscape; it also draws out questions of personal identity. Like some other roadways I have discussed, this one has both vertical and horizontal frames; it reaches into the embedded past as well as paving the way into the future. The stratified layers of the peat road suggest that, in this text, personal identity is fundamentally rooted in the landscape and in its mythic and historical substrata. Just as the deep layers of soil and time are laid in the same place, so too layers of human identity are laid one on top of the other so that they eventually become a single homogenous mass. Thus Alison, Gwyn, and Roger are subsumed into the mythic identities of Blodeuwedd, Gronw, and Lleu Llaw Gyffes. But in the present time, on the surface of the landscape, the roadway also stretches ahead, metaphorically reaching into the future, and so as Gwyn and Alison walk along the peat road they discuss their plans for the future:

> 'I can see you in about thirty years,' said Alison. 'You'll be Professor of Welsh!'
> 'Not me. I've got to get out of this place [...] At the moment the likely chance is I'll be behind a shop counter in a couple of months.'[32]

In order to escape this prescribed fate, Gwyn determines to change himself and admits he has bought 'a set of records [that] teach you how to speak properly.'[33] For Gwyn, his thick Welsh accent is the origin and embodiment of his desperate economic and social situation and believes that by changing his accent he will effect a change in his social standing. He sees this future self as a more accurate reflection of his personality and is frustrated by Alison's lack of interest in her own future. For Gwyn, the absence of a plan for the future is akin to an absence of identity and he challenges her 'to be yourself, for a change.'[34] Here, Garner draws upon the tropes and conventions of the roadway topos as a space which fosters an awareness of the landscape as a whole and encourages self-reflection and growth.

The Green Topos

The green space topos plays a major role in *The Owl Service*. The house is surrounded by expansive gardens and has a separate, hedged-in kitchen garden. The house and its gardens are set within a wide valley with a river, woods and farmlands. Several scenes are set within these green spaces and Garner appears to draw upon the conventions of the topos in his descriptions. For example:

> The wood lay still. The air throbbed with insects, and flies hovered and disappeared and hovered. Meadowsweet grew in the midst of flowers, and the sun glinted on the threads of caterpillars which hung from the trees as thick as rain.[35]

Here, Garner draws together the dialectic associations of the topos as a space of death and a space of renewal. The meadowsweet which features earlier in the novel can either be sweet and fragrant or stinking. The caterpillars, in the magical process of cocooning, are a symbol of new life and renewal but this sense of renewal is underscored by the presence of the flies which are associated with death and decay.

An image and a place Garner frequently returns to in the novel is the riverbank beside the Stone of Gronw. Initially the riverbank and the surrounding valley are presented as a version of the pleasance. Garner writes:

> Roger splashed through the shallows to the bank. A slab of rock stood out of the ground close by him, and he sprawled backwards into the foam of meadowsweet that grew thickly round its base. He gathered the stems in his arms and pulled the milky heads down over his face to shield him from the sun. [...] The mountains were gentle in the heat. The ridge above the house, crowned with a grove of fir trees, looked black against the summer light. He breathed the cool sweet air of the flowers. He felt the sun drag deep in his limbs.[36]

Here, the six essential elements of the pleasance—grass, trees, shade, flowing water, wild flowers, and a gentle breeze—are present, giving the reader the impression that this is a site for drowsy relaxation and dreaming.[37] However, Roger's idyll is soon interrupted by a scream and a cold wind.[38] We expect all aspects of the green topos to contain some hint of or reference to death but as *The Owl Service* goes on it becomes clear that the sense of death is not only pervasive but dominant in the valley. The presence of the stone of Gronw, where Lleu Llaw Gyffes and Gronw both, in turn, murdered one another, establishes deep connotations of death in the landscape. It is revealed that there are no fish in the river and that farm animals refuse to stay put within the bounds of the farms. Even the kitchen garden, which Gwyn and Alison set aside as a secret place to meet, is left unused and so becomes a sterile parody of the lovers' garden. This is a 'sick valley'[39] not a vibrant, revitalising green space. The cycles of life, death, and renewal have been interrupted and, like a broken record, are stuck in the death stage.[40] The deaths of Lleu and Gronw are 'the only thing that's ever happened in the valley.'[41]

The Lapsed Topos

The sickness of the valley is a symptom of its status as a lapsed space. The valley is not a green space, but a lapsed space, sunk in upon or perhaps gouged out of the palimpsestic layers of time. Although Butler does not recognise the underlying topoanalytical significance of the valley, he does acknowledge that it 'is not "haunted," a word that would imply an anomalous intrusion of the past into the present',[42] but suggests that in this place the past is 'still happening.'[43] Within this valley, the past is made continually present. As I discussed in Chapter Four, Butler's chief concern is with archaeology and he notes that an 'archaeological and historical focus naturally manifests itself in Garner's writing.'[44] Indeed much of the past is signalled through the appearance of artefacts such as the owl service, the fresco, the tiny kelticraft owl, and, of course, the Stone of Gronw itself. However, genealogy plays an equally important role in moderating the past within the novel and it becomes clear that Alison, Roger, and Gwyn are the inheritors of Blodeuedded, Gronw, and Lleu Llaw Gyffes just as Nancy, Huw, and Bertram were in the preceding generation. In Gwyn's case, this genealogical link is especially clear as he is Nancy and Huw Halfbacon's son and a direct descendent of Gronw. Huw tells Gwyn that he is 'the lord in blood to this valley.'[45] However, as Huw makes clear, both the archaeological and genealogical connections with the past are redundant without the framing and supporting topological connection with the past which is provided by the valley.

Meg Rosoff, *How I Live Now* (2004)

Although not written out of a British literary tradition, and therefore at a certain remove from the mythic substrata which provide Masefield, Garner, and, indeed Cooper with material for their narratives, and although it does not subscribe to the mythological and fantastic conventions and is not modelled on intertexts, Rosoff's *How I Live Now* nevertheless draws upon and functions through the same topoi as the texts examined so far. Since it is undefined historically and geographically, Rosoff's landscape is constructed out of literary commonplaces. This suggests that the topoi identified in this study have become influential and potent factors in children's literature which can be invoked without the need for direct or conscious intertexts.

The Sanctuary Topos

The early part of *How I Live Now* is centred on the home and its idyllic pastoral surroundings. Even though the building is 'practically falling down'[46] and the front door is 'left open Whenever [sic] it's not actually snowing,'[47] it is saved from ruination by a strong sense of its function as a family home and as a nexus for the care and love that Daisy and the other children feel there. The farmhouse is very much the centre of their world and of the text itself as Rosoff adheres to the home-away-home pattern typical of children's fiction as war forces the children to leave the farm and then struggle to find, or indeed retrieve, a new sense of home and belonging. This narrative patterning is repeated in many texts which deal with the alienating effects of war including Holm's *I Am David*, (1963), Bawden's *Carrie's War*, (1973) and Magorian's *Goodnight Mr. Tom*, (1981). As with other versions of the sanctuary topos, this house is described in terms of its limits with a strong emphasis on stairways and passageways, doors and windows, creating a sense of the house as a place apart from the rest of the world. The house is made up of 'funny corridors that don't seem to lead anywhere and tiny bedrooms with slanty ceilings hidden away at the top of stairs. The stairs all creak and there are no curtains on any of the windows.'[48] Daisy recognises the significance of this space immediately, knowing that it is 'the safest place I'd ever been in my life.'[49] The liminality of this house is especially appealing to Daisy as it reflects her own emotional and physical liminality. Torn with grief for her dead mother and full of resentment for her father's new wife, Daisy is emotionally insecure. Her insecurities are reflected and compounded by the instability of her body. Daisy's eating disorder causes her to wear away the limits of her body, always shrinking her personal space down. Yet she finds comfort in her new home. The perfect articulation of this is when she covers herself with a 'black-sheep blanket'[50] which, instead of masking her problems, allows them to be externalised and so to find expression. The black sheep blanket demonstrates that Daisy has come home to a place where difference is accepted and celebrated.

The Green Topos

The house is set within a farm although, like the house, the borders of the farm are slightly disturbed because the animals roam freely around the space. The garden which lies behind the house is altogether more rigid in its categorisation and spatialisation and is enclosed by high brick walls. This garden draws the twin symbols of death and rebirth together through the 'tons of flowers blooming already in all shades of white'[51] and the 'stone angel about the size of a child, very worn, with folded wings and Piper told me it was a child who lived in the house hundreds of years ago and is buried in the garden.'[52] Here, the narrative shift between the past and present tenses implies that a continuum of time is inherent in this space. The pleasance also makes an appearance when Daisy and her cousins go fishing. In keeping with the conventions of the topos Daisy lies dreaming beside a river, in the sun. Rosoff-as-Daisy writes, 'I made a nest for myself by trampling down a little patch in the tall grass and put the blanket down and lay very still and as the sun rose up in the sky I warmed up even more [...] I was thinking about almost nothing'.[53] This scene establishes the close relationship between the children and nature, and suggests that the community they will make apart from the world of adults is peaceful, organic, and idyllic. The sexual relationship between Daisy and Edmond and the abundance of references to bodies and to bodily functions like eating and drinking dissuades us from assuming that this is an Edenic or prelapsarian space.

The physicality of this space and, simultaneously, the bond between child and nature, is strengthened when Daisy makes a 'nest' for herself in the grass. Bachelard notes that a nest is 'a house built by and for the body, taking form from the inside [...] the instrument that prescribes a circular form for the nest is nothing else but the body of the bird [so that] the house is a bird's very person'.[54] Daisy impresses herself upon her environment and in so doing allows the environment to imprint itself upon her. The nest is the perfect synthesis of body and space. The nest is a sanctuary at a remove from the home and so Rosoff indicates the beginning of a shift from the built to the natural environment, from the centrality of the home to the wider world, which will prescribe the course of the narrative. Daisy's decision to make a nest indicates that, for her, the sanctuary topos is not a geographical location, but a kind of space, one that is both bodily and topological. For Daisy, as we shall see, topoi are constructed as a result of human action rather than a mere coincidence of geography. Her close relationship with her environment is bound up with her ability to impress herself upon her surroundings and to accept the impact of environmental factors on her life. It is this willingness to adopt and to adapt to her surroundings that enables Daisy to survive the dislocation and trauma of the war.

The Roadway Topos

For much of the text, Rosoff's protagonists are consciously isolated from other people, both physically and temperamentally. There is a strong cult of individuality in the text. When the street topos makes its appearance and Rosoff adheres to the conventional descriptions of the street, it is used to underline this particular aspect of the novel. In this quite properly convoluted passage (compare Barney at the carnival in Trewissick, Chapter 3), Daisy uses the street sub-topos to explain to the reader what kind of person her cousin Isaac is:

> For instance, if you were walking in town on market day and there were tons of people milling around, you would never have to worry about losing him in the crowd even if you totally forgot he was there and got separated for ages. You could zig and zag and make turns on a sudden whim and stop for tea and cut across a few back streets and decide that today would be a good time to do something totally different and try that bakery that none of you normally went to when in actual fact you had plenty of bread at home already so there'd be no reason to be in a bakery at all, and the next time you'd look up Isaac would be right at your elbow, totally casual, like he'd been there all along or possibly just followed your train of thought through the crowd.[55]

Here, Rosoff brings the carnivalesque associations of the street into play. This unusually long sentence, with its sub-clauses and convoluted structure echoes the circuitous route Daisy describes. The interplay of pronouns whereby the second person 'you' and presumably the reader is substituted for the narrative 'I' demonstrates the collapse of personal identity which is associated with the street. Paradoxically, Rosoff uses the description of the crowded street to illuminate Isaac's character. He is unlike other people and he demonstrates his unique personality by not becoming lost or confused in the crowd. Where the street breaks down other characters, it only serves to reinforce Isaac's sense of self.

Applications • 181

How I Live Now is structured as a series of journeys. The novel opens with Daisy's arrival in England from New York, and much of the central plot is given over to her journey with Piper away from, and then back towards, Gateshead Farm. The final section of the book is given over to Daisy's extradition to America and her final pilgrimage back to the farm and to her cousins. In many children's texts, as Mikkelsen notes, 'place is projected onto whatever growth patterns of character that the author is dramatizing.'[56] Rosoff's novel is no exception and so the physical journeys undertaken by Daisy and Piper are also psychological and symbolic journeys. Theirs is not simply an evacuation from and a voyage back towards home, but a journey from peace to war and from innocence to experience. Rosoff also forges a strong connection between roadways and political and administrative change; the primary effect of war is to dislocate the children from their home and the adults in the novel refer to the war euphemistically as 'the Situation On the Roads'.[57] Significantly, the occupying forces establish checkpoints all along the roads. Rosoff uses one of these checkpoints to mark the exact moment of transition between these symbolic and psychological states. On the road between an orchard where they are put to work and the house where they are billeted, Daisy and Piper witness two men being shot by enemy soldiers:

> In an almost lazy kind of way the check-point guy [...] raised his gun and pulled the trigger and there was a loud crack and part of Joe's face exploded and there was blood everywhere and he fell over out of the truck into the road. [...] I heard about a hundred shots from a machine gun and the momentum of the blasts hurled Major M. backwards across the road away from Joe with blood welling up in holes all over him [...] and our driver didn't wait around to see what might happen next but just stepped on the gas and as we drove away I thought I felt tears on my face but when I put my hand up to wipe them it turned out to be blood.[58]

At this moment the children's experience of the political situation shifts from one of hostile occupation to active conflict. After these killings the enemy soldiers begin to make house-to-house raids and to execute civilians. The escalation of violence is mirrored in the psychological and emotional developments in Daisy. By replacing the tears, which would signify sympathy and innocence, with blood, and its connotations of death and passion, Rosoff indicates that Daisy has moved from a passive acceptance of her place in the war to an active role, enabling her to make her own decisions and to fend for herself. The confirmation of this internal change is external action; following the killings, Daisy and Piper decide to run away back to Gateshead Farm where Edmond and Isaac are billeted.

Avoiding the roads which are occupied by the enemy, Daisy and Piper cannot take a prescribed route to Gateshead. They have to inscribe their own path through the countryside. In making their own way home the girls open themselves to a new connection with the landscape. They trace new paths through the fields and woods, imprinting their bodies on their surroundings. In turn the earth makes its own impression on them, leaving their feet blistered and their bodies scarred so that 'against the whiteness [of their skin] every mark standing out in bright red hieroglyphics telling the story of our journey.'[59] As when Daisy made the nest earlier in the text, the girls are in such close contact with the environment that a synthesis of human body and place is achieved. Their bodies have not only enacted the journey, but have become the journey. Daisy and Piper become a part of the roadway topos.

Indeed, Daisy and Piper's connection with the landscape runs so deep that even when they reach their farm, they do not move back into the house because, they realise, 'we'd turned a little wild and couldn't live in a normal house any more.'[60] This wildness is not the only effect of the journey; Daisy realises that the journey has forced her to forge a 'new incarnation'[61] of herself, casting herself as a fearless protector and a capable provider. Even though this 'new incarnation' is pre-emptively suggested by the nest she makes in the pleasance, Daisy only recognises it at the very end of the journey, when she and Piper finally reach the farmhouse. So, while Rosoff draws a clear connection between the completion of Daisy's newfound identity and the conclusion of her journey, she has already made it clear that Daisy always had the power and the ability to shape her environment and to allow the environment to shape her too.

The Lapsed Topos

On their journey, Daisy and Piper stay in a ruin. It 'looked like a falling-down hut and it was a little way off the path and hadn't been burned so we climbed over the wall and crashed our way through the tangled thorns and grass until we got to it and it was big enough to lie down in and fairly dry inside though it smelled like rotten wood.'[62] Here, Rosoff invokes the conventional representations of the lapsed space: the boundaries of the hut are disordered and as with the other ruined spaces I have discussed, the hut can only be accessed through unusual and ungraceful movements. If these signs were not enough to convince a reader of the hut's status as a ruin, Rosoff also draws upon the relationship between life and death which so often characterises these spaces. The rich botanical growth is a sharp contrast to the smell of rotting wood and the suggestion that the owner of the hut is now dead. Daisy and Piper, in need of a safe place to stay, seal up the gaps in the ruin's structure with a groundsheet. With its boundaries re-established the hut becomes a different kind of space; by occupying the hut and claiming it as their own, Daisy and Piper turn it into a kind of sanctuary. Daisy affirms her ownership of the space, and therefore the significance of the space, by describing it as 'our little hut' and 'our happy home'.[63]

There are other ruins in the text: Gateshead Farm is ruined through the massacre of all its inhabitants, and when Daisy and Piper finally get home they discover that the farmhouse is 'deserted, dark and silent [and] even the honey coloured stone had the feeling of something abandoned.'[64] When Daisy finally enters the house she finds that it 'was pretty well trashed [...] there were broken dishes everywhere and the ones that weren't broken were caked and filthy and the toilets were overflowing and there was mud and dirt all over the rugs.'[65] The house is effectively ruined because its connotations of safety and security have been overthrown. The disordered furniture serves as a metaphor for the disruption of domestic routine. However, Rosoff notes that none of the windows are broken and thus suggests that the house may still be salvaged and that, under the right conditions, it can become a sanctuary again. Indeed, when Daisy returns to England after the war, the house has been restored as a place of comfort and safety and it is once more 'home.'[66]

On the other hand, Edmond, who has been badly psychologically and physically damaged by the war, cannot accept that the house is a sanctuary. For him it is still a ruin because he has lost the ability to feel safe anywhere. He asserts his control over space, and over his life, through the endless reconstruction of boundaries, and in Rosoff's second description of the garden, she notes how Edmond cannot bear to see spaces run wild and so boundaries and limits are rigidly, even cruelly enforced and the flowers are 'cut and pinioned into cruel horizontals against the wall.'[67] Here, the garden retains its connotations of life and death but the process of renewal has become something artificial and enforced rather than something organic. The result is unsettling for both Daisy and the reader because Edmond's garden disrupts and subverts the tropes which make the green space a recognisable topos. Through this sense of spatial and topical unease, Rosoff invites the reader to share in Edmond's discomfort and so to sympathise with him. The reader who expects the reassurance of stable, reliable topoi is, inevitably, dismayed by this discomforting and disturbing space. Paradoxically, such discomfort could not be evoked if Rosoff had not adhered so closely to the conventions of the other topoi throughout the novel. Even though Rosoff does not follow in the mythic and literary traditions of the other authors I have discussed, she has a palpable and incontrovertible awareness of the significance of topoi, and the effect of writing back against them, which demonstrates their fundamental importance in establishing the force of her work.

Overview

Within literature, 'places mean'[68] and each kind of space has its own resonance, its own wealth of connotations. There is an organic and interactive relationship between narrative meaning and geographical space within literature. As these three short readings demonstrate, the critical models outlined in this book are readily applicable to a range of texts which, in turn, suggests that the topoi I have identified are crucial to children's literature set within the British landscape. I have demonstrated that the four fundamental topoi have remained stable in their form and symbolic function from the time of their earliest inception to that of their most recent expression. It is clear that the central topoi of children's literature have a long provenance and that the landscapes of early English literature have continued to be influential even when modern authors are not conscious of the influence of this tradition. Their stable and ubiquitous nature means that landscape topoi have become tropes, even stereotypes, which occur and recur to such an extent that even in the absence of extensive descriptions, the fictional landscape of any text may still be read topoanalytically. The reader who is aware of the significance of landscape elements and attuned to the literary conventions and traditions surrounding the representations of landscape will recognise that the same kinds of scenes take place within and are supported and upheld by the same kinds of spaces.

It is clear, then, how the scope of this study may be extended. Whereas Cooper's position in the canon and her awareness of landscape as a physical, mythopoeic, and historical space and her awareness of the importance of liminal interstices in domestic fantasy make *The Dark Is Rising Sequence* particularly fertile ground for the testing and development of such an approach, I hope I have established the generic value of my methodological critical approach by demonstrating how the topoi identified and analysed in this book may be applied to both the solid geographic and abstract human spaces in literature. In offering a means of examining landscape, topoanalysis offers a new critical method for the study and deeper understanding of children's literature. The methodology I have developed here will, I hope, assist in prompting close systematic readings of landscape elements. In tracing the development of these topoi from their earliest inception to their most recent expression, this book has highlighted the long tradition which underlies these representational conventions. The topoi I have identified and analysed have been invariably replicated and reproduced for so long that they have been assimilated almost to the point of submersion in the literary canon. In bringing landscape from a vague background presence to the forefront of critical study, this study demonstrates both the need and the potential for further structural readings of the landscapes in children's literature.

Notes

Notes to the Introduction

1. Anne H. Lundin, *Constructing the Canon of Children's Literature: Beyond Library Walls and Ivory Towers* (New York: Routledge, 2004), 112–119.
2. David Rudd, ed., *The Routledge Companion to Children's Literature* (Abingdon: Routledge, 2010), xiv.
3. Peter Hunt, 'Landscapes and Journeys, Metaphors and Maps: The Distinctive Feature of English Fantasy,' *Children's Literature Association Quarterly* 12/1 (1987): 11.
4. Stephen Daniels and Simon Rycroft, 'Mapping the Modern City: Alan Sillitoe's Nottingham Novels,' *Transactions of the Institute of British Geographers* 18/4 (1993): 460.
5. Robert Dunbar, 'It's the way we tell 'em: voices from Ulster Children's Fiction' in *Divided Worlds*, ed. Mary Shine Thompson and Valerie Coghlan (Dublin: Four Courts Press, 2007), 62.
6. Katherine Paterson, *A Sense of Wonder: On Reading and Writing Books for Children* (New York: Plume, 1995), 95.
7. Christine L. Krueger, *Functions of Victorian Culture at the Present Time* (Athens, Ohio: Ohio University Press, 2002), xi–xx.
8. Richard Muir, *Approaches to Landscape* (London: Macmillan, 1999), xiii.
9. Michel Foucault, 'Of Other Spaces,' trans. Jay Miskowiec, *Diacritics*, 16 (1986): 22.
10. Pauline Dewan, *The House as Setting, Symbol and Structural Motif in Children's Literature* (Lewiston, New York: The Edwin Mellen Press, 2004), 11.
11. Stephen Siddall, *Landscape and Literature* (Cambridge: Cambridge University Press, 2009), 7.
12. Matthew Johnson, *Ideas of Landscape* (Oxford: Blackwell, 2007), 1.
13. Mike Crang, *Cultural Geography* (London: Routledge, 1998), 43. Other geographers such as Michael Bunce (1994), Richard Muir (1999), Matthew Johnson (2007), and John Wylie (2007) have expressed similar views.
14. For instance, Gillian Tindall (1991), Pauline Dewan (2004), Margaret Drabble (2009;1979), and Stephen Siddall (2009) make no attempt to engage

with any geographical, phenomenological or environmental theories. It is, perhaps, only ecocritics such as Greg Garrard (2004) and Gillian Rudd (2007) that make any connection between literature and environment.
15. Peter Hunt, *An Introduction to Children's Literature* (Oxford: Oxford University Press, 1994), 179.
16. Tony Watkins, 'Space History and Culture: The Setting of Children's Literature' in *Understanding Children's Literature: Key Essays from the Second Edition of the International Companion Encyclopedia of Children's Literature*, ed. Peter Hunt (London and New York: Routledge, 2005), 50–72, 67.
17. Ibid.
18. Alan Gussow and Richard Wilbur, *A Sense of Place: The Artist and the American Land* (New York: Seabury, 1971), 27.
19. Bill Ashcroft, Gareth Griffiths, and Helen Tiffin, eds., *Post-Colonial Studies: The Key Concepts* (London and New York: Routledge, 1998), 182.
20. Vladimir Propp, *Morphology of the Folktale*, trans. Laurence Scott (Austin: University of Texas Press, 1968), 20.
21. Propp, *Morphology of the Folktale*, xxv.
22. Carl Ortwin Sauer, *Land and Life: A Selection from the Writings of Carl Ortwin Sauer*, ed. John Leighly (Berkeley: University of California Press, 1963), 318.
23. Carl Ortwin Sauer, quoted in E. C. Hayes, ed., *Recent Developments in the Social Sciences* (Hagerstown, Maryland: Lippincott Series in Sociology, 1927), 186.
24. Ibid., 186.
25. The natural succession of landscape history from morphology is evident in Sauer's own career. By the early 1950s he had moved away from simple morphological studies and towards integrating morphology with the principles of landscape history.
26. Jay Appleton, *The Experience of Landscape* (London: Wiley, 1975), 2.
27. Yi-Fu Tuan, *Topophilia: A Study of Environmental Perception, Attitudes and Values* (Upper Saddle River, New Jersey: Prentice Hall, 1974), 133.
28. Muir, *Approaches to Landscape*, 25.
29. W.G. Hoskins, *The Making of the English Landscape* (London: Penguin, 1985), 12.
30. Leibniz, quoted in Edward S. Casey, *Getting Back Into Place: Toward a Renewed Understanding of the Place-World* (Indianapolis: Indiana University Press, 1993), 7.
31. Simon Schama, *Landscape and Memory* (London: HarperCollins, 1995), 16.
32. Jacquetta Hawkes, *A Land* (London: The Cresset Press, 1953), 2.
33. Ibid., 4.
34. Schama, *Landscape and Memory*, 7.
35. Ibid., 16.
36. James S. Ackerman, 'Villard de Honnecourt's Drawings of Reims Cathedral: A Study in Architectural Representation,' *Artibus et Historiae*, 18/35 (1997): 41.

37. Ernst Robert Curtius, *European Literature and The Latin Middle Ages*. trans. Willard R. Trask (London and Henley: Routledge and Kegan Paul, 1953), 184.
38. See Stephen Siddall, *Landscape and Literature* , 7 and Paul Farley and Michael Symmons Roberts, *Edgelands: Journeys into England's True Wilderness* (London: Jonathan Cape, 2011), 26.
39. Genesis B in A. N. Doane, ed., *The Saxon Genesis: An Edition of the West Saxon Genesis B and the Old Saxon Vatican Genesis* (Madison, Wisconsin: University of Wisconsin Press, 1991), 212–213.
40. See Jane Suzanne Carroll, 'Its Own Place: Mindscape and Landscape in Two Children's Texts,' *The Journal of Children's Literature Studies*, 8/1 (2011): 18–33.
41. Charles Butler, *Four British Fantasists: Place and Culture in the Children's Fantasies of Penelope Lively, Alan Garner, Diana Wynne Jones and Susan Cooper* (Lanham, Maryland and Oxford: The Children's Literature Association and The Scarecrow Press, 2006), 1.
42. Margaret Parish, 'Pick of the Paperbacks: Fantasy,' *The English Journal* 66/7 (1977): 91.
43. Linda Bachelder, Patricia Kelly, Donald Kenney, and Robert Small, 'Young Adult Literature: Looking Backward: Trying to Find the Classic Young Adult Novel,' *The English Journal* 69/6 (1980): 87.
44. The most recent of these reprints was issued to coincide with the release of *The Seeker*. See note 45.
45. David L. Cunningham, Dir., *The Seeker* (Walden Media, 2007).
46. Nina Mikkelsen, *Susan Cooper* (New York: Twayne Publishers, 1998), vii.
47. Sheila Egoff, *Thursday's Child: Trends and Patterns in Contemporary Children's Literature*, (Chicago: American Library Association, 1981), 84.
48. Mikkelsen, *Susan Cooper*, viii.
49. Mary Harns Veeder, 'Gender and Empowerment in Susan Cooper's *The Dark Is Rising* Sequence,' *Children's Literature Association Quarterly* 16/1 (1991): 11–16.
50. See David Rees, *What Do Draculas Do? Essays on Contemporary Writers of Fiction for Children and Young Adults* (Methuen, New Jersey and London: The Scarecrow Press, 1990), 175–189.
51. M. Daphne Kutzer, 'Thatchers and Thatcherites: Lost and Found Empires in Three British Fantasies,' *The Lion and the Unicorn* 22/2 (1998): 209.
52. Timothy Rex Wadham, 'Light from the Lost Land: A Contextual Response to Susan Cooper's *The Dark Is Rising Sequence*' (PhD diss., University of Texas at Arlington, 1994), 11.
53. Dick Abrahamson and Barbara Kiefer, 'Young Adult Literature: Books Worth Putting on Your Summer Reading List,' *The English Journal* 73/4 (1984): 91.
54. Colin Manlove, *From Alice to Harry Potter: Children's Fantasy in England* (Christchurch: Cybereditions, 2003), 130.
55. Wadham, 'Light from the Lost Land,' 88.

56. Margaret Esmonde, Essays in *Fantasiae, The Dark Is Rising: Work in Progress*, 6, quoted Wadham, 'Light from the Lost Land,' 88.
57. Susan Cooper, email to author, August 22, 2006.
58. Leonard S. Marcus, *The Wand in the Word: Conversations with Writers of Fantasy* (Massachusetts: Candlewick Press, 2006), 43–44.
59. Susan Cooper, email to author, August 22, 2006.
60. Susan Cooper, *Dreams and Wishes: Essays on Writing for Children* (New York: McElderry, 1996): 93.
61. Butler, *Four British Fantasists*, 44.
62. Susan Cooper, Letter to Charles Butler, quoted in Butler, *Four British Fantasists*, 47.
63. L. Dudley Stamp, 'Reviews,' *Geographical Journal* 121 (1951): 512.
64. Muir, *Approaches to Landscape*, 26.
65. Butler, *Four British Fantasists*, 47.
66. Cooper, *Dreams and Wishes*, 72.
67. Ibid., 187.
68. Ibid., 73.
69. Susan Cooper's works in print are *Mandrake* (1964), *Over Sea, Under Stone* (1965), *Dawn of Fear* (1970), *The Dark Is Rising* (1973), *Greenwitch* (1974), *The Grey King* (1975), *Silver on the Tree* (1977), *Seaward* (1983), *The Boggart* (1993), *The Boggart and the Monster* (1997), *King of Shadows* (1999), *Green Boy* (2002), *Victory* (2006). Her picture books are *Jethro and the Jumbie* (1979), *The Silver Cow* (1983), *The Selkie Girl* (1986), *Matthew's Dragon* (1991), *Tam Lin* (1991), *Danny and the Kings* (1993), *Frog* (2002), and *The Magician's Boy* (2005).
70. Susan Cooper, *Over Sea, Under Stone* (London: Puffin, 1968; first published 1965), 7.
71. See Marcus, *The Wand in The Word*, 46.
72. Cooper, *Dreams and Wishes*, 193. In the same interview Cooper says that she wrote the *Sequence* with two ordnance survey maps pinned up in her study.
73. Mikkelsen, *Susan Cooper*, 97–98.
74. Susan Cooper, *The Grey King* (London: Puffin Books, 1977; first published 1975), 27.
75. The Royal Commission on the Ancient and Historical Monuments and Constructions in Wales and Monmouthshire, *An Inventory of the Ancient Monuments in Wales and Monmouthshire, VI County of Merioneth* (London: His Majesty's Stationery Office, 1921), 114.
76. Michael Drout, 'Reading the Signs of Light: Anglo-Saxonism, Education and Obedience in Susan Cooper's *The Dark is Rising*,' *The Lion and the Unicorn* 21/12 (1997): 231.
77. Donna R. White, *A Century of Welsh Myth in Children's Literature* (Westport, CT: Greenwood Press, 1998), 124.
78. Butler, *Four British Fantasists*, 15.

79. Marcus, *The Wand in the Word*, 42.
80. Butler, *Four British Fantasists*, 18.
81. I am deeply indebted to Pauline Adams, Librarian and Archivist, Somerville College, Oxford, for this information. Pauline Adams, email to author, April 1, 2009.
82. Cooper, *Dreams and Wishes*, 103.
83. Ibid.
84. Drout, 'Reading the Signs of Light,' 232.
85. Cooper, *Over Sea, Under Stone*, 71.
86. *Maxims II* in Elliott Van Kirk Dobbie, *The Anglo-Saxon Minor Poems* (New York: Columbia University Press, 1942), 55–57, lines 51–55. My translation.
87. See Colin Manlove, *From Alice to Harry Potter*, 129.
88. Susan Cooper quoted by Carmen Diana Dearden, 'Memories of Meeting Worlds or Close Encounters of the Fourth Kind,' *Bookbird: A Journal of International Children's Literature* 48/1 (2010): 60.
89. These poems and many of the others which I will refer to over the course of this study may be found in the original Old English form in George Philip Krapp and Elliott Van Kirk Dobbie, eds, *The Exeter Book* (New York: Columbia University Press, 1936).
90. Gaston Bachelard, *The Poetics of Space*, trans. Marie Jolas (Boston: Beacon Press, 1994; first published as *La poétique de l'espace*, 1958), 8.

Notes to Chapter One

1. Susan Isaacs quoted in Joseph Rykwet, *On Adam's House in Paradise: The Idea of the Primitive Hut in Architectural History*, 2nd ed. (Cambridge, Massachusetts: MIT Press, 1981), 191.
2. Yi-Fu Tuan, *Space and Place: The Perspective of Experience* (Minneapolis: University of Minnesota Press, 1977), 111–112.
3. Ibid., 108.
4. Sarah Hamilton and Andrew Spicer, 'Defining the Holy: The Delineation of Sacred Space' in *Defining the Holy: Sacred Space in Medieval and Early Modern Europe*, ed. Sarah Hamilton and Andrew Spicer (Aldershot: Ashgate Publishing, 2005), 2.
5. David Chidester and Edward Tabor Linenthal, eds, *American Sacred Space* (Indianapolis: Indiana University Press, 1995), 16.
6. Harold W. Turner, *From Temple to Meeting House: The Phenomenology and Theology of Places of Worship* (The Hague: Walter de Gruyter, 1979), 15.
7. Sharon E. J. Gerstel, Introduction, in *Thresholds of the Sacred: Architectural, Art Historical, Liturgical and Theological Perspectives on Religious Screens, East and West*, ed. Sharon E. J. Gerstel (Washington, D.C.: Harvard University Press, 2006), 1–2.
8. Richard Kieckhefer, *Theology and Stone: Church Architecture from Byzantium to Berkeley* (Oxford: Oxford University Press, 2004), 63.

9. Tuan, *Topophilia*, 146.
10. Tuan, *Space and Place*, 106.
11. Mircea Eliade, *The Sacred And the Profane: The Nature of Religion*, trans. Willard R. Trask (San Diego: Harcourt Brace Jovanovich, 1959), 59.
12. Louis P. Nelson, *American Sanctuary: Understanding Sacred Places* (Indianapolis: Indiana University Press, 2006), 70.
13. Hamilton and Spicer, 'Defining the Holy,' 6.
14. Edward Relph, *Place and Placelessness* (London: Pion, 1976), 83.
15. Le Corbusier, *Towards a New Architecture*, trans. Frederick Etchells (London: The Architectural Press, 1946; first published 1923), 100.
16. Le Corbusier, quoted by Alain de Botton in *The Architecture of Happiness: the Secret Art of Furnishing Your Life* (London: Penguin, 2007; first published 2006), 57.
17. Eliade, *The Sacred and the Profane*, 34.
18. Edward S. Casey, *Getting Back Into Place: Toward a Renewed Understanding of the Place-World* (Indianapolis: Indiana University Press, 1993), 179.
19. Eliade, *The Sacred and the Profane*, 46.
20. Bachelard, *The Poetics of Space*, 17.
21. Dewan, *The House as Setting*, 6.
22. Irene Cieraad, 'Introduction: Anthropology at Home' in *At Home: An Anthropology of Domestic Space*, ed. Cieraad (Syracuse, New York: Syracuse University Press, 1999), 4.
23. Céline Rosselin, 'The Ins and Outs of the Hall: A Parisian Example' in *At Home: An Anthropology of Domestic Space*, ed. Irene Cieraad (Syracuse, New York: Syracuse University Press, 1999), 53–59.
24. J. B. Jackson, *Landscape: Selected Writings of J. B. Jackson* (Amherst: University of Massachusetts Press, 1970), 42.
25. Bachelard, *The Poetics of Space*, 17.
26. Short, foreword, to Cieraad, *At Home: An Anthropology of Domestic Space*, x.
27. Ibid., 274.
28. Huw Benyon and Ray Hudson, 'Place and Space in Contemporary Europe: Some Lessons and Reflections,' *Antipode* 25/3 (1993): 182.
29. Naomi Wood, 'Review of *Four British Fantasists*, by Charles Butler,' *Children's Literature*, 36 (2008): 253.
30. Benyon and Hudson, 'Place and Space in Contemporary Europe,' 182.
31. Dewan, *The House as Setting*, 11.
32. James G. Watson, 'Faulkner: The House of Fiction' in *Fifty Years of Yoknapatawpha*, ed. Doreen Fowler and Ann J. Abadie (Jackson: University Press of Mississippi; 1980), 139.
33. Short, foreword to Cieraad, .*At Home: An Anthropology of Domestic Space*, x.
34. Dewan, *The House as Setting*, 36.
35. Heidi de Mare, 'Domesticity in Dispute: A Reconsideration of Sources' in *At Home: An Anthropology of Domestic Space*, ed. Irene Cieraad (Syracuse, New York: Syracuse University Press, 1999), 16.

36. Bachelard, *The Poetics of Space*, 218.
37. Eliade, *The Sacred and the Profane*, 25.
38. Homi Bhabha, *The Location of Culture* (London: Routledge, 2004), 4.
39. *The Lady of the Well* in *The Mabinogion*, trans. Sionad Davies (Oxford: Oxford University Press, 2007), 123.
40. Daniel Donoghue, *Old English Literature: A Short Introduction* (London: Blackwell, 2004), 29.
41. *Beowulf*, in F. R. Klaeber, ed., *Beowulf and The Fight at Finnsburg*, 3rd ed. (Boston: D. C. Heath, 1941), lines 1063–1159.
42. *Njal's Saga*, on the Icelandic Saga Database, Kafli 129, http://www.sagadb.org/brennu-njals_saga#121, accessed 01/09/11.
43. Both of these defence scenes may be read in the original in E. V. Gordon, *An Introduction to Old Norse* (Oxford: Oxford University Press, 1927), 100–105, 26–33. Full translations may be found in *The Saga of Grettir the Strong*, trans. Bernard Scudder and Örnolfur Thorsson (London: Penguin, 2005) and *The Saga of King Hrolf Kraki*, trans. Jesse L. Byock (London: Penguin, 1988). Both of these texts parallel Beowulf's defence of Heorot. In each case the hero confronts the monster or intruder on the threshold of the hall and the ensuing fight takes place in and around the doorway. A detailed discussion of these parallel motifs may be found where Oscar Ludvig Olson notes that 'the Grettir story and the Grendel story are essentially the same type,' in 'The Relation of the *Hrolfs Saga Kraka* and the *Bjarkarimur* to *Beowulf*: A Contribution to the History of Saga Development in England and in the Scandinavian Countries' (PhD diss., University of Chicago, 1914), 44.
44. Original Old English versions, and translations of these texts may be found in Stuart D. Lee and Elizabeth Solopova, *The Keys of Middle-Earth: Discovering Medieval Literature Through the Fiction of J.R.R. Tolkien* (London: Palgrave, 2005). *The Battle of Maldon*, 226–229; *Cynnewulf and Cynneheard*, 156–159,
45. *Beowulf*, line 82.
46. Ibid., lines 721b–724a.
47. Ibid., lines 833–836.
48. Ibid., lines 925–927.
49. Donoghue, *Old English Literature*, 29.
50. Eliade, *The Sacred and the Profane*, 25.
51. Perry Nodelman and Mavis Reimer, *The Pleasures of Children's Literature* (Boston: Allyn and Bacon, 2002), 188–191.
52. Dewan, *The House as Setting*, 2–3. Dewan does not distinguish between the term 'house' and the term 'home' in her analysis of dwelling places.
53. Beatrix Potter, *The Tale of Mrs. Tittlemouse* (London: Frederick Warne, 1910), 16.
54. Ibid., 40.
55. Ibid., 52.

56. *Beowulf*, line 727.
57. J. K. Rowling, *Harry Potter and the Philosopher's Stone* (London: Ted Smart, 1998; first published 1997), 39.
58. Ibid., 40–41.
59. The term 'domestic fantasy' and the ideas of the 'primary world' and 'secondary world' were coined by J. R. R. Tolkien in *Tree and Leaf* (London: George Allen and Unwin, 1975).
60. Tuan, *Topophilia*, 146.
61. Cooper, *Over Sea, Under Stone*, 21.
62. Ibid., 58.
63. Sigmund Freud, 'The Uncanny (1919),' *The Complete Psychological Works of Sigmund Freud, XVII (1917#1919)* trans. James Strachey (New York: W.W. Norton and Company, 1959), 218#252.
64. Cooper, *Over Sea, Under Stone*, 60.
65. Although in *The Dark Is Rising*, Cooper says there are four stones. See Cooper, *The Dark Is Rising*, 54.
66. Cooper, *Over Sea, Under Stone*, 66.
67. Ibid., 67.
68. Ibid., 72.
69. Ibid., 114.
70. Cooper, *Greenwitch*, 35–42.
71. Ibid., 25.
72. Ibid., 22.
73. Ibid., 114.
74. Cooper, *The Grey King*, 29.
75. Rhonda Lemke Sanford, *Maps and Memory in Early Modern England: A Sense of Place* (New York: Palgrave, 2002), 89.
76. Belden C. Lane, *Landscapes of the Sacred, Geography and Narrative in American Spirituality* (Baltimore: Johns Hopkins University Press, 2002), 293, n51.
77. Cooper, *The Grey King*, 27.
78. Ibid., 27.
79. Ibid.
80. Translation found in Rees Ivor Jones, *Facts and Fables from Tywyn: Some True Tales and Some Legends* (Tywyn, Gwynedd, 2001), 38.
81. Cooper, *The Grey King*, 49.
82. Susan Cooper, *Silver on the Tree* (London: Puffin, 1979; first published 1977), 205.
83. Ibid., 163, 170, 179, 188.
84. Cooper, *Silver on the Tree*, 84.
85. John F. Sears, *Sacred Places: American Tourist Attractions in the Nineteenth Century* (New York: Oxford University Press, 1989), 10.
86. Victor Turner and Edith Turner, *Image and Pilgrimage in Christian Culture* (New York: Columbia University Press, 1978), 20, 241.

87. Wayne Fife, 'British Missionaries in New Guinea' in *Intersecting Journeys: The Anthropology of Pilgrimage and Tourism,* ed. Ellen Badone and Sharon R. Roseman (Chicago: University of Illinois Press, 2004), 147.
88. Cooper, *Silver on the Tree*, 93.
89. Ibid.
90. Cooper, *Greenwitch*, 153.
91. Cooper, *Silver on the Tree*, 94.
92. Maria Nikolajeva, *From Mythic to Linear: Time in Children's Literature* (Lanham, Maryland and Oxford: The Children's Literature Association and Scarecrow Press, 2000), 8.
93. Cooper, *Silver on the Tree*, 94.
94. Ibid., 97.
95. Ibid.
96. Ibid., 97–98.
97. 'In the beginning was the Word: the Word was with God and the Word was God.' John 1:1.
98. Cooper, *Silver on the Tree*, 99. See also William Shakespeare, *The Tempest,* edited by Virginia Mason Vaughan and Alden T. Vaughan (London: Arden Shakespeare, 2003), Act 1 Scene 2, line 314.
99. Ibid.
100. Ibid.
101. Ibid., 100–101.
102. Cooper, *The Dark Is Rising*, 45.
103. Ibid., 45.
104. Ibid., 42.
105. Ibid., 43–44.
106. Ibid., 43.
107. Ibid., 42.
108. Ibid., 45.
109. Ibid., 55.
110. Ibid., 61.
111. Cooper, *The Dark Is Rising*, 163.
112. Ibid., 156.
113. Ibid.
114. Ibid.
115. Ibid., 161.
116. Ibid., 158.
117. Ibid., 157.
118. Ibid., 158.
119. Ibid., 159.
120. Ibid., 160.
121. Ibid., 99.
122. Ibid., 103.
123. Ibid., 180.

124. Ibid., 196.
125. Ibid., 200.
126. *Beowulf*, lines 712.
127. Cooper, *The Dark Is Rising*, 199.
128. Ibid. 199.
129. Ibid., 207.
130. Ibid., 11.
131. Ibid., 94–95.
132. Ibid., 179.
133. Ibid., 26–27.
134. Ibid., 265–266.
135. Ibid., 147.
136. Ibid., 148.
137. Cooper, *Silver on the Tree*, 99.
138. For a comparison between Will's attic bedroom and the other attic in the *Sequence*, the disused loft of the Grey House, which features in *Over Sea, Under Stone* see Jane Suzanne Carroll, 'Two Misconstrued Attic Spaces in Susan Cooper's The Dark Is Rising Sequence' in *Trinity College Dublin Journal of Postgraduate Research*, Vol. 7 (2008), 75–84.
139. Cooper, *The Dark Is Rising*, 20–21. Many children's domestic fantasies are characterised by the absence of parents or similar authority figures. The adventure can begin once the parents are safely out of the way. See for example, E. Nesbit's *Five Children and It* (1902), Roald Dahl's *James and the Giant Peach* (1961), or Katherine Paterson's *Bridge to Terabithia*, (1977).
140. Casey, *Getting Back into Place*, 38.
141. Muir, *Approaches to Landscape*, 275.
142. Ibid., 274.
143. Cooper, *The Dark Is Rising*, 23.
144. Ibid.
145. Ibid., 24.
146. Ibid., 23.
147. Ibid.
148. Ibid., 26.
149. Ibid.
150. Ibid.
151. Peter Davidson, *The Idea of North* (London: Reaktion Books, 2005), 21.
152. Naomi Wood, '(Em)bracing Icy Mothers: Ideology, Identity and Environment in Children's Fantasy' in *Wild Things: Children's Culture and Ecocriticism*, ed. Sidney I. Dobrin and Kenneth B. Kidd (Detroit: Wayne State University Press, 2004), 198–214.
153. Cooper, *The Dark Is Rising*, 26.
154. Ibid., 179.
155. Ibid., 25.

156. The uncanny not only reveals what has been previously hidden, but 'must oblige the reader to [...] hesitate between a natural and a supernatural explanation of the events described.' Rosemary Jackson, *Fantasy: The Literature of Subversion* (London: Routledge, 1988; first published 1981), 28.
157. Cooper, *The Dark Is Rising*, 26–28.
158. Though Paul's actions are kind, he is very much a usurper to the attic space as he is not the second eldest sibling in the house. The Stanton children are, in order of birth, Tom (who died in infancy), Stephen, Max, Glen, Paul and Robin (twins), Barbara, Mary, James, and Will. By rights either Max or Glen—who are both at home for the holidays—should lay claim to the space. In taking over the attic bedroom, Paul displaces his two elder brothers as well as Will.
159. Cooper, *The Dark Is Rising*, 182.
160. Ibid., 66.
161. Dewan, *The House as Setting*, 8.
162. Cooper, *The Dark Is Rising*, 29–30.
163. Cooper, *The Dark Is Rising*, 112. The Old Ones are 'only loosely planted within time' and within space. As an Old One, Will is able to move between places and times freely.

Notes to Chapter Two

1. Bachelard, *The Poetics of Space*, 20.
2. Martin Warnke, *Political Landscape: The Art History of Nature*, trans. David McLintock (London: Reaktion Books, 1994), 39.
3. Muir, *Approaches to Landscape*, 51.
4. R. Hartshorne, *The Nature of Geography: A Critical Survey of Current Thought in The Light of The Past* (Lancaster, Pennsylvania: Association of American Geographers, 1939), 150.
5. Curtius, *European Literature and The Latin Middle Ages*, 192n.
6. Corinne J. Saunders, *The Forest of Medieval Romance: Avernus, Broceliande, Arden* (Cambridge: D. S. Brewer, 1993), ix.
7. The association of the garden with female sexuality dates from the earliest literature and may be seen in *The Song of Songs* where the bride-to-be is referred to as 'an enclosed garden' with the garden wall substituting the hymeneal veil. Paul Shepherd, *Man in The Landscape* (New York: Knopf, 1967), 65–118 quoted in Yi-Fu Tuan, *Topophilia*, 145.
8. Frances Hodgson Burnett, *The Secret Garden*, ed. Gretchen Holbrook Gerzina (New York: W. W. Norton, 2006), 62.
9. The tendency of hermits to live in the wilderness, away from human habitation, in order to achieve enlightenment and to revive the spirit attests to this, but for a more complete discussion on the importance of the garden as a sacred space in Western and Eastern cultures, see Norris

Brock Johnson's essay "Garden as Sacred Space: Transformation of Consciousness at Tenryu Temple," in *The Power Of Place: Sacred Ground in Natural and Human Environments, An Anthology*, ed. James A. Swan (Bath: Gateway Books, 1993), 167–187.

10. Schama, *Landscape and Memory*, 529.
11. James J. Wilhelm traces this association back to classical spring lyrics of Catullus, Virgil, and Horace but also observes that the trope may be traced throughout Western literature in the work of T. S. Eliot, for example, as his title tacitly acknowledges. See James J. Wilhelm, *The Cruelest Month: Spring, Nature, and Love in Classical and Medieval Lyrics* (New Haven and London: Yale University Press, 1965).
12. Philip Robinson, ed., *The Faber Book of Gardens* (London: Faber and Faber, 2007), 153.
13. Victoria Emily Pagan, *Rome and the Literature of Gardens* (London: Duckworth, 2006), 6.
14. *The Seafarer*, lines 48–55. For a full translation see S. A. J. Bradley, *Anglo-Saxon Poetry* (London: Everyman, 2000), 333. Whereas the cuckoo is a harbinger of Spring, it is also an omen of death. A Middle Welsh homophone of 'cuckoo' means 'Where? Where?' and thus, the bird becomes a symbol of loss, *hireath*, and grief. That the cuckoo takes this mournful role in *The Seafarer* may indicate that the Anglo-Saxon poet had a good knowledge of contemporary Middle Welsh verse. See J. D. Pheifer, "*The Seafarer*, Lines 53–55," *RES* 16 (1965): 282–284. For the cuckoo as a herald of spring, see Kenneth Hurlstone Jackson, *Studies in Early Celtic Nature Poetry* (Burnham-on-Sea: Llanerch, 1995), 23; and for a discussion on the cuckoo as a herald of death, see Ifor Williams, *Lectures in Early Welsh Poetry* (Dublin: Dublin Institute for Advanced Studies 1944), 12–13.
15. Edmund Spenser, *The Faerie Queene: Books Three and Four*, ed. Dorothy Stephens (Indianapolis and Cambridge: Hackett, 2006), Book Three, Canto vi, 39.
16. Even now, Western families bury their dead in green spaces and Western societies mourn their nations' dead in gardens of remembrance, the green space acting as both a receptacle for and a monument to the dead. For a discussion on the link between public mourning, commemoration, and green spaces, see Judith R. Wasserman's essay "To Trace the Shifting Sands: Community, Ritual, and the Memorial Landscape," *Landscape Journal* 17/1 (1998): 42–62.
17. Roni Natov, *The Poetics of Childhood* (New York: Routledge, 2003), 93.
18. Ibid., 119.
19. Juliet Dusinberre, *Alice to the Lighthouse: Children's Books and Radical Experiments in Art* (London: Macmillan Press, 1999), 131.
20. Jarlath Killeen, *The Fairy Tales of Oscar Wilde* (Aldershot and Burlington: Ashgate, 2007), 75.
21. Robinson, *The Faber Book of Gardens*, xii–xiii.

22. Francis Bacon, "Of Gardens" in Robinson, *The Faber Book of Gardens*, 61.
23. Ibid., 15.
24. Gillian Rudd, *Greenery: Ecocritical Readings of Late Medieval English Literature* (Manchester: Manchester University Press, 2007), 166.
25. William Temple, 'Upon the Gardens of Epicurus or, Of Gardening, in the Year 1685', in *Five Miscellaneous Essays*, ed. Samuel Holt Monk (Ann Arbor: University of Michigan Press), 1–36, 24.
26. Robinson, *The Faber Book of Gardens*, xi.
27. Anne Van Erp-Houtepen, "The Etymological Origin of the Garden," *Journal of Garden History* 6 (1986): 229.
28. Schama, *Landscape and Memory*, 528.
29. Temple, 'Upon the Gardens of Epicurus,' 24.
30. J. B. Jackson, *The Necessity for Ruins and Other Topics* (Amherst: University of Massachusetts Press, 1980), 26.
31. Ibid., 6.
32. Michel Conan, *Sacred Gardens and Landscapes, Ritual and Agency* (Washington D.C.: Harvard University Press, 2007), 7.
33. Jackson, *The Necessity for Ruins*, 6.
34. Genesis 2:7–3:10 (NRSV).
35. Derek A. Pearsall and Elizabeth Salter, *Landscapes and Seasons of the Medieval World* (London: Elek Books, 1973), 56.
36. For example, the English versions of Genesis refer to an apple but Mediterranean and Middle Eastern traditions favour pomegranates or figs. See Robinson, *The Faber Book of Gardens*, xiii. The Hebrew word פְּרִי,' 'pěrî' simply means 'fruit.'
37. *Genesis A* in A. N. Doane, ed., *Genesis A: A New Edition* (Madison: University of Wisconsin Press, 1978), II. 947.
38. *Genesis B* in Doane, *The Saxon Genesis*, lines 840–846. There is a possible pun in this final line; for 'clothes,' the author uses 'waeda,' from 'wǽd' (MNE 'weeds') which is homophonous with 'wéod' meaning an undesirable or useless plant (MNE 'weeds'), thus implying that Adam and Eve wear 'weeds as weeds.'
39. *Genesis A*, lines 987–993, 995.
40. E. V. Gordon, *Pearl* (Oxford: Oxford University Press, 1953), line 1. For a complete translation, see J. R. R. Tolkien, *Pearl* in *Sir Gawain and the Green Knight*, ed. Christopher Tolkien (London: HarperCollins, 2006), 94–127.
41. Rudd, *Greenery*, 171–172.
42. Ibid., 172.
43. Gordon, *Pearl*, lines 42–44.
44. Ibid., lines 31–32.
45. Burnett, *The Secret Garden*, 70.
46. Philippa Pearce, *Tom's Midnight Garden* (London: Puffin Books, 1976; first published 1958), 76.

47. Ibid., 116.
48. Ibid., 212.
49. Oscar Wilde, 'The Nightingale and the Rose', in Oscar Wilde, *Stories for Children*, illus. P. J. Lynch (London: Hodder, 2000), 17.
50. Ibid., 20.
51. Oscar Wilde, 'The Selfish Giant,' in *Stories for Children*, 8.
52. Ibid., 13.
53. Natov, *The Poetics of Childhood*, 121.
54. Ibid., 93.
55. Jane Darcy, 'Wild Creatures: The Representation of Nature in *The Wind in the Willows* and *The Secret Garden*,' *The Lion and the Unicorn* 19/2 (1995): 214.
56. Burnett, *The Secret Garden*, 124.
57. http://www.oxfordjewishheritage.co.uk/projects/botanic-gardens-first-jewish-cemetery accessed 01/09/11.
58. http://www.magd.ox.ac.uk/nested_content/listings/home_-_events/events/may-day-celebrations, accessed 01/09/11.
59. Philip Pullman, *The Amber Spyglass* (London: Scholastic, 2000), 537–538.
60. Susan Cooper, *Silver on the Tree* (London: Puffin, 1979; first published 1977), 59.
61. Ibid., 57.
62. Ibid., 59.
63. Ibid.
64. Ibid., 60.
65. Ibid., 60.
66. Christian myth holds that the roses in Eden were without thorns; thus, the thorns suggest the imperfections introduced into the world by the Fall. The crown of thorns worn by Christ perfectly contrasts the thornless rose and reinforces the idea that his death atones for and undoes the harm caused by the original sin. That the immaculately conceived virgin Mary is addressed in one macaronic medieval lyric as '*rosa sine spine*' accentuates the notion that the rose without thorn is symbolic of the unfallen state. See R. T. Davies, ed., *Medieval English Lyrics* (London: Faber and Faber, 1963), 53.
67. Pagan, *Rome and the Literature of Gardens*, 15.
68. Schama, *Landscape and Memory*, 530.
69. Cooper, *Silver on the Tree*, 157.
70. Ibid., 157–160. For a discussion on manners, rudeness, and formal gardens, see Schama, *Landscape and Memory*, 538–546.
71. Cooper, *Silver on the Tree*, 159.
72. Virgil, *Georgics*, trans. Peter Fallon (Oxford: Oxford University Press, 2006), Book Two, line 398.
73. Jackson, *The Necessity for Ruins*, 31.

74. Farming is not necessarily always rooted in the immediate, as farmers still plant ahead for next season and put stores by for the winter.
75. Tuan, *Topophilia*, 96.
76. Michael Bunce, *The Countryside Ideal: Anglo-American Images of Landscape* (London and New York: Routledge, 1994), 28–29.
77. Greg Garrard, *Ecocriticism* (London and New York: Routledge, 2004), 33.
78. Tuan, *Topophilia*, 98.
79. Before the enclosures acts of the eighteenth and nineteenth centuries, boundaries between fields such as fences and walls were less common. Strip farming was practised across Europe, but animals were still penned off from plough-land, and individual farms were surrounded by ditches and hedges. The pattern and appearance of farmland in the early middle ages is detailed in W. G. Hoskins, *Fieldwork in Local History* (London: Faber and Faber, 1967). Chaucer presents a typical farm arrangement in 'The Nun's Priest's Tale' showing an enclosed yard at some remove from the domestic dwelling. Geoffrey Chaucer, *The Riverside Chaucer*, ed. F.N. Robinson (Oxford: Oxford University Press, 1988), 252–261.
80. Rudd, *Greenery*, 117.
81. Lars Lönnroth, *Njal's Saga: A Critical Introduction* (Berkeley and Los Angeles: University of California Press, 1976), 60.
82. A. F. Leach dates the book to 995. A.F. Leach, *The Schools of Medieval England* (London: Routledge, 2007; first published 1915), 87.
83. Aelfric (Abbot of Eynsham), *Aelfric's Colloquy*, ed. G. N. Garmonsway (Exeter: University of Exeter Press, 1978), 20. For a full translation see Stephen J. Harris, 'Aelfric's Colloquy' in *Medieval Literature for Children*, ed. Daniel T. Kline (London: Routledge, 2003), 112–130.
84. Aelfric, *Aelfric's Colloquy*, 22.
85. The Third Branch of the Mabinogi, *The Mabinogion*, trans. Sionad Davies (Oxford: Oxford University Press, 2007), 42.
86. Lönnroth, *Njal's Saga: A Critical Introduction*, 167.
87. Ibid., 45.
88. Derek A. Pearsall and Elizabeth Salter, *Landscapes and Seasons of the Medieval World* (London: Elek Books, 1973), 45.
89. Lönnroth, *Njal's Saga: A Critical Introduction*, 95.
90. Njal's Saga, Kafli 111, Icelandic Saga Database, http://www.sagadb.org/brennu-njals_saga#101, accessed 01/09/11.
91. Njal's Saga, Kafli 75, Icelandic Saga Database, http://www.sagadb.org/brennu-njals_saga#71 accessed 01/09/11.
92. Pearsall and Salter, *Landscapes and Seasons of the Medieval World*, 46.
93. Sylvanus Urban, 'Wright's Volume of Vocabularies,' *The Gentleman's Magazine and Historical Review* 204 (1858): 50.
94. Bunce, *The Countryside Ideal*, 63–64.
95. Dick King-Smith, *The Sheep-Pig* (London: Puffin, 2003; first published 1983), 113–114.

96. Steve Augarde, *The Various* (London: Corgi Books, 2003), 15–16.
97. Virgil, *Georgics*, line 398.
98. Genesis 3:23 (NRSV).
99. Susan Price, *The Sterkarm Handshake* (London: Scholastic, 1998), 83.
100. Ibid., 453.
101. Terry Pratchett, *The Wee Free Men* (London: Corgi, 2004; first published 2003), 16.
102. Ibid., 19.
103. Ibid., 131.
104. Tuan, *Topophilia*, 98.
105. Cooper, *The Grey King*, 25.
106. Cooper, *The Dark Is Rising*, 14–15.
107. Cooper, *Silver on the Tree*, 30.
108. Ibid., 31.
109. Ibid., 30.
110. Ibid., 32.
111. Ibid.
112. Ibid., 33.
113. Virgil, *Georgics*, line 200.
114. Norman John Grenville Pounds, *The Culture of the English People: Iron Age to the Industrial Revolution* (Cambridge: Cambridge University Press, 1994), 189.
115. Ibid., 386.
116. Cooper, *The Dark Is Rising*, 15.
117. Cooper, *The Grey King*, 30.
118. Ibid., 31.
119. Cooper, *The Grey King*, 31.
120. Cooper, *The Dark Is Rising*, 112.
121. Cooper, *The Grey King*, 136.
122. Ibid., 136.
123. Ibid., 104.
124. Garrard, *Ecocriticism*, 59.
125. Rudd, *Greenery*, 93.
126. Roderick Nash, *Wilderness and the American Mind* (New Haven and London: Yale University Press, 1973; first published 1967), 5
127. Schama, *Landscape and Memory*, 520.
128. Albertus Magnus quoted in Rolf Toman, ed., *European Garden Design: From Classical Antiquity to the Present Day* (Oxford: Tandem Verlag, 2005), 27.
129. Ernst Robert Curtius, *European Literature and the Latin Middle Ages*, trans. Willard R. Trask (London and Henley: Routledge and Kegan Paul, 1953), 186. See also Pearsall and Salter, *Landscapes and Seasons of the Medieval World*, 50.

130. Jay Appleton, *The Experience of Landscape* (London: Wiley, 1975), 73.
131. See *Sir Orfeo* in Donald B. Sands, ed., *Middle English Verse Romances* (Exeter: University of Exeter Press, 1986), lines 33–50.
132. Oscar Wilde, 'The Happy Prince' in *Stories for Children*, illus. P. J. Lynch (London: Hodder, 2000), 53.
133. Natov, *The Poetics of Childhood*, 119.
134. Ibid.
135. Catherine A. M. Clarke, *Literary Landscapes and the Idea of England, 700–1400* (Cambridge: D.S. Brewer, 2008), 36–7.
136. Ibid., 41.
137. Herman Pleijj, *Dreaming of Cockaigne* trans. Diane Webb (New York: Columbia University Press, 2001), 216.
138. *Sir Orfeo*, lines 48–52.
139. William Langland, *The Vision of William Concerning Piers the Ploughman*, edited by Walter W. Skeat (Oxford: Clarendon Press, 1869), lines 1–11. For a complete translation see William Langland, *Piers the Ploughman*, trans. J. F. Goodridge (London: Penguin, 1966).
140. John David Moore, "Pottering about in the Garden: Kenneth Grahame's Version of the Pastoral in *The Wind in the Willows*," *The Journal of the Midwest Modern Language Association* 23/1 (1990): 47.
141. Lewis Carroll, *The Annotated Alice: Alice's Adventures in Wonderland and Through the Looking Glass*, ed. Martin Gardner (London: Penguin, 1963; first published 1960), 21. It is interesting that the stories about Alice were first composed during a boating trip on July 4th 1862 from Oxford to Godstow, (see Lewis Carroll, The Annotated Alice, 21 n.1) a place name possibly derived from the Old English 'gód stowe' meaning 'lovely place'.
142. Manlove, *From Alice to Harry Potter*, 49.
143. Humphrey Carpenter, *Secret Gardens: A Study of the Golden Age of Children's Literature* (London: Allen and Unwin, 1985), 155.
144. Kenneth Grahame, *The Wind in the Willows* (London: Penguin, 2005; first published 1908), 9.
145. Cooper, *Silver on the Tree*, 11.
146. Ibid., 13.
147. Ibid..
148. Ibid.,13–14.
149. Langland, *Piers the Ploughman*, 25.
150. Ibid., 25.
151. Ibid., 18–19.
152. Ibid., 18.
153. Ibid., 18–19.
154. Cooper, *Silver on the Tree*, 14.
155. Ibid., 15.

156. Cooper, *The Dark Is Rising*, 249.
157. The link between sleep and death is familiar. Sleep is often described as a lesser form of death—for instance as 'death's brother' in Oscar Wilde's 'The Happy Prince' in *Stories for Children*, 53.
158. Cooper, *The Dark Is Rising*, 250.
159. William Empson notes that the marriage-bed and the grave may be treated 'as identical'—see William Empson, *Some Versions of Pastoral* (London: Chatto and Windus, 1935), 215—but it is Cooper's recurring use of the phrase 'blanketing snow,' which clinches this association.
160. Garrard, *Ecocriticism*, 59.
161. Ibid.
162. Schama, *Landscape and Memory*, 540.
163. Garrard, *Ecocriticism*, 61.
164. Ibid., 63.
165. Nash, *Wilderness and the American Mind*, 3.
166. Anders Andrén 'Landscape and Settlement as Utopian Space,' in *Settlement and Landscape: Proceedings of a Conference in Arhus, Denmark, May 4–7 1998*, eds. Charlotte Fabech and Jytte Rintveld (Moesgard: Jutland Archaeological Society, 1999), 386.
167. See Saunders, *The Forest of Medieval Romance*, 13.
168. Roland Bechmann, *Trees and Man: The Forest in the Middle Ages* (New York: Paragon House, 1990; first published 1984), 280.
169. Ibid., ix.
170. Schama, *Landscape and Memory*, 450.
171. A notable exception to this genre is Jean Craighead George's *My Side of the Mountain* (London: Puffin, 1959).
172. Nash, *Wilderness and the American Mind*, 2.
173. Ibid., 1.
174. *Maxims II*, The Complete Corpus of Anglo-Saxon Poetry, http://www.sacred-texts.com/neu/ascp/a15.htm, lines 42b–43a. Accessed 01/09/11.
175. F. R. Klaeber, ed., *Beowulf* in *Beowulf and the Fight at Finnsburg*, 3rd ed. (Boston: D. C. Heath, 1922), line 103.
176. Ibid., lines 702–704, 710–711.
177. Pearsall and Salter, *Landscapes and Seasons of the Medieval World*, 43.
178. *Beowulf,* lines 1357–1361.
179. Pearsall and Salter, *Landscapes and Seasons of the Medieval World*, 44.
180. The description of Hell in the Anglo-Saxon *Genesis B* closely mirrors the Beowulf poet's description of Grendel's mere. *Genesis B*, lines 356–388 in Doane, *The Saxon Genesis*, 212–213.
181. *Beowulf,* lines 1368—1371.
182. Rudd, *Greenery*, 110.
183. Ibid., 111.
184. Ibid,, 114.
185. Ibid., 111.

186. Ibid., 115.
187. J. R. R. Tolkien and E. V. Gordon, eds., *Sir Gawain and the Green Knight* (Oxford: Oxford University Press, 1925), lines 701, 709–712. For a full translation, see Tolkien, *Sir Gawain and the Green Knight*, 17–93.
188. Tolkien and Gordon, *Sir Gawain and the Green Knight*, lines 2172–2174, 2180–2183.
189. Jacques Le Goff, *The Medieval Imagination*, trans. Arthur Goldhammer (Chicago and London: University of Chicago Press, 1998), 58.
190. Peter Bramwell, *Pagan Themes in Modern Children's Fiction: Green Man, Shamanism, Earth Mysteries* (Basingstoke and New York: Palgrave Macmillan, 2009), 38.
191. Darcy, *Wild Animals*, 215.
192. Bramwell, *Pagan Themes in Modern Children's Fiction*, 39.
193. Rudyard Kipling, *Puck of Pook's Hill* (London: Penguin, 1994; first published 1906), 11.
194. See K. M. Briggs, *Hobberdy Dick* (Harmondsworth: Kestrel Books, 1955), 199–202 and J. K. Rowling, *Harry Potter and the Chamber of Secrets* (London: Bloomsbury, 1998), 248–249 for a comparison.
195. Grahame, *The Wind in the Willows*, 82.
196. Pratchett, *The Wee Free Men*, 13.
197. David Almond, *The Savage*, illus. Dave McKean (London: Walker Books, 2008), 9.
198. Ibid., 67.
199. Ibid., 76–77.
200. It is worth noting that these spirits are gendered. Cooper describes Tethys as a goddess and as a female embodiment of the wilderness. Even though Herne and the Brenin Llwyd are expressly male, the Greenwitch is described as neither male nor female——a fact which has led some critics to condemn the weak position of the female gender within Cooper's work—but nevertheless is closely associated with women and often referred to as female by other characters. Only women are admitted to the making ceremony and Jane Drew—who is repeatedly associated with the moon in the *Sequence*—befriends the monstrous creature. The Greenwitch is often figured as a child—she is the child of Tethys, the water goddess, and Jane describes her as childlike on several occasions. Susan Cooper, *Greenwitch*, (London: Puffin Books, 1977; first published 1974), 58, 106. Despite its desexualised nature, the women of Trewissick refer to the Greenwitch as 'she' and I have chosen to follow suit.
201. Cooper, *The Grey King*, 125.
202. Ibid., 141.
203. Cooper, *Silver on the Tree*, 176.
204. Cooper, *The Grey King*, 125.

204 • Notes

205. Ibid., 126.
206. This obliqueness is appropriate as a quirk of the localised weather systems means that, in reality, the peak of Cader Idris is never totally free from mist, and it is almost impossible to make out the true shape of the mountain.
207. Bechmann, *Trees and Man*, 288.
208. Ibid., 283.
209. Jennifer Westwood, *Albion: A Guide to Legendary Britain*, (London: Granada, 1985), 75.
210. See Nigel Pennick, *Celtic Sacred Landscapes* (London: Thames and Hudson, 1996), 170.
211. The First Branch of the Mabinogi, *The Mabinogion*, trans. Sionad Davies (Oxford: Oxford University Press, 2007), 3.
212. Bechmann, *Trees and Man*, 285.
213. Bramwell, *Pagan Themes in Modern Children's Fiction*, 45.
214. Cooper, *The Dark Is Rising*, 247–248.
215. Ibid., 248.
216. Cooper, *Greenwitch*, 27.
217. Clive Hicks, *The Green Man: A Field Guide* (Fakenham: Compass Books, 2000), v.
218. Cooper, *Greenwitch*, 37.
219. Susan Cooper "In Defense of the Artist" in *Signposts to the Criticism of Children's Literature*, ed. Robert Bator (Chicago: American Library Association, 1983), 102.
220. James Frazer, *The Golden Bough: A Study in Magic and Religion* (Oxford: Oxford University Press, 1994; first published 1922), 273–299.
221. Terri Windling, *The Green Man: Tales from the Mythic Forest* (London: Penguin, 2002), 5. See also Ralph Whitlock, *A Calendar of Country Customs* (London: B. T. Batsford, 1978) for a collection of green-man customs practised in twentieth-century Britain.
222. Ibid., 654–655.
223. Ibid., 300.
224. There are suggestions that these effigies were once people and that blood sacrifices were used to sate the spirits. but, either through necessity or changes in law, the customs were gradually amended to the ritualised 'murder' of inanimate greenery or green figure. See Frazer, *The Golden Bough*, 744.
225. Cooper, *Greenwitch*, 38.
226. Ibid., 38.
227. Ibid.
228. Ibid., 38–39. A reader of the *Sequence* will recall that rowan or mountain ash is sacred to the forces of the Light and that hazel and hawthorn are repeatedly noted for their magical properties. Robert Graves notes that the hawthorn is 'in general an unlucky tree' (171) and that

it 'may not be introduced to the house lest [the fairies] destroyed the children inside' (63). He suggests the hazel is 'inimical to the vine' in classical mythology and that it carries Bacchic, carnivalesque overtones. See Robert Graves, *The White Goddess: A Historical Grammar of Poetic Myth*, ed. Grevel Lindop (London: Faber and Faber, 1948). The hawthorn also features in Arthurian myth as Merlin is imprisoned in a hawthorn tree by Vivian, the Lady of the Lake. See Dan Nastali, "Swords, Grails and Bag-Puddings: A Survey of Children's Poetry and Plays," in *Adapting the Arthurian Legends for Children: Essays on Arthurian Juvenilia*, ed. Barbara Tepa Lupack (New York: Palgrave, 2004), 193n.
229. Windling, *The Green Man*, 5.
230. Ibid., 43.
231. Ibid., 38, 41.
232. Ralph Whitlock, *A Calendar of Country Customs* (London: B. T. Batsford, 1978), 78.
233. Ibid., 79.
234. Christina Hole, *British Folk Customs* (London: Hutchinson, 1976), 10.
235. Ibid,, 45.
236. Pennick, *Celtic Sacred Landscapes*, 23. Great trees are a common feature in Northern European mythology such as Yggdrasill, the ash-tree that supports the world in Norse myth—see Kevin Crossley-Holland, *The Norse Myths* (New York: Pantheon Books, 1980), xxiii–xxiv.
237. Frazer, *The Golden Bough*, 86–88.
238. Cooper, *Greenwitch*, 40.
239. Windling, *The Green Man*, 10.
240. Tempting as it is to find meanings for these words, they do not have any simple correspondences in Celtic or Teutonic mythology. Lir may correspond to Lir, a Celtic sea god, whereas Reck may be a version of Rig, a pseudonym taken on by the Norse god of gateways Heimdall when he went down into the world to beget the race of men. It is more likely that Cooper's source is Jessie L. Weston's *From Ritual To Romance* (Princeton, New Jersey: Princeton University Press, 1993; first published 1920). Weston refers to Mana as a relic associated with the worship of tree-spirits (9–10) and to the Rig-veda as a Hindu 'nature ritual' (36). Thus the connection between the Greenwitch and earth, vegetation and sea is reiterated.
241. Cooper, *Greenwitch*, 108.
242. Ibid., 123.
243. Ibid., 111.
244. Ibid., 123.
245. Ibid., 39. These features recall the stone heads on Easter Island and pumice figures from New Zealand which are characterised by a 'narrow rectangular head, jutting brow and long curving nose,' John Flenley and

Paul G. Bahn, *The Enigmas of Easter Island: Island on the Edge* (Oxford: Oxford University Press, 2003), 104.
246. Robert MacFarlane, *The Wild Places* (London: Granta Books, 2007), 144.

Notes to Chapter Three

1. Perry Nodelman, *The Pleasures of Children's Literature* (London: Longman, 1992), 192. Later editions are co-edited with Mavis Reimer, but for the purposes of my discussion, I examine the writers' separate contributions to the study of journey-patterns in children's literature.
2. Pauline Dewan, *The Art of Place in Literature for Children and Young Adults: How Locale Shapes a Story* (Lewiston, Queenston, Lampeter: The Edwin Mellen Press, 2010), 13.
3. Mavis Reimer, ed., *Home Words: Discourses of Children's Literature in Canada* (Waterloo, Ontario: Wilfrid Laurier University Press, 2008), xviii.
4. Hunt, "Landscapes and Journeys, Metaphors and Maps," 13.
5. Tuan, *Topophilia*, 174.
6. Ibid., 148.
7. Ibid., 149.
8. Casey, *Getting Back into Place*, 273.
9. From the Old French *jornee* or *journee*, which becomes the Modern French *journée* meaning a day, a day's space, day's travel and work or employment.
10. Walter Benjamin, *The Arcades Project*, trans. Howard Eiland and Kevin McLaughlin (Cambridge, Massachusetts and London: The Belknap Press of Harvard University Press, 1999), 399.
11. M. M. Bakhtin, *The Dialogic Imagination: Four Essays*, trans. Michael Holquist (Austin: University of Texas Press, 1981), 98.
12. Ibid., 84.
13. Robyn McCallum, *Ideologies of Identity in Adolescent Fiction: The Dialogic Construction of Subjectivity* (London: Routledge, 1999), 186.
14. Bhabha, *The Location of Culture* (London: Routledge, 2004), 5.
15. Ibid.
16. Paul Shepard, *Nature and Madness* (San Francisco: Sierra Club Books, 1982), 24.
17. Benjamin, *The Arcades Project*, 423.
18. Ibid., 423.
19. Henri Lefebvre, *The Production of Space*, trans. Donald Nicholson-Smith, (Oxford: Blackwell, 2009; first published 1974), 223.
20. Virginia Woolf, "Street Haunting: A London Adventure," in *The Death of the Moth and Other Essays* (London: The Hogarth Press, 1942), 19.
21. Bakhtin, *The Dialogic Imagination*, 145.
22. Benjamin, *The Arcades Project*, 423.

23. Mikhail Bakhtin, *Rabelais and His World*, trans. Helene Iswolsky (London: Bloomington, 1965).4.
24. Benjamin, *The Arcades Project*, 423.
25. Ibid., 7.
26. Richard Lehan, *The City in Literature: An Intellectual and Cultural History* (Berkeley: University of California Press, 1998), 239.
27. Bakhtin, *Rabelais and His World*, 12.
28. Ibid., 13.
29. Ibid., 18.
30. Ibid., 32.
31. Ibid., 26.
32. Ibid., 21.
33. Ibid., 9.
34. This cyclical movement evokes the Ouroboros, the self-consuming serpent, which in turn recalls both the cyclical time-scale of the carnival and the consumption of the individual by the collective. The Ouroboros is a complex symbol, but one that may help in creating an understanding of the civic street. The self-eating snake or tail-biting serpent prefigures the destruction of the world and yet holds the world in place.
35. Louis Althusser, *Lenin and Philosophy and Other Essays*, trans. Ben Brewster (London: New Left Books, 1971), 104.
36. David Wallace, *Chaucerian Polity: Absolutist Images and Associational Forms in England and Italy* (Stanford: Stanford University Press, 1977), 179.
37. Clarke, *Literary Landscapes and the Idea of England, 700–1400*, 90.
38. Maurice Sendak, *Where the Wild Things Are* (London: Scholastic, 1963).
39. P. L. Travers, *Mary Poppins* (London: Peter Davies, 1934), 137.
40. Ibid., 133.
41. Bakhtin, *Rabelais and His World*, 7.
42. Neil Gaiman, *The Graveyard Book* (London: HarperCollins, 2008), 158.
43. Ibid., 158–159.
44. Ibid., 162.
45. Lammas is the Harvest Festival, traditionally held on August 1, and although at the time of writing it is still observed as a quarter day in Scotland, elsewhere it has been subsumed into the August bank holiday.
46. Susan Cooper, *Over Sea, Under Stone* (London: Puffin, 1968; first published 1965), 122–123.
47. Ibid., 123.
48. Benjamin, *The Arcades Project*, 400.
49. Ibid., 121.
50. Bakhtin, *Rabelais and His World*, 39.
51. Cooper, *Over Sea, Under Stone*, 123.
52. Bakhtin, *Rabelais and His World*, 32.
53. Cooper, *Greenwitch*, 376.

54. Bakhtin, *Rabelais and His World*, 10.
55. Cooper, *Over Sea, Under Stone*, 123.
56. Cooper, *Greenwitch*, 111–112.
57. Ibid.
58. Ibid., 113.
59. Ibid., 114–115.
60. See J. K. Rowling, *Harry Potter and the Philosopher's Stone* (London: Bloomsbury, 1997), 12–13.
61. Richard Lehan, *The City In Literature: An Intellectual and Cultural History* (Berkeley: University of California Press, 1998), 260.
62. Ibid., 144.
63. Benjamin, *The Arcades Project*, 423.
64. Cooper, *Greenwitch*, 117.
65. Ibid., 118.
66. Ibid., 120–121.
67. Will Stanton also falls prey to animalistic fear when his sense of identity is threatened by the Dark. See Cooper, *The Dark Is Rising*, 26.
68. Cooper, *Greenwitch*, 126.
69. Ibid., 127.
70. Ibid.
71. Ibid.
72. Ibid.
73. Ibid,, 128.
74. McCallum, *Ideologies of Identity in Adolescent Fiction*, 68.
75. Casey, *Getting Back into Place*, 275.
76. Christopher Booker, *The Seven Basic Plots: Why We Tell Stories* (London: Continuum, 2004), 83.
77. Reimer, *Home Words*, xviii.
78. Bachelard, *The Poetics of Space*, 11.
79. Wolfgang Schivelbusch, *The Railway Journey: The Industrialisation of Space and Time*, (Berkeley and Los Angeles: University of California Press, 1986; first published as *Geschichte der Eisenbahnreise*, 1977), 55.
80. Ibid., 55.
81. Ibid., 37.
82. Ibid.
83. Alice Jenkins, "Getting to Utopia: Railways and Heterotopia in Children's Literature" in *Utopian and Dystopian Writing for Children and Young Adults*, ed. Carrie Hintz and Elaine Ostry (London: Routledge, 2003), 27.
84. Foucault, 'Of Other Spaces,' 25.
85. Jenkins, "Getting to Utopia: Railways and Heterotopia in Children's Literature," 23.
86. Cooper, *The Dark Is Rising*, 11.

87. Jenkins, "Getting to Utopia: Railways and Heterotopia in Children's Literature," 33.
88. Cooper, *Silver on the Tree*, 238.
89. Ibid., 238.
90. Ibid., 244.
91. Ibid., 250.
92. Margery Hourihan, *Deconstructing the Hero: Literary Theory and Children's Literature* (London: Routledge, 1997), 233.
93. Paul Hindle, *Medieval Roads and Tracks* (Princes Risborough: Shire Publications, 1982), 8.
94. Hindle notes that there were some 10,000 miles of Roman roads in Britain by AD 150. See Hindle, *Medieval Roads and Tracks*, 6.
95. Geoffrey Chaucer, *The Canterbury Tales* in Robinson, *The Riverside Chaucer*.
96. See, for instance, the stories of *Peredur Son of Efrog* and *The Lady of the Well* in Davies, *The Mabinogion*.
97. Hourihan, *Deconstructing the Hero*, 9.
98. Ibid., 10.
99. Tolkien and Gordon, *Sir Gawain and The Green Knight*, line 632.
100. Ibid., line 692.
101. Ibid., line 693.
102. Ibid., lines 709, 713.
103. Casey, *Getting Back into Place*, 276.
104. Tolkien and Gordon, *Sir Gawain and the Green Knight*, line 2502.
105. Ibid., lines 2505–2508.
106. Ibid., line 638.
107. Ibid. line 2509.
108. Hunt, "Landscapes and Journeys," 11.
109. Reimer, *Home Words*, xix.
110. J. R. R. Tolkien, *The Hobbit: Or, There and Back Again*, (London: HarperCollins, 1998; first published 1937).
111. Bakhtin, *The Dialogic Imagination*, 120.
112. Ibid., 150.
113. Tolkien, *The Hobbit*, 361.
114. Robert Westall, *The Kingdom by the Sea* (London: Methuen, 1990), 168.
115. Cooper, *Over Sea, Under Stone*, 66.
116. Cooper, *The Dark Is Rising*, 64.
117. Ibid., 29.
118. Ibid., 31.
119. Ibid.
120. Ibid., 66.
121. Ibid., 31–32.
122. Ibid., 64.
123. Ibid., 48.

124. Ibid., 52.
125. Ibid., 31.
126. Ibid., 217.
127. Ibid..
128. Ibid.
129. Ibid.
130. Ibid., 219.
131. Ibid., 261.
132. Ibid., 260.
133. Ibid., 141.
134. Ibid., 142.
135. Ibid., 147.
136. Ibid., 153.
137. Cooper, *Silver on the Tree*, 214.
138. Throughout T. H. White's *The Once and Future King* (1958), Arthur calls Guinevere 'Jenny-oh.' By having Bran use this name, Cooper multiplies ideas of intertextuality and heritage and reinforces the idea that Bran is the Pendragon and the proper heir to Arthur's power.
139. Ibid., 226.
140. Ibid., 200.
141. Cooper, *Silver on the Tree,* 185–9.
142. Robert Graves, *The White Goddess: A Historical Grammar of Poetic Myth*, ed. Grevel Lindop (London: Faber and Faber, 1948), 71.
143. *The Lady of the Well* in Davies, *The Mabinogion,* 116–139.
144. Cooper, *Silver on the Tree,* 150.
145. See Casie Hermansson, *Bluebeard: A Reader's Guide to the English Tradition* (Jackson: University of Mississippi Press, 2009) 9–10.
146. Jessie L. Weston, *From Ritual to Romance* (Princeton, New Jersey: Princeton University Press, 1993; first published 1920), 60.
147. Ibid., 13.
148. J. J. Jusserand, *English Wayfaring Life in the Middle Ages* (London: Methuen, 1961; first published 1889), 128.
149. Ibid., 141.
150. A.N. Doane, ed., *Genesis A: A New Edition.* (Madison: University of Wisconsin Press, 1978), lines 1050–1051.
151. Ibid., lines 1013b——1021.
152. Ibid., lines 1037–1049.
153. *Beowulf* in Klaeber, *Beowulf and The Fight at Finnsburg,* line 711b.
154. Ibid., line 103.
155. Ibid., line 721a.
156. Ibid., lines 703–725. Among these, Grendel is attributed with *cóm*, coming (702), and *'gongan*, walking (711), *wód*, wending (714) and is elegantly described as *sceadu-genga*, one who moves in shadow (703).

157. Ibid., line 703.
158. *The Wanderer* is found in the Exeter Book, folios 76v to 78r and is reprinted in the original Old English in T. P. Dunning and A. J. Bliss, eds., *The Wanderer* (London: Methuen and Co., 1978) and in George Philip Krapp and Elliott Van Kirk Dobbie, eds., *The Exeter Book* (New York: Columbia University Press, 1936), 134–137.
159. R. F. Leslie, ed., *The Wanderer* (Manchester: Manchester University Press, 1966), lines 5, 32.
160. Ibid., lines 15–24.
161. Also found in the Exeter book. See Krapp and Dobbie, *The Exeter Book*, 143–147.
162. Leslie, *The Wanderer*, line 55.
163. Ibid., lines 56–57.
164. Cooper, *The Dark Is Rising*, 112.
165. See Rosemary Jackson, *Fantasy: The Literature of Subversion* (London: Routledge, 1981), 86.
166. Cooper, *The Dark Is Rising*, 74.
167. Ibid., 76.
168. Ibid., 38–39.
169. Bakhtin, *The Dialogic Imagination*, 177–178.
170. Ibid., 238.
171. Cooper, *The Dark Is Rising*, 74.
172. Ibid., 250.
173. Ibid., 198.
174. Ibid., 128.
175. Genesis 4: 11–14 (NRSV).
176. Marie-France Rouart, 'The Myth of The Wandering Jew' in *Companion to Literary Myths, Heroes and Archetypes*, ed. Pierre Brunel (London: Routledge, 1995), 826–834.
177. Cooper, *The Dark is Rising*, 250.
178. Ibid., 180.
179. In Exodus, the Promised Land is referred to as 'a good broad land, a land flowing with milk and honey' (Exodus 3:8) and when the Israelites cross the desert, God provides them with bread. See Exodus 16.4–16. Thus, bread and honey are associated with both the promise and the process of salvation.
180. Cooper, *The Dark Is Rising*, 14.
181. Ibid., 197.
182. Ibid., 198.
183. A. E. Housman, *A Shropshire Lad* (New York: Henry Holt, 1922).
184. Cooper, *The Dark is Rising*, 38–39.
185. Leslie, *The Wanderer*, line 24.
186. Cooper, *The Dark is Rising*, 167.
187. Ibid., 14.
188. Ibid., 73.

189. Ibid., 76.
190. Reimer, *Home Words*, xviii.
191. Cooper, *The Dark Is Rising*, 253.
192. McCallum, *Ideologies of Identity in Adolescent Fiction*, 189.
193. Muir, *Approaches to Landscape*, 37.
194. Hunt, "Landscapes and Journeys," 11.
195. See Butler, *Four British Fantasists*, 44.
196. Penelope Lively, *The Presence of the Past* (London: Collins, 1976), 7.
197. Penelope Lively, *The Driftway* (London, Heinemann, 1972), 27.
198. Alfred Watkins, *The Old Straight Track: Its Mounds, Beacons, Moats, Sites and Mark Stones* (London: Methuen, 1925).
199. Will identifies John Smith as Wayland (46). Wayland's Smithy, 'a Neolithic long barrow, surrounded by trees, is perhaps the most famous landmark of the Ridgeway and attracts many thousands of visitors annually.' Howard Clarke and Vera Burden, *Discovering the Ridgeway* (London: Osprey, 2002; first published 1976), 53–54.
200. Cooper, *The Dark Is Rising*, 41. The white horse that Will encounters at Wayland's forge could well be the White Horse of Uffington come to life as Wayland's Forge is barely two miles from the chalk horse.
201. Ibid., 31–32.
202. Ibid., 35.
203. Ibid., 38.
204. Rees Ivor Jones, *Facts and Fables From Tywyn: Some True Tales and Some Legends* (Tywyn: Gwynedd, 2001) 37.
205. The Royal Commission on the Ancient and Historical Monuments and Constructions in Wales and Monmouthshire, *An Inventory of the Ancient Monuments in Wales and Monmouthshire, VI County of Merioneth* (London: His Majesty's Stationery Office, 1921), 114. Llwybr Cadfan is no longer in use and it seems to have passed out of memory. When I visited Tywyn in April 2010, no one I spoke to knew of Cadfan's Way.
206. Cooper, *The Grey King*, 36.
207. Ibid., 113.
208. Cooper, *The Dark Is Rising*, 71.
209. Ibid.
210. Ibid., 79.
211. Ibid., 80–81.
212. A similarly important etymological link with the past is seen when Jane Drew realises that 'Kenmare Head' was once 'King Mark's Head.' See Cooper, *Over Sea, Under Stone*, 49.
213. Lively, *The Presence of the Past*, 199.
214. Carl Ortwin Sauer, "Cultural Geography," in E. C. Hayes, ed., *Recent Developments in the Social Sciences* (Hagerstown, Maryland: Lippincott Series in Sociology, 1927), 186.

Notes to Chapter Four

1. Cooper, *Dreams and Wishes*, 187.
2. Jacquetta Hawkes, *A Guide to the Prehistoric and Roman Monuments in England and Wales* (London: Chatto and Windus, 1951), 31–32.
3. David Staines "Crouched in Dark Caves: The Post-Colonial Narcissism of Canadian Literature," *The Yearbook of English Studies* 13, (1983): 268. http://www.jstor.org/stable/3508125. Accessed: 02/11/2009.
4. Tuan, *Space and Place*, 187.
5. Ibid., 187.
6. Muir, *Approaches to Landscape*, 37.
7. Tim Edensor, *Industrial Ruins* (Oxford, Berg, 2005), 88.
8. David Lowenthal, *The Past Is a Foreign Country* (Cambridge: Cambridge University Press, 1985), xxiii.
9. Charles Butler, *Four British Fantasists* (Lanham, Maryland and Oxford: The Children's Literature Association and The Scarecrow Press, 2006), 145.
10. Edensor, *Industrial Ruins*, 126.
11. Butler, *Four British Fantasists*, 44.
12. Ibid., 44, 48.
13. Cooper, *The Dark Is Rising*, 255.
14. Cooper, *Over Sea, Under Stone*, 198.
15. Ibid., 201.
16. Cooper, *The Dark Is Rising*, 24.
17. Drout, 'Reading the Signs of Light,' 230–250.
18. See C. S. Lewis, *The Lion, the Witch and the Wardrobe* (London: HarperCollins, 1980; first published 1950), 43.
19. Cooper, *Over Sea, Under Stone*, 218.
20. Drout, 'Reading the Signs of Light,' 242.
21. Ibid.
22. Cooper, *The Dark Is Rising*, 24.
23. Lois R. Kuznets, "High Fantasy in America: A Study of Lloyd Alexander, Ursula Le Guin, and Susan Cooper," *The Lion and the Unicorn* 9 (1985): 27.
24. Christine Wilkie-Stibbs, 'Intertextuality and the Child Reader' in *Understanding Children's Literature: Key Essays from the Second Edition of the International Companion Encyclopedia of Children's Literature*, ed. Peter Hunt (London and New York: Routledge, 2005), 168–179, 175.
25. Drout, 'Reading the Signs of Light,' 230.
26. The Sutton Hoo ship-burial dates from the seventh century. See Martin Carver, *Sutton Hoo: A Seventh-Century Princely Burial Ground and Its Context* (London: The British Museum Press, 2005), 186–189.
27. Butler, *Four British Fantasists*, 57.
28. Booker, *The Seven Basic Plots*, 23–25.

29. For these terms and for many other regional variations, see Elizabeth Atwood Lawrence, *Hunting the Wren: Transformation of Bird to Symbol: A Study in Human–Animal Relationships* (Knoxville: University of Tennessee Press, 1997), 23.
30. Iona Opie and Peter Opie, *The Lore and Language of Schoolchildren* (Oxford: Oxford University Press, 1960), 288.
31. Butler, *Four British Fantasists*, 47.
32. Hawkes, *A Land*, 4.
33. The normal modern representative of OE *græf* would be *graff*; the ME disyllabic *grave*, from which the standard modern form descends, was probably due to the especially frequent occurrence of the word in the dative (locative) case.
34. Note that my discussion of chthonic spaces does not include animal burrows or subterranean houses; the presence of a resident animal means that these spaces must be considered as domestic spaces rather than chthonic spaces. Mole's house in Grahame's *The Wind in the Willows* (1908), Bilbo Baggins' Hobbit-hole in Tolkien's *The Hobbit* (1937), and Mr. Fox's den in Dahl's *Fantastic Mr. Fox* (1970) are some examples of the subterranean domestic space.
35. Of course, the intertext is still there, and those informed readers that can intuit, guess, or recall the reference will garner a fuller reading of the scene than the naive reader but, most importantly, nobody is left out.
36. Booker, *The Seven Basic Plots*, 69.
37. Cooper, *Over Sea, Under Stone*, 131.
38. For example, see G. P. Taylor, *Wormwood* (2004); Marcus Sedgwick, *My Swordhand Is Singing* (2006); and Neil Gaiman, *The Graveyard Book* (2008).
39. Examples of underworld as fairyland include Lewis Carroll's *Alice's Adventures in Wonderland* (1865) and Terry Pratchett's *The Wee Free Men* (2003). Examples of underworld as the realm of the dead include Garth Nix's *Sabriel* (1995) and Philip Pullman's *The Amber Spyglass* (2000).
40. Booker, *The Seven Basic Plots*, 76.
41. Clare Bradford, *Unsettling Narratives: Postcolonial Readings of Children's Literature* (Waterloo, Ontario: Wilfred Laurier University Press, 2007), 97–100.
42. Bhabha, *The Location of Culture*, 160.
43. Ibid., 160.
44. Most commonly a male figure enters the chthonic space. The cave enters into, penetrates the surface of the earth which, in many mythologies, is figured as feminine. Hervor, the notable exception, professes her willingness to become Angantyr's Son rather than his daughter; she proves herself to have a virile, masculine, de-feminised role. A full translation of *The Waking of Angantyr* may be found in Patricia Terry, *Poems of the Vikings* (Indianapolis: Bobbs-Merrill, 1969), 249–254.

45. Mines are, obviously, full of treasure, even made of treasure, and there are often references to people having 'mined too deeply' and awaking furious underground spirits—J. R. R. Tolkien's *The Fellowship of the Ring* (London: HarperCollins, 2001; first published 1954) or Alan Garner's *The Weirdstone of Brisingamen* (London" William Collins Sons and Co., 1960), for example.
46. Philip Pullman, *The Amber Spyglass* (London: Scholastic, 2000), 281–285.
47. J. R. R. Tolkien, *The Hobbit* (London: HarperCollins, 1998; first published 1937), 201.
48. Cooper, *Over Sea, Under Stone*, 194–195.
49. Ibid., 75.
50. 'The First Branch,' *The Mabinogion*, 5.
51. Snorri Sturluson, *Snorra Edda ásamt Skaldu og þarmeð fylgjandi ritgjörðum*, ed. R. Kr. Rasdk, (Stockholm: Elmen, 1818), 67. A translation of *Snorra Edda* may be found in Kevin Crossley-Holland, *The Norse Myths*, (New York: Pantheon, 1980).
52. The figure of Hel, with her rotting lower body, bears some resemblance to the figure of Sin in Milton's *Paradise Lost*. John Milton, *Paradise Lost, A Poem in Twelve Books*, 2nd ed. (London: Thomas Newton, 1750) Book II, lines 760–802.
53. 'Gylfaginning,' in Sturlson, *Snorra Edda ásamt Skaldu og þarmeð fylgjandi ritgjörðum*, 68.
54. Euripides, *Heracles* in *Medea and Other Plays*, trans. Philip Vellacott (London: Penguin, 1963), lines 12–50. The Orpheus myth may be found in Ovid, *Metamorphoses*, trans. Mary Innes (London: Penguin, 1955), 225–226. The Orpheus myth has a direct descendent in *Sir Orfeo*, the Middle English verse romance. However, in *Sir Orfeo*, the chthonic space is not a route to the past but the entrance to fairyland. *Sir Orfeo* in Donald B. Sands, ed., *Middle English Verse Romances* (Exeter: University of Exeter Press, 1993; first published 1986), 185–201.
55. E. V. Gordon, note on 'Grettis saga,' *An Introduction to Old Norse*, 100.
56. *Njal's Saga*, Kafli 78, Icelandic Saga Database, http://www.sagadb.org/brennu-njals_saga#71 accessed 01/09/11
57. *Grettir's Saga*, Kafli 35, Icelandic Saga Database, http://www.sagadb.org/grettis_saga#31 accessed 01/09/11.
58. 'The Waking of Angantyr' in Gordon, *An Introduction to Old Norse*, lines 35–41. A full translation of 'The Waking of Angantyr' can be found in Terry, *Poems of the Vikings*, 249–254.
59. Tofa gives birth to Hervor after Angantyr's death and, up until this point, she has been unable to prove her parentage. Hervor knows that she will in turn pass the sword on to her own children.

60. 'The Waking of Angantyr' in Gordon, *An Introduction to Old Norse*, lines 50–51. It is interesting to note that the Old Norse word for 'anthill' translates literally as 'ant-barrow' or 'ant-grave.'
61. *The Wife's Lament* in Krapp and Van Kirk Doobie, *The Exeter Book*, 210–211, line 29.
62. Ibid., lines 27–28.
63. Ibid., lines 38–41.
64. Ibid., lines 32–33.
65. F. R. Klaeber, ed. *Beowulf and The Fight at Finnsburg*. 3rd ed. (Boston: D. C. Heath and Co., 1941), lines 2267–2270.
66. Ibid., lines 2247–2248.
67. Ibid., lines 2252–2254.
68. Ibid., lines 103–104.
69. Ibid., line 1513. The *niðsele* stands in direct opposition to the *wínsele*, the joy-hall, Heorot. The poet clearly invites a comparison between the two halls, describing the cave as *hrófsele*, a vaulted hall in which firelight gleams (1515–1517). Heorot is described as 'towering, high and horn-gabled' (81–82).
70. Ibid. lines 1663.
71. Ibid. lines 1558.
72. Ibid., lines 1694–1698.
73. Ibid., lines 2799–2800.
74. A corresponding episode from the *Mabinogion* sees Peredur enter a cave to slay a dragon. Although there is no gold here, the treasure, in the form of a bride, waits patiently outside for him to slay the monster.
75. F. R. Klaeber, ed. *Beowulf*, lines 2758–2762.
76. Nolan Dalrymple, 'North East Childhoods,' PhD diss., Newcastle University, 2008, 285–286.
77. Ibid., 278–279.
78. Michael Rosen, *We're Going on a Bear Hunt* (London: Walker, 1989) opening 11.
79. Alan Garner, *The Weirdstone of Brisingamen* (London: William Collins Sons and Co., 1960), 32.
80. Ibid., 42.
81. Ibid., 40–41.
82. Bill Griffiths, *Meet the Dragon: An Introduction to Beowulf's Adversary* (Loughborough: Heart of Albion Press, 1996), 9.
83. C. S. Lewis, *The Voyage of the Dawn Treader* (London: HarperCollins, 1994; first published 1955), 92–7.
84. J. K. Rowling, *Harry Potter and the Deathly Hallows* (London: Bloomsbury, 2007), 432.
85. Neil Gaiman, *The Graveyard Book* (London: HarperCollins, 2008), 56.
86. Tolkien, *The Hobbit*, 68.
87. Ibid., 67.
88. Ibid., 68.

89. Ibid., 77.
90. Ibid., 112.
91. Ibid., 198.
92. Ibid., 202.
93. Cooper, *Over Sea, Under Stone* 132; Cooper, *The Grey King*, 181–183.
94. The female figure, Tethys, is not out of place as Cooper posits powerful female figures throughout the *Sequence* in *The Lady*, Miss Greythorne, and (as I have argued) the *Greenwitch*.
95. Cooper, *Over Sea, Under Stone*, 132.
96. Ibid., 35.
97. It should be noted that the map is not an authentic connection to the past because it is a copy of an earlier manuscript.
98. Cooper, *Over Sea, Under Stone*, 82.
99. Ibid., 136.
100. Ibid..
101. Ibid., 139–140.
102. Hawkes, *A Land*, 17.
103. Cooper, *Over Sea, Under Stone*, 185.
104. Ibid., 185–186.
105. Ibid., 186.
106. Ibid., 190.
107. Ibid., 191.
108. Ibid., 192.
109. Ibid., 75.
110. Ibid., 194.
111. Ibid., 195.
112. Ibid., 196.
113. Cooper, *The Dark Is Rising*, 234.
114. Ibid., 235. Michael Drout notes that the ship and the treasure provide an intertextual link with medieval literature and, through the mention of the ship-burial and the boar-helmet which the king wears, evoke the Sutton-Hoo ship burial. See Michael C. Drout, 'Reading the Signs of Light: Anglo-Saxonism, Education and Obedience in Susan Cooper's *The Dark Is Rising*,' *The Lion and the Unicorn* 21/2 (1997): 234. The Sutton-Hoo ship burial, excavated during the 1930s, provides clear archaeological evidence for this kind of ship-burial in the East and South of England. Among the many treasures found during the excavation was a great gold buckle of seventh-century East-Anglian craftsmanship found in the very centre of the coffin. Whether this buckle lay on the breast of the deceased or was placed on top of the coffin lid remains unclear. See Carver, *Sutton Hoo*, 186–189. If the Sutton Hoo ship-burial is a true source for Cooper's ship of the Light, then the great buckle may be read——especially considering its position——as a source for the Sign of Water.

115. *Beowulf* in Klaeber, *Beowulf and The Fight at Finnsburg*, lines 26–46.
116. Snorri Sturluson, *Snorra Edda ásamt Skaldu og þarmeð fylgjandi ritgjörðum*, 64–67.
117. Roberta Frank, "Beowulf and Sutton Hoo: The Odd Couple" in *Voyage to the Other World: The Legacy of Sutton Hoo*, ed. Calvin B. Kendall and Peter S. Wells (Minneapolis: University of Minnesota Press, 1992), 47–65.
118. Cooper, *The Dark Is Rising*, 234–235.
119. Cooper, *The Grey King* (London: Puffin Books, 1977; first published 1975), 86.
120. Ibid., 88. Riddle-tests are common in literature, but the ones most readers of children's literature are familiar with are the riddles in Lewis Carroll's *Alice's Adventures in Wonderland* and the games played by Bilbo, Gollum, and Smaug in Tolkien's *The Hobbit*, both of which take place underground. While Gollum's cave, like the cave at Craig yr Aderyn, is deeply embedded in time, Wonderland is a place where time is continually disrupted.
121. Cooper, *Over Sea, Under Stone*, 75.
122. Cooper, *Greenwitch*, 88.
123. Ibid., 85.
124. Ibid., 84.
125. Ibid., 85.
126. Ibid., 87.
127. Ibid., 85.
128. Ibid., 88.
129. Cooper, *Silver on the Tree*, 683.
130. Ibid., 687.
131. Ibid., 663.
132. Ibid., 663.
133. W. Jenkyn Thomas, *The Welsh Fairy Book* (London: Dover, 2001; first published 1907), 22.
134. Robin Gwyndaf, *Welsh Folk Tales* (Cardiff: National Museum Wales, 1989), 77.
135. Cooper, *Silver on the Tree*, 43.
136. Ibid., 44.
137. Ibid., 49.
138. Ibid., 46–47.
139. Ibid., 47.
140. Ibid., 51.
141. Ibid., 44
142. Ibid., 49.
143. Ibid..
144. Edensor, *Industrial Ruins*, 139.
145. Ibid.

146. For a discussion of the uneasy and uncanny association of ruins see David Watkin, 'Built Ruins: The Hermitage as a Retreat' in *Visions of Ruin: Architectural Fantasies and Designs for Garden Follies,* ed. Margaret Richardson (London: Sir John Soane's Museum, 1999), 14.
147. Edensor, *Industrial Ruins,* 25.
148. Claire Sponsler, 'Beyond the Ruins: The Geopolitics of Urban Decay and Cybernetic Play,' *Science Fiction Studies* 20/ 2 (1993): 256.
149. W. J. T. Mitchell, "Imperial Landscape" in W. J. T. Mitchell, *Landscape and Power* , 2nd ed. (Chicago: University of Chicago Press, 2002), 18.
150. Peter Nicholls, '"The Pastness of Landscapes": Susan Howe's *Pierce-Arrow,*' *Contemporary Literature* 43/3 (2002): 449.
151. Edensor, *Industrial Ruins,* 41.
152. Csaba Toth, 'Like Cancer in the System: Industrial Gothic, Nine Inch Nails and Videotape,' in *Gothic: Transmutations of Horror in Late Twentieth Century Art,* edited by Christoph Grunenberg (Boston: Institute of Contemporary Art, 1997), 90–80 (pagination runs in reverse), 89.
153. Bhabha, *The Location of Culture,* 163.
154. Edensor, *Industrial Ruins,* 43.
155. Mike Crang and Penny Tavlou, "The city and topologies of memory," in *Environment and Planning D: Society and Space* 19 (2001): 161.
156. Edensor, *Industrial Ruins,* 17.
157. R. Kabbani, *Europe's Myths of Orient* (London: Pandora, 1986) quoted in Edensor, *Industrial Ruins,* 55.
158. Bhabha, *The Location of Culture,* 234.
159. Anne Janowitz, *England's Ruins* (Oxford: Blackwell, 1990),108.
160. David Punter, *The Literature of Terror: A History of Gothic Fictions from 1765 to the Present Day* (London: Longman, 1980), 97.
161. Anthony Vidler, *The Architectural Uncanny* (Cambridge, Massachusetts: Massachusetts Institute of Technology, 1992), 6–7.
162. Christoph Grunenberg, "Unsolved Mysteries: Gothic Tales from *Frankenstein* to the Hair-Eating Doll," in *Gothic: Transmutations of Horror in Late Twentieth-Century Art,* ed. Christoph Grunenberg (Boston: The Institute of Contemporary Art and Cambridge, Massachusetts: The MIT Press, 1997), 195.
163. Watkin, "Built Ruins: The Hermitage as a Retreat," 10.
164. David Punter, *The Gothic* (Malden, Massachussetts and Oxford : Blackwell, 2004), 9–10.
165. Ibid., 88–89.
166. Patrick McGrath, "Transgression and Decay" in *Gothic: Transmutations of Horror in Late Twentieth-Century Art,* ed. Christoph Grunenberg (Boston: The Institute of Contemporary Art and Cambridge, Massachusetts: The MIT Press, 1997), 154.
167. Janowitz, *England's Ruins,* 6.

220 • Notes

168. Stuart D. Lee and Elizabeth Solopova, *The Keys of Middle Earth* (London: Palgrave, 2005), 135.
169. S. A .J. Bradley, *Anglo-Saxon Poetry* (London: Everyman, 2000), 202.
170. F. R. Klaeber, ed., *Beowulf*, lines 2249–2266.
171. Ibid., line 2462.
172. Ibid., lines 70–87.
173. Ibid., line 113.
174. Ibid., line 727.
175. Ibid., lines 409–413.
176. B. J. Muir, ed., *The Exeter Anthology of Old English Poetry: An Edition of Exeter Dean and Chapter MS3501*, 2 vols. (Exeter: University of Exeter Press, 1994; first published 1994), 699.
177. 'The Ruin' in Krapp and Van Kirk Dobbie, *The Exeter Book*, 227–229, lines 8–9.
178. Ibid., line 1.
179. Ibid., lines 5–6.
180. Ibid., line 10.
181. Ibid., lines 3–4.
182. Ibid., lines 29–31.
183. Edensor, *Industrial Ruins*, 11
184. Cooper, *Dreams and Wishes*, 187.
185. C. S. Lewis, *Prince Caspian* (London: HarperCollins, 2005; first published 1951), 19–22.
186. Robert Westall, *Ghost Abbey* (London: Corgi, 2004; first published 1988), 215–216.
187. Ibid., 217.
188. Ibid., 120–121.
189. Crang and Travlou, "The City and Topologies of Memory, " 161.
190. Edensor, *Industrial Ruins*, 126.
191. J. K. Rowling, *Harry Potter and the Prisoner of Azkaban* (London: Bloomsbury, 1999), 248.
192. Ibid., 277.
193. Terry Pratchett, *Nation* (London: Doubleday, 2008), 30.
194. Pullman, *The Amber Spyglass*, 267–271.
195. Gaiman, *The Graveyard Book*, 15–16.
196. Edensor, *Industrial Ruins*, 152.
197. Pratchett, *Nation*, 34.
198. Ibid., 141.
199. Edensor, *Industrial Ruins*, 55.
200. Fred Botting, *Gothic* (London: Routledge, 1996), 2.
201. Cooper, *Greenwitch*, 138–9.
202. Ibid., 143.
203. Ibid., 142.
204. Ibid., 142–143.

205. Cooper, *Silver on the Tree*, 186.
206. The magical and mythic associations of the hawthorn are detailed in Chapter 2, n. 228.
207. Cooper, *The Grey King*, 148–149.
208. Ibid., 155.
209. Ibid., 148.
210. Ibid., 149.
211. Ibid., 160.
212. Ibid., 164.
213. Ibid., 167.
214. Ibid., 164.
215. Bhabha, *The Location of Culture*, 234.
216. Cooper, *The Grey King*, 165.
217. Ibid., 168.
218. Ibid,.173.
219. Ibid,.172–173.
220. Cooper, *Dreams and Wishes*, 187.
221. Tuan, *Space and Place*, 18.

Notes to Chapter Five

1. For a discussion of the relationship between mindscape and landscape see Jane Suzanne Carroll, 'Its Own Place: Mindscape and Landscape in Two Children's Texts,' *The Journal of Children's Literature Studies*, 8/1 (2011): 18–33.
2. Peter Bramwell, *Pagan Themes in Modern Children's Fiction: Green Man, Shamanism, Earth Mysteries* (Basingstoke and New York: Palgrave Macmillan, 2009), 38–83.
3. Butler, *Four British Fantasists*, 45.
4. Susan Cooper in interview with Marcus in Marcus, *The Wand in the Word*, 38–39.
5. Mikkelsen, *Susan Cooper*, 123.
6. John Masefield, *The Box of Delights* (London: Egmont, 2000; first published 1935), 35.
7. Ibid., 37.
8. Ibid., 42.
9. Manlove, *From Alice to Harry Potter*, 58.
10. Masefield, *The Box of Delights*, 303.
11. Ibid., 83.
12. Ibid., 85–86.
13. See Davies, *The Mabinogion*, 47–64. This kind of physical transformation is a common folkloric trope and Vladimir Propp classes it as function T1 of the folktale. See Propp, *Morphology of the Folktale*, 154.

14. Bramwell, *Pagan Themes in Modern Children's Fiction*, 52.
15. Masefield, *The Box of Delights*, 68.
16. Ibid., 12.
17. For a discussion of the hanged man archetype in modern children's literature, see James Holt McGavran, *Literature and the Child: Romantic Continuations, Postmodern Contestations* (Iowa City: University of Iowa Press, 1999), 244–246.
18. Masefield, *The Box of Delights*, 32.
19. Ibid.,194.
20. Ibid.,192.
21. Neil Philip, *A Fine Anger: A Critical Introduction to the Work of Alan Garner* (New York: Philomel, 1981), 12.
22. Hunt, 'Landscapes and Journeys,' 13.
23. Ibid., 11.
24. Garner, *The Owl Service*, 9–10.
25. Ibid., 138.
26. Ibid., 52.
27. Ibid., 52–53.
28. Ibid., 55.
29. Ibid.
30. Ibid., 124–125.
31. Ibid., 125.
32. Ibid., 128.
33. Ibid., 143.
34. Ibid., 127.
35. Ibid., 58.
36. Ibid., 13.
37. See Pearsall and Salter, *Landscapes and Seasons of the Medieval World*, 50.
38. Garner, *The Owl Service*, 13–14.
39. Ibid., 140.
40. Butler, *Four British Fantasists*, 155.
41. Garner, *The Owl Service*, 72.
42. Butler, *Four British Fantasists*, 88.
43. Garner, *The Owl Service*, 51.
44. Butler, *Four British Fantasists*, 47.
45. Garner, *The Owl Service*, 192.
46. Meg Rosoff, *How I Live Now* (London: Penguin, 2004), 8.
47. Ibid., 9.
48. Ibid.
49. Ibid., 11.
50. Ibid., 12.
51. Ibid., 9.
52. Ibid., 9.

53. Ibid., 21.
54. Bachelard, *The Poetics of Space*, 101.
55. Rosoff, *How I Live Now*, 40.
56. Mikkelsen, *Susan Cooper*, 122.
57. Rosoff, *How I Live Now*, 104.
58. Ibid., 112–113.
59. Ibid., 141.
60. Rosoff, *How I Live Now*, 159.
61. Ibid., 156.
62. Ibid., 134–135.
63. Ibid., 136.
64. Ibid., 156.
65. Ibid., 162.
66. Ibid., 190.
67. Ibid., 207.
68. Hunt, 'Landscapes and Journeys, Metaphors and Maps,' 11.

Bibliography

Abrahamson, Dick, and Barbara Kiefer. 'Young Adult Literature: Books Worth Putting on Your Summer Reading List.' *The English Journal* 73/4 (1984): 90–92.
Abrams, J., ed. *Reclaiming the Inner Child*. New York: G. P. Putnam's Sons, 1990.
Ackerman, James S. 'Villard de Honnecourt's Drawings of Reims Cathedral: A Study in Architectural Representation.' *Artibus et Historiae* 18/35 (1997): 41–49.
Adams, Richard. *Watership Down*. London: Rex Collings, 1972.
Aelfric (Abbot of Eynsham). *Aelfric's Colloquy*. Edited by G. N. Garmonsway. Exeter: University of Exeter Press, 1978.
Almond, David. *Clay*. London: Hodder, 2005.
———. *Kit's Wilderness*. London: Hodder, 1999.
———. *The Savage*. Illustrated by Dave McKean. London: Walker Books, 2008.
Althusser, Louis. *Lenin and Philosophy and Other Essays*. Translated by Ben Brewster. London: New Left Books, 1971.
Althusser, Louis, and Étienne Balibar. *Reading Capital*. Translated by Ben Brewster. London: Verso, 1997.
Aiken, Joan. *The Wolves of Willoughby Chase*. London: Jonathan Cape, 1963.
Andrén, Anders. 'Landscape and Settlement as Utopian Space.' In *Settlement and Landscape: Proceedings of a Conference in Arhus, Denmark, May 4–7 1998*, edited by Charlotte Fabech and Jytte Rintveld, 383–393. Moesgard: Jutland Archaeological Society, 1999.
Anderson, Benedict. *Imagined Communities: Reflections on the Origin and Spread of Nationalism*. London: Verso, 1983.
Appleton, Jay. *The Experience of Landscape*. London: Wiley, 1975.
Ashcroft, Bill, Gareth Griffiths, and Helen Tiffin, eds. *Post-Colonial Studies: The Key Concepts*. London and New York: Routledge, 1998.
Attenborough, Richard. Dir. *Shadowlands*. Price Entertainment, 1993.
Augarde, Steve. *The Various*. London: Corgi Books, 2003.
Bachelard, Gaston. *The Poetics of Reverie: Childhood, Language and the Cosmos*. Translated by Daniel Russell. Boston: Beacon Press, 1969.
———. *The Poetics of Space*. Translated by Marie Jolas. Boston: Beacon Press, 1994; first published as *La poétique de l'éspace*, 1958.
Bachelder, Linda, Patricia Kelly, Donald Kenney, and Robert Small. 'Young Adult Literature: Looking Backward: Trying to Find the Classic Young Adult Novel.' *The English Journal* 69/6 (1980): 86–89.
Bacon, Francis. *The Essays*. London: Penguin Books, 1986.
Badone, Ellen, and Sharon R. Roseman, eds. *Intersecting Journeys: The Anthropology of Pilgrimage and Tourism*. Chicago: University of Illinois Press, 2004.
Bakhtin, M. M. *The Dialogic Imagination: Four Essays*. Translated by Michael Holquist. Austin: University of Texas Press, 1981.
———. *Rabelais and His World*. Translated by Helene Iswolsky. London: Bloomington, 1965.
Barrell, John. *The Idea of Landscape and the Sense of Place 1730–1840: An Approach to the Poetry of John Clare*. Cambridge: Cambridge University Press, 1972.

226 • Bibliography

Bator, Robert, ed. *Signposts to the Criticism of Children's Literature*. Chicago: American Library Association, 1983.
Bawden, Nina. *Carrie's War*. London: Victor Gollancz, 1973.
Bechmann, Roland. *Trees and Man: The Forest in the Middle Ages*. New York: Paragon House, 1990; first published 1984.
Benjamin, Walter. *The Arcades Project*. Translated by Howard Eiland and Kevin McLaughlin. Cambridge, Massachusetts and London: The Belknap Press of Harvard University Press, 1999.
Beynon, Huw, and Ray Hudson. 'Place and Space in Contemporary Europe: Some Lessons and Reflections.' *Antipode* 25/3 (1993): 177–190.
Bhabha, Homi. *The Location of Culture*. London: Routledge, 2004.
Blanchot, Maurice. *The Infinite Conversation*. Translated by Susan Hanson. Minneapolis: University of Minnesota Press, 1993.
Bloom, Harold. *Charlotte Bronte's Jane Eyre*. London: Chelsea House, 1987.
Blyton, Enid. *Adventures of the Wishing Chair*. London: Newnes, 1950.
———. *The Children of Cherry-Tree Farm*. London: Merlin, 1947; first published 1940.
———. *Five go to Finniston Farm*. London: Hodder and Stoughton, 1960.
Booker, Christopher. *The Seven Basic Plots: Why We Tell Stories*. London: Continuum, 2004.
Boston, Lucy M. *The Children of Green Knowe*. London: Faber and Faber, 2006; first published 1954.
Botting, Fred. *Gothic*. London: Routledge, 1996.
Bradford, Clare. *Unsettling Narratives: Postcolonial Readings of Children's Literature*. Waterloo, Ontario: Wilfred Laurier University Press, 2007.
Bradley, S. A. J. *Anglo-Saxon Poetry*. London: Everyman, 2000.
Bramwell, Peter. *Pagan Themes in Modern Children's Fiction: Green Man, Shamanism, Earth Mysteries*. Basingstoke and New York: Palgrave Macmillan, 2009.
Briggs, K. M. *Hobberdy Dick*. Harmondsworth: Kestrel Books, 1955.
Briggs, Raymond. *The Snowman*. London: Hamish Hamilton, 1978.
Brontë, Charlotte. *Jane Eyre*. London: J. M. Dent and Sons, 1922; first published 1847.
Bunce, Michael. *The Countryside Ideal: Anglo-American Images of Landscape*. London and New York: Routledge, 1994.
Burnett, Frances Hodgson. *A Little Princess*. London: Puffin, 2008; first published 1905.
———. *The Secret Garden*. Edited by Gretchen Holbrook Gerzina. New York: W. W. Norton, 2006.
Butler, Charles. *Four British Fantasists: Place and Culture in the Children's Fantasies of Penelope Lively, Alan Garner, Diana Wynne Jones and Susan Cooper*. Lanham, Maryland and Oxford: The Children's Literature Association and The Scarecrow Press, 2006.
Butler, Judith. *Gender Trouble: Feminism and the Subversion of Identity*. New York and London: Routledge, 1999.
Byock, Jesse L., trans. *The Saga of King Hrolf Kraki*. London: Penguin, 1988.
Carpenter, Humphrey. *Secret Gardens: A Study of the Golden Age of Children's Literature*. London: Allen and Unwin, 1985.
Carroll, Jane Suzanne. 'Its Own Place: Mindscape and Landscape in Two Children's Texts.' *Journal of Children's Literature Studies*, 8/1 (2011): 18–33.
———. 'Two Misconstrued Attic Spaces in Susan Cooper's The Dark Is Rising Sequence.' *Trinity College Dublin Journal of Postgraduate Research*, 7 (2008): 75–84.
Carroll, Lewis. *The Annotated Alice: Alice's Adventures in Wonderland and Through the Looking Glass*. Edited by Martin Gardner. London: Penguin, 1963; first published 1960.
Carver, Martin. *Sutton Hoo: A Seventh-Century Princely Burial Ground and Its Context*. London: The British Museum Press, 2005.
Casey, Edward S. *Getting Back into Place: Toward a Renewed Understanding of the Place-World*. Indianapolis: Indiana University Press, 1993.
Chaucer, Geoffrey. *The Riverside Chaucer*. Edited by F. N. Robinson. Oxford: Oxford University Press, 1988.
Chidester, David, and Edward Tabor Linenthal, eds. *American Sacred Space*. Indianapolis: Indiana University Press, 1995.
Cieraad, Irene, ed. *At Home: An Anthropology of Domestic Space*. Syracuse, New York: Syracuse University Press, 1999.
Cixous, Hélène. *The Cixous Reader*. Edited by Susan Sellers. New York and London: Routledge, 1994.
Clarke, Catherine A. M. *Literary Landscapes and the Idea of England, 700–1400*. Cambridge: D. S. Brewer, 2008.

Clarke, Howard, and Vera Burden. *Discovering the Ridgeway*. London: Osprey, 2002; first published 1976.
Clausen, Wendell. *A Commentary on Virgil Eclogues*. Oxford: Clarendon Press, 1994.
Cole, David. 'Abstract Spaces: A Workshop Approach.' *The Drama Review* 22/4 (1978): 43–54.
Colfer, Eoin. *Artemis Fowl*. London: Viking, 2001.
Conan, Michel. *Sacred Gardens and Landscapes, Ritual and Agency*. Washington, D.C.: Harvard University Press, 2007.
Cooper, Susan. *The Boggart*. Harmondsworth: Puffin, 1994; first published 1993.
———. *The Boggart and the Monster*. Harmondsworth: Puffin, 2000; first published 1997.
———. *Danny and the Kings*. Illustrated by Jos A. Smith. New York: McElderry, 1993.
———. *The Dark Is Rising*. London: Puffin Books, 1976; first published 1973.
———. *Dawn of Fear*. London: Puffin Books, 1970.
———. *Dreams and Wishes: Essays on Writing for Children*. New York: McElderry, 1996.
———. *Frog*. Illustrated by Jane Browne. London: Bodley Head, 2002.
———. *Green Boy*. London: Puffin Books, 2002.
———. *Greenwitch*. London: Puffin Books, 1977; first published 1974.
———. *The Grey King*. London: Puffin Books, 1977; first published 1975.
———. 'In Defense of the Artist.' In *Signposts to the Criticism of Children's Literature*, edited by Robert Bator, 98–102. Chicago: American Library Association, 1983.
———. *Jethro and the Jumbie*. Illustrated by Ashley Bryan. New York: Atheneum, 1979.
———. *King of Shadows*. London: Bodley Head, 1999.
———. *The Magician's Boy*. Illustrated by Serena Riglietti. New York: McElderry, 2005.
———. *Mandrake*. Harmondsworth: Penguin, 1966; first published 1964.
———. *Matthew's Dragon*. Illustrated by Jos A. Smith. New York: McElderry, 1991.
———. *Over Sea, Under Stone*. London: Puffin Books, 1968; first published 1965.
———. *Seaward*. Harmondsworth: Puffin, 1985; first published 1983.
———. *The Selkie Girl*. Illustrated by Warick Hutton. London: Hodder and Stoughton, 1987; first published 1986.
———. *The Silver Cow*. Illustrated by Warwick Hutton. London: Chatto and Windus, 1983.
———. *Silver on the Tree*. London: Puffin Books, 1979; first published 1977.
———. *Tam Lin*. Illustrated by Warwick Hutton. New York: McElderry, 1991.
———. *Victory*. London: Bodley Head, 2006.
Crang, Mike. *Cultural Geography*. London: Routledge, 1998.
Crang, Mike, and Penny Travlou. 'The City and Topologies of Memory.' *Environment and Planning D: Society and Space* 19 (2001): 161–177.
Croce, Benedetto. *History: Its Theory and Practice*. New York: Harcourt, 1921.
Crossley-Holland, Kevin. *Gatty's Tale*. London: Orion, 2006.
———. *The Norse Myths*. New York: Pantheon Books, 1980.
Cunningham-Burley, Sarah, and Kathryn Backett-Milburn, eds. *Exploring the Body*. London: Palgrave, 2001.
Cunningham, David L. Dir. *The Seeker*. Walden Media, 2007.
Curtius, Ernst Robert. *European Literature and The Latin Middle Ages*, translated by Willard R. Trask. London and Henley: Routledge and Kegan Paul, 1953.
Dahl, Roald. *Fantastic Mr. Fox*. London: Allen and Unwin, 1970.
———. *James and the Giant Peach*. New York: Alfred A. Knopf, 1961.
Dalrymple, Nolan. 'North East Childhoods.' PhD diss., Newcastle University, 2008.
Daniels, Stephen, and Simon Rycroft. 'Mapping the Modern City: Alan Sillitoe's Nottingham Novels.' *Transactions of the Institute of British Geographers* 18/4 (1993): 460–480.
Darcy, Jane. 'Wild Creatures: The Representation of Nature in *The Wind in the Willows* and *The Secret Garden*.' *The Lion and The Unicorn* 19/2 (1995): 211–222.
Davidson, Peter. *The Idea of North*. London: Reaktion, 2005.
Davies, R. T., ed. *Medieval English Lyrics*. London: Faber and Faber, 1963.
Davies, Sionad, trans. *The Mabinogion*. Oxford: Oxford University Press, 2007.
Dearden, Carmen Diana. 'Memories of Meeting Worlds or Close Encounters of the Fourth Kind.' *Bookbird: A Journal of International Children's Literature* 48/1 (2010): 51–60.
de Botton, Alain. *The Architecture of Happiness: the Secret Art of Furnishing Your Life*. London: Penguin, 2007; first published 2006.
de Mare, Heidi. 'Domesticity in Dispute: A Reconsideration of Sources.' In *At Home: An Anthropology of Domestic Space*, edited by Irene Cieraad, 13–30. Syracuse, New York: Syracuse University Press, 1999.

Derrida, Jacques. *Writing and Difference*. London: Routledge and Kegan Paul, 1968; first published 1967.
Dewan, Pauline. *The House as Setting, Symbol and Structural Motif in Children's Literature*. Lewiston, New York: The Edwin Mellen Press, 2004.
———. *The Art of Place in Literature for Children and Young Adults: How Locale Shapes a Story*. Lewiston, Queenston, Lampeter: The Edwin Mellen Press, 2010.
DiTerlizzi, Tony, and Holly Black. *The Field Guide*. New York: Simon and Schuster, 2003.
Doane, A. N., ed. *Genesis A: A New Edition*. Madison: University of Wisconsin Press, 1978.
———. *The Saxon Genesis: An Edition of the West Saxon Genesis B and the Old Saxon Vatican Genesis*. Madison: University of Wisconsin Press, 1991.
Donoghue, Daniel. *Old English Literature: A Short Introduction*. London: Blackwell, 2004.
Dowd, Siobhan. *Solace of the Road*. Oxford: David Fickling Books, 2007.
Drabble, Margaret. *A Writer's Britain*. London: Thames and Hudson, 2009; first published as *A Writer's Britain: Landscape in Literature*, 1979.
Drout, Michael. 'Reading the Signs of Light: Anglo-Saxonism, Education, and Obedience in Susan Cooper's *The Dark Is Rising*.' *The Lion and the Unicorn* 21/2 (1997): 230–250.
Dunbar, Robert. 'It's the way we tell 'em: voices from Ulster Children's Fiction.' In *Divided Worlds*, edited by Mary Shine Thompson and Valerie Coghlan, 61–75. Dublin: Four Courts Press, 2007.
Dunning, T. P., and A. J. Bliss, eds. *The Wanderer*. London: Methuen and Co., 1978.
Duroche, Leonard L. 'A 'Landscape' Approach to Teaching Poetry.' *Die Unterrichtspraxis/Teaching German* 11/1 (1978): 20–6.
Dusinberre, Juliet. *Alice to the Lighthouse: Children's Books and Radical Experiments in Art*. London: Macmillan Press, 1999.
Edensor, Tim. *Industrial Ruins*. Oxford: Berg, 2005.
Edwards, J.M, trans. and ed. *The Greek Bucolic Poets*. Cambridge: Cambridge University Press, 1986.
Egoff, Sheila. *Thursday's Child: Trends and Patterns in Contemporary Children's Literature*. Chicago: American Library Association, 1981.
Eliade, Mircea. *The Sacred And the Profane: The Nature of Religion*. Translated by Willard R. Trask. San Diego: Harcourt Brace Jovanovich, 1959.
Eliot, T. S. *Collected Poems, 1909–1962*. London: Faber and Faber, 1974.
Empson, William. *Some Versions of Pastoral*. London: Chatto and Windus, 1935.
Euripides. *Medea and Other Plays*. Translated by Philip Vellacott. London: Penguin, 1963.
Farley, Paul, and Michael Symmons Roberts. *Edgelands: Journeys into England's True Wilderness*. London: Jonathan Cape, 2011.
Fife, Wayne. 'British Missionaries in New Guinea.' In *Intersecting Journeys: The Anthropology of Pilgrimage and Tourism*, edited by Ellen Badone and Sharon R. Roseman, 140–59.Chicago: University of Illinois Press, 2004.
Flenley, John, and Paul G. Bahn. *The Enigmas of Easter Island: Island on the Edge*. Oxford: Oxford University Press, 2003.
Foucault, Michel. *The Order of Things: An Archaeology of the Human Sciences*. Abingdon and New York: Routledge, 2002; first published as *Les mots et les choses*, 1966.
———. 'Of Other Spaces.' Translated by Jay Miskowiec. *Diacritics* 16 (1986): 22–27.
Frank, Roberta. 'Beowulf and Sutton Hoo: The Odd Couple.' In *Voyage to the Other World: The Legacy of Sutton Hoo*, edited by Calvin B. Kendall and Peter S. Wells, 47–65. Minneapolis: University of Minnesota Press, 1992.
Frazer, James. *The Golden Bough: A Study in Magic and Religion*. Oxford: Oxford University Press, 1994; first published 1922.
Freud, Sigmund. *The Complete Psychological Works of Sigmund Freud, XVII (1917–1919)*. Translated by James Strachey. New York: W. W. Norton, 1959.
Gaiman, Neil. *The Graveyard Book*. London: HarperCollins, 2008.
———. *Stardust*. London: Headline, 1999.
Gallagher, Winifred. *The Power of Place*. New York: HarperCollins, 1993.
Garner, Alan. *The Owl Service*. London: HarperCollins, 2007; first published 1967.
———. *The Weirdstone of Brisingamen*. London: William Collins Sons and Co., 1960.
Garrard, Greg. *Ecocriticism*. London and New York: Routledge, 2004.
George, Jean Craighead. *My Side of the Mountain*. London: Puffin, 1959.
Gerstel Sharon E. J., ed. *Thresholds of the Sacred: Architectural, Art Historical, Liturgical and Theological Perspectives on Religious Screens, East and West*. Washington, D.C.: Harvard University Press, 2006.

Glotfelty, Cheryll, and Harold Fromm, eds. *The Ecocriticism Reader: Landmarks in Literary Ecology*. Athens and London: University of Georgia Press, 1996.
Godwin, Joscelyn. *The Pagan Dream of the Renaissance*. London: Thames and Hudson, 2002.
Gordon, E. V. *An Introduction to Old Norse*. Oxford: Oxford University Press, 1927.
———. *Pearl*. Oxford: Oxford University Press, 1953.
Goudge, Elizabeth. *The Little White Horse*. London: University of London Press, 1946.
Grahame, Kenneth. *The Wind in the Willows*. London: Penguin, 2005; first published 1908.
Graves, Robert. *The White Goddess: A Historical Grammar of Poetic Myth*. Edited by Grevel Lindop. London: Faber and Faber, 1948.
Griffiths, Bill. *Meet the Dragon: An Introduction to Beowulf's Adversary*. Loughborough: Heart of Albion Press, 1996.
Grunenberg Christoph, ed. *Gothic: Transmutations of Horror in Late Twentieth-Century Art*. Boston: The Institute of Contemporary Art and Cambridge, Massachusetts: The MIT Press, 1997.
Gussow, Alan, and Richard Wilbur. *A Sense of Place: The Artist and the American Land*. New York: Seabury, 1971.
Gwyndaf, Robin. *Welsh Folk Tales*. Cardiff: National Museum Wales, 1989.
Haddon, Mark. *The Curious Incident of the Dog in the Night-Time*. Oxford: David Fickling, 2003.
Haggard, H. Rider. *King Solomon's Mines*. London: Cassell and Co., 1885.
Hamilton, Sarah, and Andrew Spicer, eds. *Defining the Holy: Sacred Space in Medieval and Early Modern Europe*. Aldershot: Ashgate Publishing, 2005.
Handler, Daniel. *The Basic Eight*. New York: St. Martin's Press, 1999.
Harris, Stephen J. 'Aelfric's Colloquy.' In *Medieval Literature for Children*. Edited by Daniel T. Kline, 112–130. London: Routledge, 2003.
Harrison, Stephen, Steve Pile, and Nigel Thrift, eds. *Patterned Ground: Entanglements of Nature and Culture*. London: Reaktion, 2004.
Hartshorne, R. *The Nature of Geography: A Critical Survey of Current Thought in The Light of The Past*. Lancaster, Pennsylvania: Association of American Geographers, 1939.
Hawkes, Jacquetta. *A Guide to the Prehistoric and Roman Monuments in England and Wales*. London: Chatto and Windus, 1951.
———. *A Land*. London: The Cresset Press, 1953.
Hayes, E. C., ed. *Recent Developments in the Social Sciences*. Hagerstown, Maryland: Lippincott Series in Sociology, 1927.
Hermansson, Casie. *Bluebeard: A Reader's Guide to the English Tradition*. Jackson: University of Mississippi Press, 2009.
Hicks, Clive. *The Green Man: A Field Guide*. Fakenham: Compass Books, 2000.
Hindle, Paul. *Medieval Roads and Tracks*. Princes Risborough: Shire Publications, 1982.
Hole, Christina. *British Folk Customs*. London: Hutchinson, 1976.
Crossley-Holland, Kevin. *The Norse Myths*. New York: Pantheon, 1980.
Holm, Anne. *I Am David*. Translated by L. W. Kingsland. London: Methuen, 1965; first published 1963.
Hoskins, W. G. *Fieldwork in Local History*. London: Faber and Faber, 1967.
———. *The Making of the English Landscape*. London: Penguin, 1985.
Hourihan, Margery. *Deconstructing the Hero: Literary Theory and Children's Literature*. London: Routledge, 1997.
Housman, A. E. *A Shropshire Lad*. New York: Henry Holt, 1922.
Hughes, Shirley. *Alfie Gets in First*. New York: Lothrop, Lee and Shepard, 1981.
Hunt, Peter. 'Landscapes and Journeys, Metaphors and Maps: The Distinctive Feature of English Fantasy.' *Children's Literature Association Quarterly* 12/1 (1987): 11–14.
———. *An Introduction to Children's Literature*. Oxford: Oxford University Press, 1994.
Hunter, Lynette, ed. *Toward a Definition of Topos: Approaches to Analogical Reasoning*. Basingstoke: Macmillan, 1991.
Ingold, Tim. *The Perception of The Environment*. London: Routledge, 2000.
Jackson, J. B. *Landscape: Selected Writings of J. B. Jackson*. Amherst: University of Massachusetts Press, 1970.
———. *The Necessity for Ruins and Other Topics*. Amherst: University of Massachusetts Press, 1980.
———. *A Sense of Place, A Sense of Time*. New Haven: Yale University Press, 1994.
Jackson, Kenneth Hurlstone. *Studies in Early Celtic Nature Poetry*. Burnham-on-Sea: Llanerch, 1995.

Jackson, Rosemary. *Fantasy: The Literature of Subversion*. London: Routledge, 1988; first published 1981.
Janowitz, Anne. *England's Ruins*. Oxford: Blackwell, 1990.
Jekyll, Gertrude. *Children and Gardens*. Suffolk: Antique Collector's Club, 1982; first published 1908.
Jenkins, Alice. 'Getting to Utopia: Railways and Heterotopia in Children's Literature.' In *Utopian and Dystopian Writing for Children and Young Adults*, edited by Carrie Hintz and Elaine Ostry, 23–7. London: Routledge, 2003.
Johnson, Mark. *The Body in The Mind*. Chicago: Chicago University Press, 1987.
Johnson, Matthew. *Ideas of Landscape*. Oxford: Blackwell, 2007.
Johnson, Norris Brock. 'Garden as Sacred Space: Transformation of Consciousness at Tenryu Temple.' In *The Power of Place: Sacred Ground in Natural and Human Environments, An Anthology*, edited by James A. Swan, 167–187. Bath: Gateway Books, 1993.
Jones, Diana Wynne. *The House of Many Ways*. London: HarperCollins, 2008.
——. *Howl's Moving Castle*. London: Methuen, 1986.
Jones, Lawrence. 'Thomas Hardy and the Cliff Without a Name.' In *Geography and Literature: A Meeting of the Disciplines*, edited by William E. Mallory and Paul Simpson-Housley, 169–77. Syracuse, New York: Syracuse University Press, 1987.
Jones, Rees Ivor. *Facts and Fables from Tywyn: Some True Tales and Some Legends*. Tywyn: Gwynedd, 2001.
Jung, Carl Gustav. *Psychology and Alchemy*. Translated by R. F. C. Hull. 2nd ed. London: Routledge, 2000; first published 1953.
Jusserand, J. J. *English Wayfaring Life in the Middle Ages*. London: Methuen, 1961; first published 1889.
Kabbani, R. *Europe's Myths of Orient*. London: Pandora, 1986.
Kerr, Judith. *The Tiger Who Came to Tea*. London: Collins, 1968.
Kieckhefer, Richard. *Theology and Stone: Church Architecture from Byzantium to Berkeley*. Oxford: Oxford University Press, 2004.
Killeen, Jarlath. *The Fairy Tales of Oscar Wilde*. Aldershot and Burlington: Ashgate, 2007.
King-Smith, Dick. *The Sheep-Pig*. London: Puffin, 2003; first published 1983.
Kipling, Rudyard. *Puck of Pook's Hill*. London: Penguin, 1994; first published 1906.
Klaeber, F. R., ed. *Beowulf and The Fight at Finnsburg*. 3rd ed. Boston: D. C. Heath and Co., 1941.
Kline, Daniel T. *Medieval Literature for Children*. London: Routledge, 2003.
Krapp, George Philip, and Elliott Van Kirk Dobbie, eds. *The Exeter Book*. New York: Columbia University Press, 1936.
Krueger, Christine L. *Functions of Victorian Culture at the Present Time*. Athens, Ohio: Ohio University Press, 2002.
Kutzer, M. Daphne. 'Thatchers and Thatcherites: Lost and Found Empires in Three British Fantasies.' *The Lion and the Unicorn* 22/2 (1998): 196–210.
Kuznets, Lois R. 'High Fantasy in America: A Study of Lloyd Alexander, Ursula Le Guin, and Susan Cooper.' *The Lion and the Unicorn* 9 (1985): 19–35.
Landry, Donna. *The Invention of the Countryside: Hunting, Walking and Ecology in English Literature, 1671–1831*. New York: Palgrave, 2001.
Lane, Belden C. *Landscapes of the Sacred, Geography and Narrative in American Spirituality*. Baltimore: Johns Hopkins University Press, 2002.
Langland, William. *The Vision of William Concerning Piers the Ploughman*. Edited by Walter W. Skeat. Oxford: Clarendon Press, 1869.
——. *Piers the Ploughman*. Translated by J. F. Goodridge. London: Penguin, 1966.
Lawrence, Elizabeth Atwood. *Hunting the Wren: Transformation of Bird to Symbol: A Study in Human–Animal Relationships*. Knoxville: University of Tennessee Press, 1997.
Leach, A. F. *The Schools of Medieval England*. London: Routledge, 2007; first published 1915.
Le Corbusier. *Towards a New Architecture*. Translated by Frederick Etchells. London: The Architectural Press, 1946; first published 1923.
Lee, Stuart D., and Elizabeth Solopova. *The Keys of Middle Earth: Discovering Medieval Literature Through the Fiction of J.R.R. Tolkien*. London: Palgrave, 2005.
Lefebvre, Henri. *The Production of Space*. Translated by Donald Nicholson-Smith. Oxford: Blackwell, 2009; first published 1974.
Le Goff, Jacques. *The Medieval Imagination*. Translated by Arthur Goldhammer. Chicago and London: University of Chicago Press, 1998.

Lehan, Richard. *The City in Literature: An Intellectual and Cultural History*. Berkeley: University of California Press, 1998.
Leslie, Michael. 'Gardens of Eloquence: Rhetoric, Landscape and Literature in the English Renaissance.' In *Toward a Definition of Topos: Approaches to Analogical Reasoning*, edited by Lynette Hunter, 17–44. Basingstoke: Macmillan, 1991.
Leslie, R. F., ed. *The Wanderer*. Manchester: Manchester University Press, 1966.
Lewis, C. S. *The Lion, the Witch and the Wardrobe*. London: HarperCollins, 1980; first published 1950.
———. *The Magician's Nephew*. London: Lion, 1980; first published 1955.
———. *Prince Caspian*. London: HarperCollins, 2005; first published 1951.
———. *The Voyage of the Dawn Treader*. London: HarperCollins, 1994; first published 1955.
Lively, Penelope. *The Driftway*. London: William Heinemann, 1972.
———. *The Ghost of Thomas Kempe*. London: William Heinemann. 1973.
———. *The House in Norham Gardens*. London: William Heinemann, 1974.
———. *The Presence of the Past*. London: Collins, 1976.
———. *The Whispering Knights*. London: William Heinemann, 1971.
Lönnroth, Lars. *Njal's Saga: A Critical Introduction*. Berkeley and Los Angeles: University of California Press, 1976.
Lowenthal, David. *The Past Is a Foreign Country*. Cambridge: Cambridge University Press, 1985.
Lundin, Anne H. *Constructing the Canon of Children's Literature: Beyond Library Walls and Ivory Towers*. New York: Routledge, 2004.
MacFarlane, Robert. *The Wild Places*. London: Granta Books, 2007.
McCallum, Robyn. *Ideologies of Identity in Adolescent Fiction: The Dialogic Construction of Subjectivity*. London: Routledge, 1999.
McGavran, James Holt. *Literature and the Child: Romantic Continuations, Postmodern Contestations*. Iowa City: University of Iowa Press, 1999.
McGrath, Patrick. 'Transgression and Decay.' In *Gothic: Transmutations of Horror in Late Twentieth-Century Art*, edited by Christoph Grunenberg, 159–62. Boston: The Institute of Contemporary Art and Cambridge, Massachusetts: The MIT Press, 1997.
McIntosh, Christopher. *Gardens of the Gods: Myth, Magic and Meaning*. London: I. B. Tauris, 2005.
McKee, David. *Not Now Bernard*. London: Anderson, 1980.
The Mabinogion, trans. Sionad Davies. Oxford: Oxford University Press, 2007 .
Manlove, Colin. *From Alice to Harry Potter: Children's Fantasy in England*. Christchurch: Cybereditions, 2003.
Marcus, Leonard S. *The Wand in the Word: Conversations with Writers of Fantasy*. Somerville, Massachusetts: Candlewick Press, 2006.
Masefield, John. *The Box of Delights*. London: Egmont, 2000; first published 1935.
———. *The Midight Folk*. London: Macmillan, 1927.
Mikkelsen, Nina. *Susan Cooper*. New York: Twayne Publishers, 1998.
Milton, John. *Paradise Lost: A Poem in Twelve Books*. 2nd ed. London: Thomas Newton, 1750.
Mitchell, W. J. T., ed. *Landscape and Power*. 2nd ed. Chicago: University of Chicago Press, 2002; first published 1994.
Moore, John David. 'Pottering about in the Garden: Kenneth Grahame's Version of the Pastoral in *The Wind in the Willows*.' *The Journal of the Midwest Modern Language Association* 23/1 (1990): 25–60.
Moynihan, Elizabeth. *Paradise as a Garden*. New York: Braziller, 1980.
Muir. B. J., ed. *The Exeter Anthology of Old English Poetry: An Edition of Exeter Dean and Chapter MS3501*. 2 vols. Exeter: University of Exeter Press, 2000; first published 1994.
Muir, Richard. *Approaches to Landscape*. London: Macmillan, 1999.
———. *History and Wildlife*. London: Michael Joseph, 1987.
Naramore Mahe r, Susan. 'Review of *The House As Setting Symbol and Structural Motif in Children's Literature* by Pauline Dewan.' *The Lion and the Unicorn* 29/2 (2005): 286–289.
Nash, Roderick. *Wilderness and the American Mind*. New Haven and London: Yale University Press, 1973; first published 1967.
Nastali, Dan. 'Swords, Grails and Bag-Puddings: A Survey of Children's Poetry and Plays.' In *Adapting the Arthurian Legends for Children: Essays on Arthurian Juvenilia*, edited by Barbara Tepa Lupack, 171–96. New York: Palgrave, 2004.

Natov, Roni. *The Poetics of Childhood*. New York: Routledge, 2003.
Nelson, Louis P. *American Sanctuary: Understanding Sacred Places*. Indianapolis: Indiana University Press, 2006.
Nesbit, E. *Five Children and It*. London: T. Fisher Unwin, 1902.
———. *The Phoenix and the Carpet*. London: Newnes, 1904.
———. *The Story of the Treasure Seekers*. London: Puffin, 1996; first published 1899.
Ness, Patrick. *A Monster Calls*. London: Walker, 2011.
Nicholls, Peter "'The Pastness of Landscapes': Susan Howe's *Pierce-Arrow*,' *Contemporary Literature* 43/3 (2002): 441–460.
Nikolajeva, Maria. *From Mythic to Linear: Time in Children's Literature*. Lanham, Maryland and Oxford: The Children's Literature Association and The Scarecrow Press, 2000.
Nix, Garth. *Sabriel*. London: HarperCollins, 1995.
Nodelman, Perry. *The Pleasures of Children's Literature*. London: Longman, 1992.
Nodelman, Perry, and Mavis Reimer. *The Pleasures of Children's Literature*. Boston: Allyn and Bacon, 2002.
Ockman, Joan. 'Review of *The Poetics of Space* by Gaston Bachelard.' *Harvard Design Magazine*, 6 (1998): 1–4.
Olson, Oscar Ludvig. 'The Relation of the *Hrolfs Saga Kraka* and the *Bjarkarimur* to *Beowulf*: A Contribution to the History of Saga Development in England and in the Scandinavian Countries.' PhD diss., University of Chicago, 1914.
Opie, Iona, and Peter Opie. *The Lore and Language of Schoolchildren*. Oxford: Oxford University Press, 1960.
Ovid, *Metamorphoses*. Translated by Mary Innes. London: Penguin, 1955.
Owen-Crocker, Gale R. *The Four Funerals in Beowulf*. Manchester: Manchester University Press, 2000.
Pagan, Victoria Emily. *Rome and the Literature of Gardens*. London: Duckworth, 2006.
Parish, Margaret. 'Pick of the Paperbacks: Fantasy.' *The English Journal* 66/7 (1977): 90–93.
Paterson, Katherine. *Bridge to Terabithia*. London: Puffin Books, 1980; first published 1977.
———. *A Sense of Wonder: On Reading and Writing Books for Children*. New York: Plume, 1995.
Pearce, Philippa. *Tom's Midnight Garden*. London: Puffin, 1976; first published 1958.
Pearce, Susan, and Alexandra Bounia. *The Collector's Voice: Ancient Voices*. Vol. 1. Aldershot and Burlington, Vermont: Ashgate, 2000.
Pearsall, Derek A., and Elizabeth Salter. *Landscapes and Seasons of the Medieval World*. London: Elek Books, 1973.
Pennick, Nigel. *Celtic Sacred Landscapes*. London: Thames and Hudson, 1996.
Petroff, Elizabeth. 'Landscape in 'Pearl': The Transformation of Nature.' *The Chaucer Review* 16/2 (1981): 181–193.
Pheifer, J. D. 'The Seafarer,' Lines 53–55.' *RES* 16 (1965): 282–284.
Philip, Neil. *A Fine Anger: A Critical Introduction to the Work of Alan Garner*. New York: Philomel, 1981.
Pleijj, Herman. *Dreaming of Cockaigne*. Translated by Diane Webb. New York: Columbia University Press, 2001.
Potter, Beatrix. *The Tale of Mrs. Tittlemouse*. London: Frederick Warne, 1910.
Pounds, Norman John Grenville. *The Culture of the English People: Iron Age to the Industrial Revolution*. Cambridge: Cambridge University Press, 1994.
Pratchett, Terry. *Nation*. London: Doubleday, 2008.
———. *The Wee Free Men*. London: Corgi, 2004; first published 2003.
Prest, John. *The Garden of Eden: The Botanic Garden and the Recreation of Paradise*. New Haven: Yale University Press, 1981.
Price, Susan. *The Sterkarm Handshake*. London: Scholastic, 1998.
Propp, Vladimir. *Morphology of the Folktale*. Translated by Laurence Scott. Austin: University of Texas Press, 1968.
Pullman, Philip. *The Amber Spyglass*. London: Scholastic, 2000.
———. *Northern Lights*. London: Scholastic, 1995.
Punter, David. *The Gothic*. Malden, Massachusetts and Oxford: Blackwell, 2004.
———. *The Literature of Terror: A History of Gothic Fictions from 1765 to the Present Day*. London: Longman, 1980.
Quinn, John. *The Summer of Lily and Esme*. Dublin: Poolbeg, 1991.
Reeve, Philip. *No Such Thing as Dragons*. London: Scholastic, 2009.

Reimer, Mavis, ed. *Home Words: Discourses of Children's Literature in Canada*. Waterloo, Ontario: Wilfrid Laurier University Press, 2008.
Relph, Edward. *Place and Placelessness*. London: Pion, 1976.
Rees, David. *What Do Draculas Do? Essays on Contemporary Writers of Fiction for Children and Young Adults*. Methuen, New Jersey and London: The Scarecrow Press, 1990.
Richardson, Margaret, ed. *Visions of Ruin: Architectural Fantasies and Designs for Garden Follies*. London: Sir John Soane's Museum, 1999.
Robinson, Philip, ed. *The Faber Book of Gardens*. London: Faber and Faber, 2007.
Rosen, Michael. *The Attic: Fear*. Illustrated by Agusti Asensio. London: Firefly, 1989.
———. *We're Going on a Bear Hunt*. London: Walker, 1989.
Rosoff, Meg. *How I Live Now*. London: Penguin, 2004.
Rosselin, Céline. 'The Ins and Outs of the Hall: A Parisian Example.' In *At Home: An Anthropology of Domestic Space*, edited by Irene Cieraad, 53–9. Syracuse, New York: Syracuse University Press, 1999.
Rouart, Marie-France. 'The Myth of The Wandering Jew.' In *Companion to Literary Myths, Heroes and Archetypes*, edited by Pierre Brunel, 826–34. London: Routledge, 1995.
Rowling, J. K. *Harry Potter and the Chamber of Secrets*. London: Bloomsbury, 1998.
———. *Harry Potter and the Deathly Hallows*. London: Bloomsbury, 2007.
———. *Harry Potter and the Half-Blood Prince*. London: Bloomsbury, 2005.
———. *Harry Potter and the Philosopher's Stone*. London: Ted Smart, 1998.
———. *Harry Potter and the Prisoner of Azkaban*. London: Bloomsbury, 1999.
The Royal Commission on the Ancient and Historical Monuments and Constructions in Wales and Monmouthshire. *An Inventory of the Ancient Monuments in Wales and Monmouthshire, VI County of Merioneth*. London: His Majesty's Stationery Office, 1921.
Rudd, David, ed. *The Routledge Companion to Children's Literature*. Abingdon: Routledge, 2010.
Rudd, Gillian. *Greenery: Ecocritical Readings of Late Medieval English Literature*. Manchester: Manchester University Press, 2007.
Ryder, Frank Glessner. *The Song of the Nibelungs, A Verse Translation from Middle High German*. Detroit: Wayne State University Press, 1962.
Rykwet, Joseph. *On Adam's House in Paradise: The Idea of the Primitive Hut in Architectural History*. 2nd ed. Cambridge, Massachusetts: The MIT Press, 1981.
Sands, Donald B., ed. *Middle English Verse Romances*. Exeter: University of Exeter Press, 1986.
Sanford, Rhonda Lemke. *Maps and Memory in Early Modern England: A Sense of Place*. New York: Palgrave, 2002.
Sauer, Carl Ortwin. *Land and Life: A Selection from the Writings* of Carl Ortwin Sauer. Edited by John Leighly. Berkeley: University of California Press, 1963.
Saunders, Corinne, J. *The Forest of Medieval Romance: Avernus, Broceliande, Arden*. Cambridge: D. S. Brewer, 1993.
Schama, Simon. *Landscape and Memory*. London: HarperCollins, 1995.
Schivelbusch, Wolfgang. *The Railway Journey: The Industrialisation of Space and Time*. Berkeley and Los Angeles: University of California Press, 1986; first published as *Geschichte der Eisenbahnreise*, 1977.
Scudder, Bernard, and Örnolfur Thorsson, trans. *The Saga of Grettir the Strong*. London: Penguin, 2005.
Sears, John F. *Sacred Places: American Tourist Attractions in the Nineteenth Century*. New York: Oxford University Press, 1989.
Seddon, George. *Landprints: Reflections on Place and Landscape*. Cambridge: Cambridge University Press, 1997.
Sedgwick, Marcus. *My Swordhand Is Singing*. London: Orion, 2006.
Sendak, Maurice. *In the Night Kitchen*. London: Bodley Head, 1971.
———. *Where the Wild Things Are*. London: Scholastic, 1963.
Sessions, George. *Deep Ecology for the Twenty-First Century: Readings on the Philosophy and Practice of the New Environmentalism*. London: Shambhala, 1995.
Shakespeare, William. *The Tempest*. Edited by Virginia Mason Vaughan and Alden T. Vaughan. London: Arden Shakespeare, 2003.
Shepard, Paul. *Man in the Landscape*. New York: Knopf, 1967.
———. *Nature and Madness*. San Francisco: Sierra Club Books, 1982.
Shippey, Tom. *J. R. R. Tolkien: Author of the Century*. London: Harper Collins, 2000.
Shippey, Tom, ed. *Poems of Wisdom and Learning in Old English*. Cambridge: D. S. Brewer, 1976.

234 • Bibliography

Short, John Rennie. Foreword to Irene Cieraad, ed. *At Home: An Anthropology of Domestic Space*, ix–x. Syracuse, New York: Syracuse University Press, 1999.
Siddall, Stephen. *Landscapes and Literature*. Cambridge: Cambridge University Press, 2009.
Skelton, Matthew. *Endymion Spring*. London: Puffin, 2006.
Solnit, Rebecca. *A Field Guide to Getting Lost*. Edinburgh: Canongate, 2005.
Spenser, Edmund. *The Faerie Queene: Books Three and Four*. Edited by Dorothy Stephens. Indianapolis and Cambridge: Hackett, 2006.
Spirn, Anne Whiston. *The Language of Landscape*. New Haven: Yale University Press, 1998.
Sponsler, Claire. 'Beyond the Ruins: The Geopolitics of Urban Decay and Cybernetic Play.' *Science Fiction Studies* 20/2 (1993): 251–265.
Staines, David. 'Crouched in Dark Caves: The Post-Colonial Narcissism of Canadian Literature.' *The Yearbook of English Studies* 13 (1983): 259–269.
Stamp, L. Dudley. 'Reviews.' *Geographical Journal* 121 (1951): 511–13.
Storr, Catherine. *Marianne Dreams*. London: Faber and Faber, 2000; first published 1958.
Sturluson, Snorri. *The Prose Edda: Norse Mythology*. Translated by Jesse L. Byock. London: Penguin, 2005.
———. *Snorra Edda ásamt Skaldu og þarmeð fylgjandi ritgjörðum*. Edited by R. Kr. Rasdk. Stockholm: Elmen, 1818.
Sutcliffe, Rosemary. *The Eagle of the Ninth*. London: Anthony Lawton, 1954.
Swan, James A, ed. *The Power of Place: Sacred Ground in Natural and Human Environments, An Anthology*. Bath: Gateway Books, 1993.
Talib, Ismail S. *The Language of Postcolonial Literatures: An Introduction*. New York and London: Routledge, 2002.
Taylor, G. P. *Wormwood*. London: Faber and Faber, 2004.
Temple, William. 'Upon the Gardens of Epicurus or, Of Gardening, in the Year 1685.' In *Five Miscellaneous Essays*, edited by Samuel Holt Monk, 1–34. Ann Arbor: University of Michigan Press.
Terry, Patricia. *Poems of the Vikings*. Indianapolis: Bobbs-Merrill, 1969.
Thacker, Christopher. *History of Gardens*. London: Croom Helm, 1985.
Tindall, Gillian. *Countries of the Mind: The Meaning of Place to Writers*. London: Hogarth Press, 1991.
Thomas, W. Jenkyn. *The Welsh Fairy Book*. London: Dover, 2001; first published 1907.
Thompson, Kate. *Annan Water*. London: Bodley Head, 2004.
Thompson, Mary Shine, and Valerie Coghlan, eds. *Divided Worlds*. Dublin: Four Courts Press, 2007.
Tolkien, J. R. R. *The Fellowship of the Ring*. London: HarperCollins, 2001; first published 1954.
———. *The Hobbit: Or, There and Back Again*. London: HarperCollins, 1998; first published 1937.
———. *Sir Gawain and the Green Knight*. Edited by Christopher Tolkien. London: HarperCollins, 2006.
———. *Tree and Leaf*. London: George Allen and Unwin, 1975.
Tolkien, J. R. R., and E. V. Gordon, eds. *Sir Gawain and the Green Knight*. Oxford: Oxford University Press, 1925.
Toman, Rolf, ed. *European Garden Design: From Classical Antiquity to the Present Day*. Oxford: Tandem Verlag, 2005.
Toth, Csaba. 'Like Cancer in the System: Industrial Gothic, Nine Inch Nails and Videotape.' In *Gothic: Transmutations of Horror in Late Twentieth Century Art*, edited by Christoph Grunenberg, 90–80 (pagination runs in reverse). Boston: Institute of Contemporary Art, 1997.
Travers, P. L. *Mary Poppins*. London: Peter Davies, 1934.
Tuan, Yi-Fu. *Space and Place: The Perspective of Experience*. Minneapolis: University of Minnesota Press, 1977.
———. *Topophilia: A Study of Environmental Perception, Attitudes and Values*. Upper Saddle River, New Jersey: Prentice Hall, 1974.
Turner, Harold W. *From Temple to Meeting House: The Phenomenology and Theology of Places of Worship*. The Hague: Walter de Gruyter, 1979.
Turner, Victor, and Edith Turner. *Image and Pilgrimage in Christian Culture*. New York: Columbia University Press, 1978.

Urban, Sylvanus. 'Wright's Volume of Vocabularies.' *The Gentleman's Magazine and Historical Review* 204 (1858): 48–54.
Van Erp-Houtepen, Anne. 'The Etymological Origin of the Garden.' *Journal of Garden History* 6 (1986): 227–231.
Van Kirk Dobbie, Elliott. *The Anglo-Saxon Minor Poems*. New York: Columbia University Press, 1942.
Vidler, Anthony. *The Architectural Uncanny*. Cambridge, Massachusetts: The MIT Press, 1992.
Virgil *Georgics*. Translated by Peter Fallon. Oxford: Oxford University Press, 2006.
Veeder, Mary Harns. 'Gender and Empowerment in Susan Cooper's *The Dark Is Rising* Sequence.' *Children's Literature Association Quarterly* 16/1 (1991): 11–16.
Wadham, Timothy Rex. 'Light from the Lost Land: A Contextual Response to Susan Cooper's *The Dark Is Rising Sequence*.' PhD diss., University of Texas at Arlington, 1994.
Wallace, David. *Chaucerian Polity: Absolutist Images and Associational Forms in England and Italy*. Stanford: Stanford University Press, 1977.
Warnke, Martin. *Political Landscape: The Art History of Nature*. Translated by David McLintock. London: Reaktion, 1994.
Wasserman, Judith R. 'To Trace the Shifting Sands: Community, Ritual, and the Memorial Landscape.' *Landscape Journal* 17/1 (1998): 42–62.
Watkin, David. 'Built Ruins: The Hermitage as a Retreat.' In *Visions of Ruin: Architectural Fantasies and Designs for Garden Follies*, edited by Margaret Richardson, 5–15. London: Sir John Soane's Museum, 1999.
Watkins, Alfred. *The Old Straight Track: Its Mounds, Beacons, Moats, Sites and Mark Stones*. London: Methuen, 1925.
Watkins, Tony. 'Space History and Culture: The Setting of Children's Literature.' In *Understanding Children's Literature: Key Essays from the Second Edition of the International Companion Encyclopedia of Children's Literature*, edited by Peter Hunt, 50–72. London and New York: Routledge, 2005.
Watson, James G. 'Faulkner: The House of Fiction.' In *Fifty years of Yoknapatawpha*, edited by Doreen Fowler and Ann J. Abadie, 134–58. Jackson: University Press of Mississippi, 1980.
Westall, Robert. *Ghost Abbey*. London: Corgi, 2004; first published 1988.
———. *The Kingdom by the Sea*. London: Methuen, 1990.
Weston, Jessie L. *From Ritual To Romance*. Princeton, New Jersey: Princeton University Press, 1993; first published 1920.
Westwood, Jennifer. *Albion: A Guide to Legendary Britain*. London: Granada, 1985.
White, Donna R. *A Century of Welsh Myth in Children's Literature*. Westport, Connecticut: Greenwood Press, 1998.
White. T. H. *The Once and Future King*. London: Collins, 1958.
Whitlock, Ralph. *A Calendar of Country Customs*. London: B. T. Batsford, 1978.
Wilde, Oscar. *Stories for Children*. Illustrated by P. J. Lynch. London: Hodder, 2000; first published 1990.
Wilhelm, James J. *The Cruelest Month: Spring, Nature, and Love in Classical and Medieval Lyrics*. New Haven and London: Yale University Press, 1965.
Wilkie-Stibbs, Christine. 'Intertextuality and the Child Reader.' In *Understanding Children's Literature: Key Essays from the Second Edition of the International Companion Encyclopedia of Children's Literature*, edited by Peter Hunt, 168–179. London and New York: Routledge, 200.
Williams, M. "'The Apple of My Eye': Carl Sauer and Cultural Geography." *Journal of Historical Geography* 9 (1983): 1–28.
Williams, Ifor. *Lectures in Early Welsh Poetry*. Dublin: Dublin Institute for Advanced Studies 1944.
Windling, Terri. *The Green Man: Tales from the Mythic Forest*. London: Penguin, 2002.
Wood, Naomi. 'Review of *Four British Fantasists*, by Charles Butler.' *Children's Literature* 36 (2008): 251–256.
Wood, Naomi. '(Em)bracing Icy Mothers: Ideology, Identity and Environment in Children's Fantasy.' In *Wild Things: Children's Culture and Ecocriticism*, edited by Sidney I. Dobrin and Kenneth B. Kidd, 198–214. Detroit, Michigan: Wayne State University Press, 2004.
Woolf, Virginia. 'Street Haunting: A London Adventure.' In *The Death of the Moth and Other Essays*, 19–29. London: The Hogarth Press, 1942.
Wylie, John. *Landscape*. Abingdon: Routledge, 2007.

Other Media

http://www.oxfordjewishheritage.co.uk/projects/botanic-gardens-first-jewish-cemetery. Accessed 01/09/11.

http://www.magd.ox.ac.uk/nested_content/listings/home_-_events/events/may-day-celebrations. Accessed 01/09/11.

Maxims II, The Complete Corpus of Anglo-Saxon Poetry, http://www.sacred-texts.com/neu/ascp/a15.htm. Accessed 01/09/11.

Njal's Saga, Icelandic Saga Database, http://www.sagadb.org/brennu-njals_saga#121. Accessed 01/09/11.

Index

Adams, Richard, *Watership Down*, 112
Aelfric Bata, *Colloquy of the Occupations*, 61
Aiken, Joan, *The Wolves of Willoughby Chase*, 110
Alfred Jewel, 11
Alice Stanton, 64–65, 67, 89
Almond, David, 146–147, 148; *Clay*, 23, 147; *Kit's Wilderness*, 147; *The Savage*, 80, 147
Althusser, Louis, 98
Arawn, King of Annwfn, 83, 143
Archaeology, 134, 135, 136, 138, 139, 148, 155, 166, 173, 178
Attic, 19, 42, 43, 44, 45, 46, 174, 194
Augarde, Steve, *The Various*, 63

Bachelard, Gaston, 13, 14, 20, 49, 179
Bakhtin, Mikhail, 93, 96, 97, 99, 105, 109, 113, 122
Barbara Stanton, 56–57
Barney Drew, 9, 28, 34, 143, 164; and the grail, 149–152, 153, 154; and carnival, 100–103, 105, 180
'Battle of Maldon, The', 22
'Battle at Stamford Bridge, The', 22
Bawden, Nina, *Carrie's War*, 24, 110
Benjamin, Walter, 93, 96, 101
Beowulf, 11, 14, 22, 60, 77, 120, 135, 145–146, 147, 152, 160, 191n43; Beowulf, 136, 146, 24, 40; burial of Scyld Shefing, 152; fight with Grendel, 22–23; fight with Dragon, 146; Finn episode, 21; Grendel, 22, 24, 40, 77, 120–121, 123, 125, 145, 148, 160; lament of the last survivor, 145
Bird Rock. *See* Craig yr Aderyn
Black Rider. *See* Mitothin

Blyton, Enid, *Adventures of the Wishing Chair*, 112; *The Children of Cherry-Tree Farm*, 62; *Five go to Finniston Farm*, 62
Boston, Lucy, 13, *The Children of Greenknowe*, 24, 170
Bran Davies, 32, 33, 34, 67, 82, 163, 165–167; in Craig Yr Aderyn 152–153; in the Lost Land 154–155, 165; as Pendragon, 117–119, 136, 139
Brenin Llwyd, 32, 50, 80, 81, 82, 83, 84, 88, 105, 139
Brigg, Raymond, *The Snowman*, 98
Briggs, Katherine, *Hobberdy Dick*, 80
Buckinghamshire, 8
Burnett, Frances Hodgson, *The Secret Garden*, 54–55

Cader Idris, 9, 32, 33, 37, 82, 149
Cadfan's Way. *See* Llwybr Cadfan
Caerleon, 136, 138, 149, 153, 155, 156, 163
Cafall, 67, 166
Cain, 60, 120, 121, 123
Cantr'er Gwaelod, 7, 32, 33, 56, 57–58, 82, 117, 118, 119, 139, 149, 153, 154, 155, 165
Captain Toms, 27, 105–106
Carnival, 84, 89, 97–98; in children's literature 98–100; in *The Dark is Rising Sequence*, 100–108, 175, 180
Carroll, Lewis (C.L. Dodgson), *Alice's Adventures in Wonderland* 72, 74, 201n141, 218n120
Cave, 32, 80, 134, 136, 139, 141–143. *See also* chthonic space.
Cernunnos. *See* Herne the Hunter
Chthonic space, 140–153; in medieval literature, 143–146; in children's

238 · Index

literature, 146–148; in *The Dark is Rising Sequence*, 138–139, 148–153; anomalous chthonic spaces 153–157
Church, 10, 18, 19, 32, 38, 39, 40, 44, 76, 124, 125, 171, 172. *See also* sanctuary topos
Church-yard, 126
Cockaigne, 71
Colonisation, 142, 158, 161, 165
Cornwall, 8, 85, 113, 139, 149. *See also* Kenmare Head; The Gravestones; Trewissick
Craig yr Aderyn, 138, 149, 152, 154
Crossley-Holland, Kevin, *Gatty's Tale*, 113
Cwm Maethlon, 33
Cynnewulf and Cynneheard, 22

Death, 14, 49, 50, 52, 53, 54, 55, 56, 58, 61, 64, 65, 66, 67, 70, 71, 73, 74, 75, 78, 82, 83, 84, 86, 87, 89, 97, 98, 99, 100, 102, 104, 142, 143, 144, 145, 152, 158, 160, 163, 164, 172, 177, 179, 181, 182, 183
Defence in the Doorway trope 22–23, 24, 36, 38, 39
Diachronic time 94, 100, 108, 121, 126, 128, 131
Dowd, Siobhan, *Solace of the Road*, 112
Dronke, Ursula, 11, 12
Drowned Hundred. *See* Cantr'er Gwaelod
Dūstscēawung poetry, 13, 159, 160
Dyfi, 9

Echoes, 34–35
Ecocriticism, 76
Eden, 49, 51–53, 54, 57, 60, 70, 179, 198n66
Edmund Spenser, *The Faerie Queene*, 50, 119

Farm, 59–67; in children's literature, 62–64; in *The Dark is Rising Sequence*, 64–67; in medieval literature, 60–62
Fear, 18, 40, 45, 50, 60, 74, 76, 79, 119, 143, 151, 154, 159; and carnival 98, 105
Fisher King. *See* Gwyddno Garanhir
Follies, 159
Forest, 46, 49, 53, 76–78, 83–84, 87, 92, 171
Foucault, Michel, 1
Frazer, Sir James, 86, 87

Gaiman, Neil, *The Graveyard Book*, 13, 99–100, 147, 162; *Stardust*, 113
Garden, 51–58; in medieval literature, 53–54; in children's literature, 54–56; in *The Dark is Rising Sequence*, 56–58
Garner, Alan, 148, 169; *The Owl Service*, 136, 173–178; *The Weirdstone of Brisingamen*, 23, 109, 135, 147
Genealogy, 134, 135, 136–139, 148, 155, 165, 166, 173, 178
Genesis 63
Genesis A, 53, 120
Genesis B, 5, 77
Genius locus, 32, 79–81, 84, 126
Ghosts, 28
Goudge, Elizabeth, *The Little White Horse*, 79
Grahame, Kenneth, *The Wind in the Willows*, 23, 72–73, 79, 80, 170
Grail, 80, 86, 113, 135, 138, 150–151, 163; Grail legends, 119
Grave, 139, 141–142, 144–145, 149, 150, 158, 159, 161. *See also* chthonic space
Gravestones, 10, 27, 28–30, 149
Green Topos 49–89
Greenwitch, 9, 31, 50, 80, 81, 84, 85–89, 104, 105–106, 174; Greenwitch ceremony, 30, 85–88, 100, 102
Grendel. *See* Beowulf
Grettir Saga. *See* The Saga of Grettir the Strong
Grey King. *See* Brenin Llwyd
Greythorne Manor, 39–40, 44, 123, 124
Gwion, 118
Gwyddno Garanhir, 119, 155

Haggard, H. Rider, *King Solomon's Mines*, 141
Happy Valley. *See* Cwm Maethlon
Hawkes, Jacquetta: and Landscape History 4, 5, 8, 9; influence on Cooper, 8, 12, 134, 141
Hawkin, 67, 75, 121–126, 129, 152, 170
Hedges, 66, 89
Herne the Hunter, 50, 80, 81, 83–84, 139, 169–172, 174
Hervorsaga, 144–145
Heterotope, 109–110
Hoskins, W.G., 4, 5
Hrolfs Saga Kraka, 22, 25
Hughes, Shirley, *Alfie Gets in First*, 24
Huntercombe Church, 39–42

Huntercombe Lane, 114–116, 117, 128, 130

Initiation Rites, 45, 54, 114, 142, 154, 156

James Stanton, 41, 65, 73, 110, 115, 128
Jane Drew, 28, 29, 31, 42, 135, 151; and the Greenwitch 85–88, 100, 103–105; as Guinevere, 118; and the Lady 33–35
John Rowlands, 66–67, 89, 165
Jones, Diana Wynne, *The House of Many Ways*, 24; *Howl's Moving Castle*, 24

Kenmare Head, 27, 28, 138, 149, 151, 154
Kenneth Grahame, *The Wind in the Willows*, 23, 72–73, 79–80
Kerr, Judith, *The Tiger Who Came to Tea*, 98
King Arthur, 10, 23, 34, 75, 78, 79, 80, 84, 139, 152, 172
King Mark 100, 139, 149, 150; King Mark's Head *see* Kenmare Head
King-Smith, Dick, *The Sheep-Pig*, 62
Kipling, Rudyard, *Puck of Pook's Hill*, 26, 72

Lady, the, 35, 37
Landscape History, 4, 8–9, 10, 12, 13, 14
Langland, *Piers the Plowman*, 71–72, 74, 121
Lapsed Topos, 133–68
Lewis, C.S., 10–11, *The Chronicles of Narnia*, 136; *The Lion, The Witch and the Wardrobe*, 26, 135; *Prince Caspian*, 161; *The Voyage of the Dawn Treader*, 147; influence on Cooper, 10–11
Leys, 126–131
Lively, Penelope, 13, 126; *The Driftway*, 127–128; *The Ghost of Thomas Kempe*, 24; *The Whispering Knights*, 23
Llwybr Cadfan, 10, 129, 212 n. 205
Llyn Barfog, 33, 34, 37
Locus amoenus, 49, 63, 70–71, 72, 75, 159. *See also* Pleasance
Locus horribilus, 159
Lost Land. *See* Cantr'er Gwaelod

Mabinogion, 14, 111, 118; The First Branch, 83, 139, 143; The Third Branch, 61; The Fourth Branch, 172; and *The Owl Service* 176–178; The Lady of the Well, 21, 119

Mari Llwyd, 82, 118, 119, 154, 165
Mary Stanton, 123
Masefield, John, 11, 169; *The Box of Delights*, 170–173
Maxims II, 12, 77
McKee, Dave, *Not Now Bernard*, 98
Mearcstapa, 46, 77, 120, 125, 170
Merlin, 136. *See also* Merriman Lyon
Merriman Lyon, 9, 12, 28, 29, 31, 37, 85, 104, 106, 110, 115, 117, 130–131, 134, 135–136, 152, 153–154, 155, 156
Mevagissey, 10
Mikkelsen, Nina, 7, 170
Mink, 64–65
Miss Greythorne, 39, 136
Mitothin, 40, 41, 45, 58, 80, 129, 152, 154
Morphology, 3
Mr Beaumont 38–39
Mr Jackson, 24

Names: 139, 146, 166; naming rituals; 78, 152; nicknames, 61–62; substitutions, 53, 78, 118, 210 n 138; and Hawkin, 121–122, 126; and the Greenwitch, 86; place-names, 10, 101, 128, 129, 130–131
Nesbit, Edith, *The Phoenix and the Carpet*, 112
Ness, Patrick, *A Monster Calls*, 24
Njal's Saga, 61; burning-in of Njal, 21; murder of Hoskuld, 62; Gunnar of Hlidarendi, 62, 144

Old English (language) 11, 12, literature 12, 40, 71, 159. *See also* individual titles
Old Norse (language) 11
Old Ones, 29, 38, 39, 40, 106, 116–117, 135, 156; and time, 47, 114–115, 121, 153; and death, 66, 82, and memory, 134, 166; and Oldway Lane, 131
Oldway Lane, 129–131
Oxford, 10–11; Cooper in 10–12; Botanical Gardens, 55; Magdalen Tower, 56

P.L. Travers, *Mary Poppins*, 99
Paul Stanton, 45, 116, 123, 125
Pearce, Philippa, *Tom's Midnight Garden*, 54
Pearl, 53, 54
Pilgrimage, 33, 62, 111, 113, 181
Plants: blossom, 55, 58, 87; grass, 56, 58, 70, 73, 77, 164, 177, 179, 182;

hawthorn, 87, 165; hazel, 66, 87; holly, 41, 78; roses, 56, 57, 58; rowan, 87
Pleasance, 70–75; 71–72; in children's literature, 72–73; in *The Dark is Rising Sequence*, 73–75; in medieval literature
Potter, Beatrix, *The Tale of Mrs Tittlemouse*, 23
Pratchett, Terry; *Nation*, 162; *The Wee Free Men*, 63–64, 80
Price, Susan, *The Sterkarm Handshake*, 63, 161
Primary world/secondary world 26–27, 29, 32, 36–37, 38, 41, 44–45, 142
Propp, Vladimir, 3, 13
Prospect-refuge theory, 70
Pullman, Philip, *The Amber Spyglass*, 55–56, 143, 162; *Northern Lights*, 27

Quest, 46, 53, 76, 79; and the lapsed topos, 141, 147, 154, 165; and the roadway topos; 110, 111, 112–113, 114, 116, 118–119, 133, 135

Rage, 42, 88, 104, 106, 147
Riddles, 152–153, 218n120
Ridgeway, 128–129
Roadway Topos, 91–131; anomalous ways, 109–111. See also train
Roads, 108–119; in children's literature, 112–113; in *The Dark is Rising Sequence*, 113–119; Old Roads and Magic Roads, 126–131; in medieval literature, 111–112;
Romanticism, 33, 62, 63
Rosoff, Meg, *How I Live Now*, 63, 169–170, 178–183
Rowling, J.K., *Harry Potter and the Deathly Hallows*, 147; *Harry Potter and the Half-Blood Prince*, 135; *Harry Potter and the Philosopher's Stone*, 24, 104, 110; *Harry Potter and the Prisoner of Azkaban*, 162
'Ruin, The', 13, 160–161
Ruins 157–158; in children's literature 161–163; in *The Dark is Rising Sequence*, 163–167; in medieval literature 158–161

Saga of Grettir the Strong, The, 22, 40, 144, 145
Saga of the Niebelungs, The, 21

Sanctuary Topos 17–18; in children's literature, 23–25; domestic space, 18–23; in medieval literature, 21–23; in *The Dark is Rising Sequence*, 26–47
Sauer, Carl Ortwin, 3, 5, 13
'Seafarer', 13, 50, 121, 124, 160
Sedgewick, Marcus, *My Swordhand is Singing*, 24
Sendak, Maurice, *In the Night Kitchen*, 99; *Where the Wild Things Are*, 98
Shakespeare, William, *Hamlet*, 9; *Merry Wives of Windsor*, 84; *The Tempest*, 34
Simon Drew, 28, 33, 34, 135, 150, 151, 164–165
Sir Gawain and the Green Knight, 78, 79, 80, 112
Sir Orfeo, 70, 71, 74
Skelton, Matthew, *Endymion Spring*, 99
Sleep, 70–72, 74, 75
Sleepers, The, 23, 75, 139, 147
Snorra Edda, 14, 143–144, 146, 152
Snow, 38, 40, 41, 43, 44–45, 46, 75, 88, 114, 124, 125–126, 130, 171
Stephen Stanton, 43–44, 56–57, 73
Stone circle, 10, 23, 27, 28–30, 37
Storr, Catherine, *Marianne Dreams*, 24
Street, 96–108; in children's literature, 98–100; in *The Dark is Rising Sequence*, 100–108
Sutcliff, Rosemary, *The Eagle of the Ninth*, 112–113
Sutton Hoo, 138, 152
Swearing, 122
Synchronic time 94, 100, 114, 119, 121, 126, 128, 131, 141

Taplow, 152
Tethys, 80, 149, 153–154
Thompson, Kate, *Annan Water*, 63
Threshold, 19–20, 24, 26, 31, 33–34, 37, 114, 119; as focus of rituals, 19, 22–23; reinforcement of, 40, 41; disruptions of, 41, 170
Tolkien, J.R.R., 10–11, *The Hobbit*, 23, 112–113, 143, 147–148; *The Fellowship of the Ring*, 141; influence on Cooper, 10–11
Tourism, 2, 33–34
Train, 9, 109–110, 113, 172
Treasure, 135–6, 138, 139, 142, 143, 144, 145, 146, 147–148, 149–150, 151, 152, 153, 154, 156, 161

Index • 241

Trewissick, 10, 31, 81, 84, 85, 87, 88, 89, 100, 101, 102, 104, 105, 106, 139, 149; and carnival 100–108
Tywyn, 10, 32, 129

Uncanny 28, 44, 156, 159, 161, 163; doubles 164–165

Virgil, 5, 60, 65

'Waking of Angantyr, The'. *See Hervorsaga*
Wales, 8, 82, 113. *See also*, Cader Idris; Llwybr Cadfan; Craig yr Aderyn; Cwm Maethlon; Dyfi; Llyn Barfog; Tywyn; Cantr'er Gwaelod
Walker. *See* Hawkin
Wandering and Exile 119–126; in medieval literature, 120–121; in *The Dark is Rising Sequence* 121–126
Wandering Jew, 121
'Wanderer, The', 13, 121, 122–123, 125, 160
Wayland, 117, 129; Wayland's Smithy, 128
Westall, Robert, *Ghost Abbey*, 161–162; *The Kingdom by the Sea*, 113
'Wife's Lament, The', 145, 160

Wild Hunt. *See* Herne
Wilde, Oscar, 'The Selfish Giant', 54–55, 64; 'The Nightingale and the Rose', 54, 64; 'The Young King', 54
Wilderness, 19, 22, 50, 52, 60–61, 67, 68–69, 70, 76–89, 123; in medieval literature, 76–79; in children's literature, 79–80; in *The Dark is Rising Sequence*, 80–89
Will Stanton, 8, 10, 27, 31, 33–34, 35, 56–57, 64, 65–66, 73–75, 82–83, 84, 88–89, 105–106, 129, 139, 152–154, 164; and awareness of space, 37, 38, 41, 45, 114–117, 129–131, 165; encounters with Hawkin, 122–126; as guide, 33, 117–119, 154, 165; as mearcstapa, 32, 46, 77; as Old One, 36–39, 40, 41, 42, 66–67, 115, 116–117, 129, 135–136, 155–156; and relationship with domestic space 40–46; as Seeker, 75, 135, 138, 152; and synchronic time, 117
Window, 19, 24, 28, 163, 164, 165, 170, 171, 174, 178, 179, 183
Wren, 139; Wren-boys, 139